CASE STUDIES IN
CULTURAL ANTHROPOLOGY

GENERAL EDITORS
George and Louise Spindler
STANFORD UNIVERSITY

THE PEASANTS OF CENTRAL RUSSIA

MAP OF CENTRAL RUSSIA

GORKII OBLAST

KOSTROMA OBLAST

VOLOGDA OBLAST

IVANOVO OBLAST

VLADIMIR OBLAST

TAMBOV OBLAST

VIRIATINO

RYAZAN OBLAST

VORONEZH OBLAST

LAKE RYBINSK

YAROSLAVL OBLAST

LIPETSK OBLAST

LAKE BELOYE

MOSCOW

TULA OBLAST

BELGOROD OBLAST

KALININ OBLAST

KALUGA OBLAST

OREL (ORLOVSKAIA OBLAST)

KURSK OBLAST

LAKE LADOGA

NOVGOROD OBLAST

LENINGRAD

SMOLENSK OBLAST

BRYANSK OBLAST

LAKE IL'MEN'

PSKOV OBLAST

LAKE CHUD

ESTONIA

LATVIA

LITHUANIA

THE PEASANTS
OF CENTRAL RUSSIA

By

STEPHEN P. DUNN AND ETHEL DUNN

HOLT, RINEHART AND WINSTON

NEW YORK   CHICAGO   SAN FRANCISCO   TORONTO   LONDON

Editors' Foreword

About the Series

These case studies in cultural anthropology are designed to bring to students in the social sciences insights into the richness and complexity of human life as it is lived in different ways and in different places. They are written by men and women who have lived in the societies they write about, and who are professionally trained as observers and interpreters of human behavior. The authors are also teachers, and in writing their books they have kept the students who will read them foremost in their minds. It is our belief that when an understanding of ways of life very different from one's own is gained, abstractions and generalizations about social structure, cultural values, subsistence techniques, and other universal categories of human social behavior become meaningful.

About the Authors

Stephen P. Dunn received his doctorate in anthropology from Columbia University in 1959 with a dissertation on the present Jewish community of Rome.

Ethel Dunn received an M. A. in History and a certificate of the Russian Institute from Columbia University in 1956.

Since 1959, the authors have been studying directed culture change in the Soviet Union. This work was supported from 1963 to 1966 by grants from the National Science Foundation, administered first by Fordham University, and in 1964 by the University of California. The authors are currently associates at the Center for Slavic Studies, University of California, Berkeley. In 1964, they attended the Seventh International Congress of Anthropological and Ethnographic Sciences in Moscow with the aid of a grant from the Wenner-Gren Foundation for Anthropological Research. The Dunns have written articles on culture change in Central Russia, the Far North, Central Asia, and the Baltic (this last Stephen Dunn's alone), as well as many reviews and translations of Soviet sociological and ethnographic literature. Stephen Dunn has also had an article published in *Sovetskaia etnografiia,* a Russian journal.

Stephen Dunn also edited the English translation, *The Peoples of Siberia* (1964). He is currently editor of *Soviet Sociology* and *Soviet Anthropology and Archeology.*

About the Book

Our comments here will be brief, since Professor Alex Vucinich has provided a foreword. This case study by the Dunns makes readily available for the first time to beginning students an authoritative ethnographic description of significant aspects of Russian peasant life. The description is internally coherent and meaningful despite the fact that fieldwork could not be done and therefore the study was based upon secondary sources in Russian, written by Soviet ethnographers. The case study is remarkable in this respect and also in that the Dunns' rich knowledge of Soviet institutions has allowed them to show how socialist designs have been adapted to the cultural patterns of the folk and at the same time how the folk culture has been changed by the influence of the state.

GEORGE AND LOUISE SPINDLER
General Editors

Stanford, California
December 1966

Acknowledgments

In writing this book we received the help of many individuals and institutions for which we render thanks now. First of all, we were supported by the National Science Foundation through grants administered by Fordham University Institute of Contemporary Russian Studies and University of California Institute of International Studies. Our superior at Fordham was the Reverend Walter C. Jaskievicz, S. J. Our superiors at the University of California have been Professors E. A. Hammel, G. D. Berreman, Gregory Grossman, and Benjamin Ward. All of these gentlemen have the important gift of knowing how to support without interfering. The Wenner-Gren Foundation for Anthropological Research gave us a grant-in-aid which enabled us to attend the Seventh International Congress of Anthropological and Ethnographic Sciences in Moscow, August 1964, and to meet and speak personally with our Soviet colleagues. William A. Cox also made this trip possible through his devoted efforts as our assistant. William Mandel, translator and writer, was always available for consultation and was our guide through the thickets of Soviet affairs and the interpretation of Soviet sources. Though he is not responsible for the end result, which is ours alone, we are most grateful to him. Miss Carolyn Fowler, Mrs. G. E. Pratty, and Mrs. Joseph Fabry typed and read earlier versions of this book. Geoffrey E. Pratty, our assistant during the writing, helped by keeping us calm. A. A. Podobedova gave us valuable insights into Russians; Professor D. B. Shimkin assured us that we could write the book, and we took him at his word. Professor Alexander Vucinich made very useful criticisms and has written a foreword to the book, for which we are grateful. Last but not least, we thank the editors of the series for their patience and encouragement.

STEPHEN P. DUNN AND ETHEL DUNN

December 1966

FOREWORD

During the 1920s the famous Russian ethnographer V. G. Bogoraz edited three ethnographic symposia—*Revolution in the Village, The Old and New Life,* and *The Transformed Village*—which marked the beginning of a systematic study of the socialist transformation of the Soviet rural community. The Bogoraz volumes were actually completed before the mass collectivization of agriculture was undertaken and before the Soviet government adopted the kolkhoz as the principal model of socialist farm communities. The papers were written mostly by university students majoring in ethnography who did fieldwork during summer vacations, and who found the unsettled reality of the countryside and the undeveloped methodology of community studies equally baffling.

During the 1930s and most of the 1940s Soviet ethnographers showed very little interest in the current socialization processes in the rural community. The research emphasis shifted to the ethnic origin and traditional customs of the non-Slavic national groups which have added to the great cultural diversity of the Soviet Union. Ethnographers stayed away from the modern problems of a sociological nature and developed a "historical science" concerned equally with the grand process of cultural evolution and the unique historical destinies of individual peoples. In this, they cooperated with the archeologists and historians in gathering the data necessary for a historical reconstruction of the cultural histories of those Soviet ethnic and national groups for which limited written documentary material was preserved.

It was not until 1948 that the Institute of Ethnography—a subsidiary of the Soviet Academy of Sciences and the guiding and coordinating agency of Soviet ethnographic research—began sending teams of fieldworkers to the rural community to gather data depicting the new realities of village life. At first the ethnographers studied individual kolkhozy or specific institutions, particularly the family. More recently, the emphasis has been on the comparative study of all the kolkhozy of a district or a province. Direct observation, systematic interviews, the local press, questionnaires, and family budgets have been the basic sources of information.

Soviet scholars are the first to admit the kolkhoz ethnography is still a wandering discipline unsupported by coherent and articulated theory, and that its methodology does not meet the rigorous criteria of scientific inquiry. Their contributions, however, are an inexhaustible source of cultural data virtually untapped by Western scholars.

Whether dealing with an individual kolkhoz or the farm communities of an entire province, a typical Soviet ethnographic study of the rural world covers the following topics: pre-Soviet local history; ecological setting and material culture; economic processes and organization; administrative organization and internal order;

mass organizations; family; and sacred and secular ceremonialism. Permeating these general categories are valuable data related to social stratification, the interplay of traditional customs and "socialist customs," the loci of informal power, the kinship systems (and their function in linking the rural and urban communities), the sociology of leisure, the conflict between generations, and the division of labor between the sexes. The fact that rural sociology—or any sociology for that matter—was outlawed in the Soviet Union until the 1960s, makes the contributions of kolkhoz ethnography virtually the only source of information on the dynamics of the rural community.

Officially, one of the most vital functions of the kolkhoz ethnographer is to scrutinize the unexpected results of socioeconomic planning and to tell the authorities what went awry with their rural schemes. His job is to explain how and why local institutions are bent under the pressure of local needs and traditions. Of all Soviet social scientists, he is the least expected to adhere to a legalistic interpretation of Soviet institutions.

The work of the kolkhoz ethnographer is not limited to examination of the realities of rural living; he also helps change these realities in accordance with communist plans. His task is to guard the structural principles of Soviet society by recognizing and interpreting informal groups, latent functions of individual institutions, and deviations from social norms that show the unplanned and undirected side of the Soviet universe. He is also called upon to make concrete recommendations for remedial planning in the countryside.

One of the more important functions of the Soviet ethnographer is to provide government authorities with reliable intelligence on the nature, scope, and social significance of religious behavior in the rural community. Although rural religion has lost much of its traditional doctrinal identification, it is of tangible consequence as a custom-sustaining cultural force. It provides a background for the rise of public opinion and public pressure unsanctioned and untutored by the authorities. As a source of social unity in the village, it thwarts a smooth and predictable functioning of the institutions of government control.

The ethnographer does not have a monopoly on the study of the kolkhoz community. But while the economists, political scientists, demographers, and other experts study specific aspects of rural life, the ethnographer is interested in rural culture as a whole. Kolkhoz ethnography supplies more thorough and basic information on both the triumphs and dilemmas of rural socialism than any other social science or social philosophy. It shows that the perennial problem of agricultural production is too complex to be explained in terms of economics alone. An unequal distribution of the sexes in the working force of the kolkhozy, for example, has been a serious impediment in creating a sound basis for the collective farm as a social and economic unit. In most kolkhozy, men are dominant in administrative positions and women in working brigades. Selective migration to urban communities has added to the plight of the village. Even today—as shown by the study of the Kalinin province—boys tend to follow educational interests that guarantee them urban employment, while most girls attend schools that assure them of professional positions in the village. Large-scale underemployment of the rural population (almost one half

of the Soviet population lives in village communities) has been an important dis-
organizing factor in the rural community. Uneven technological development of
agriculture has prevented a more efficient implementation of socialist rural designs.
Only one tenth of the total agricultural production has been fully mechanized; most
of the work is still done by primitive manual techniques. Frequent organizational
mutations—particularly in the administrative network that connects the kolkhoz
with the government—have been a constant source of managerial confusion, institu-
tional ambivalence, and, in general, rural alienation.

Soviet ethnography shows conclusively that the structural changes in the
countryside have not produced corresponding changes in the psychological make up
of kolkhozniks. On ideological grounds, the ethnographers endorse Khrushchev's
statement that "the [psychological] survivals of the past are a dreadful force—a
nightmare which presses heavily on human minds," and continues "to have deep
roots in the way of life and in the consciousness of the millions of people long after
the disappearance of the economic conditions responsible for their emergence."

Soviet ethnographic studies provide particularly rich descriptions of the
growth of new folkways and mores in the rural community which stand as a buffer
between the peasant and the state and between rural traditionalism and the Soviet
designs for the urbanization of the rural community. Many spontaneous customs,
tightly woven into the rich fabric of rural tradition, emerge for every "socialist custom," sanctioned by the authorities and sanctified by "Soviet ethics." However, the
changes in the family structure, the urbanization of leisure, the spread of education
and reading habits, the organization of work, and the modernization of technology
testify to a gradual disappearance of peasant culture and the growing domination of
the urban way of life. Kolkhoz ethnography is primarily a study of the transformation of the Soviet *peasant*—to whom agriculture is not only an economic pursuit but
also a way of life, a total culture—into a modern *farmer* (of a socialist variety) to
whom agriculture is essentially an occupation anchored to urban culture. The slow-
ness of this transformation has been responsible for the richness and the diversity
of empirical material gathered and examined by Soviet ethnographers.

The present work of Stephen and Ethel Dunn shows the great value of Soviet
ethnographic material when it is carefully and critically processed in the light of
modern anthropological theory. The authors have adduced ample evidence to show
how the sweeping socialist designs are remolded to fit the unique cultural traditions
of the countryside of Central Russia. They have been singularly successful in pointing
out and dissecting the complexities and intricacies of the local implementation of
socialist designs. In Raymond Firth's terminology, they have shown both the fine
details and principles of the social *structure,* which remains stable over a relatively
long period of time, and the social *organization,* which reflects the daily contingen-
cies and produces new modes of behavior. The Dunns have stripped the Soviet theory of "psychological lag" of its ideological overtones and have shown that many
of the so-called psychological survivals of the *ancien regime* have actually been bred
by the Soviet system.

In utilizing the inexhaustible cultural data supplied by Soviet ethnography,
the Dunns have carefully avoided the pitfalls of the doctrinal commitments of the

Soviet theory of culture change, that combine the elements of nineteenth century evolutionism with historical materialism. This theory supplies Soviet ethnographers with two ideological doctrines: one placing Soviet society at the highest point in the upward development of universal culture and the second regarding economic and technological developments as pure indices of cultural advancement. The first doctrine eliminates all considerations of cultural relativity from the thinking of Soviet ethnographers, who judge cultures not in terms of their intrinsic value patterns and individualities but in terms of the position they occupy on the grand line of cultural evolution. The second doctrine prevents Soviet ethnographers from doing any work in ethnopsychology. Using their own society as an example, they operate on the assumption that since social structure (and its dominant values) may change faster than personality, the latter is not necessarily a reliable reflection of the existing culture. Despite their awareness of the importance of theory, Soviet ethnographers make no effort to elucidate or refine such basic concepts of cultural change as "acculturation," "assimilation," and "urbanization." It is to the Dunns' credit that they have tried to cast the empirical data provided by Soviet ethnographers into the modern concepts of culture change.

ALEXANDER VUCINICH

Urbana, Illinois
December 1966

Contents

THE PEASANTS OF CENTRAL RUSSIA

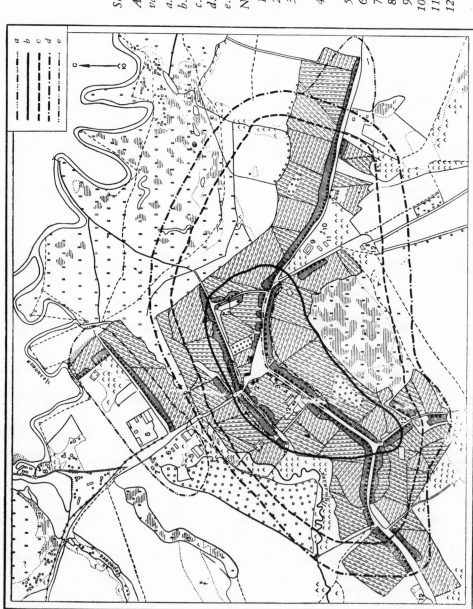

Sketch Map of Viriatino
Approximate boundaries at various times:

a. mid-nineteenth century
b. 1880
c. 1900
d. before 1917
e. after 1917.

Numbered locations:

1. *club-house*
2. *school*
3. *headquarters of village Soviet*
4. *offices of the "Path of Lenin" kolkhoz*
5. *animal-husbandry farm*
6. *hay barn*
7. *brickyard*
8. *hydroelectric station*
9. *garage*
10. *smithy*
11. *drying yard*
12. *brigade headquarters*

Introduction

THE STUDY that follows describes the present-day culture of the peasants of Central Great Russia. It has been reconstructed from Soviet ethnographic and other sources and from the accounts of a few Western travelers and scholars in such special fields as demography and economics. Geographically, the account embraces an area running from Novgorod Oblast in the north to the border of the Ukraine in the south, and from Smolensk Oblast in the west to the Volga in the east. The term Central Russia is used in an ethnic and historical sense rather than a strictly geographical one. It is intended to include those areas which are occupied predominantly by Great Russians and have been more or less so occupied throughout history. In other words, we omit regions such as the east bank of the Volga, the Urals, the Kuban, and Siberia which were colonized by Russians during the Middle Ages or later.

The account is dynamic. That is, it describes the changes that have taken place and are now taking place in Central Russian peasant culture, and it focuses on the factors which are determining the force and direction of these changes.

Every culture, and every cultural process, is at one and the same time the result of certain unique historical factors—the combination of which has not occurred before and probably will not occur again—and an exemplar of certain laws of development, which apply universally given similar conditions. This remains true even though at any moment the laws of development may be perceived incorrectly or not at all. The peasant culture of Central Russia is no exception to this general rule. We find that the same problems arise in this area as in many other parts of the world where similar processes—let us call them, for the sake of convenience, industrialization, urbanization, and secularization—are taking place. We also find that the solutions to these problems are affected by unique historical and ecological factors.

Apart from the scientific problems which are inescapable in a work of this kind, we had an additional problem because this study, unlike the others in this series, is based on secondary sources rather than on firsthand field data. These secondary sources (mostly in Russian) have their own built-in biases, some of which are

1

frankly stated by the authors, while others are implicit and even unconscious. In drawing conclusions from this sort of secondary evidence, we made allowances for both types of bias, insofar as our knowledge permitted us to do so. We also specify the points at which, and the manner in which, our own approach differs from that of the authors whose works we used.

Concepts Used and Their Derivation

By referring in our title to the peasants of Central Russia, we have already raised one basic question: What do we mean by a peasant? The usual image of the peasant is that of a person of little or no education and rude manners, who makes his living by agriculture and resides far from the centers of culture and population. Certainly not all of the people mentioned in this study would fit this definition. Fortunately, social science provides another concept of the peasant which is more precise and more widely applicable. According to this definition, the peasant is a person who lives on the outskirts of an economically complex, politically-organized society, with a corresponding highly developed culture, and participates in both of these, albeit in a limited fashion. Economically, he is specialized in farming (on a wholly or partially subsistence basis), fishing, hunting, handicrafts or combinations of these, usually with little or no mechanization. He is thus intermediate between the primitive tribesman and the modern city-dweller, possessing characteristics of both. Like the tribesman, he lives from day to day in a face-to-face society—that is, one where he personally knows and is known to everyone with whom he ordinarily comes into contact, and where the standards which govern his behavior are set (at least in large part and over considerable areas of social life) by tradition and tacit consent rather than by formal statute and regulation. Unlike the tribesman and like the city-dweller, he participates in a whole, larger than the face-to-face society in which he lives, and conducts at least part of his economic and social life in terms of cash and in accordance with formal regulations. It is evident that the peasant is a man in transition, in a way in which the tribesman is not. He feels the influence of the larger culture, whose elements are diffused to him through a screen made up of geographical, economic, and social (class) factors. This screen filters out certain elements completely (for instance, academic philosophy or complex musical forms) and lets others seep through after varying delays and in more or less simplified forms—for instance, urban modes of dress, specific dances, songs and stories, and innovations in technology or religion.[1]

In modern times, the peasant is in transition in still another sense. Not only does he feel the influence of the larger urban culture in various specified ways, but

---

[1] Of course, each individual's own personal screen determines the factors in his culture of which he will be aware, and which ones will remain foreign to him. However, when the screens of many people coincide in large part—that is, when a group is cut off by social, ethnic, or other factors from full participation in the culture within which it is located—they show one of the important characteristics of peasants, and may show others as well. In fact, when an urban group is cut off from full cultural participation—for example, the inhabitants of the former ghetto in Rome (Dunn 1959, 1960), of New York's Harlem, or of the Jewish quarters of North African cities (Briggs and Guède 1964) it may be spoken of, though with qualifications and somewhat paradoxically, as an urban peasantry.

he is increasingly coming to resemble the city-dweller. That is, the points at which the urban culture touches his life are increasing in number, and the contact is growing more intense. It is with this process that we are largely concerned in this study. Obviously, the Russian peasant of the early 1920s, as described by Fenomenov (1925), differed from his descendants who live in the same places now, just as he differed from his ancestors who lived in those same places before the abolition of serfdom. Nevertheless, the culture of all three exhibits certain continuities and common elements (Soviet writers call them "survivals") which form the second main concern of this study. This is why, at this time of writing, we continue to call the rural inhabitant of Central Russia a peasant. His contact with the larger society and culture in which he participates is still subject to screening even though the screen is less dense than it was for his father and grandfather and operates in different ways.

The Folk Institutions

Later in this study we speak of folk institutions. By these we mean those institutions which express the values and regulate the affairs of the face-to-face community, as distinct from those which express the values of the larger society and transmit its influence to the face-to-face community. Folk institutions in the Russian context would thus include the family and (historically) the *skhod,* or gathering of heads of families in a village, as well as, in another sense, the ceremonial cycle that centers on marriage. Other institutions, such as the school, the local Communist Party unit, the kolkhoz or *sovkhoz,* and the local government structure, with its decision-making processes and allocation of responsibility, are not folk institutions, although some of them may be in process of becoming so. This process is one of the main focuses of our study.

Finally, our study makes use of an important distinction which applies particularly to "developing" societies and nations. The changes which we observed in the Great Russian context and in many others can be divided into two categories: "culture change," meaning change in the economic base of the culture and the fundamental structure of the society, accompanied by shifts in the people's values and in the direction in which the culture is moving; and "cultural development," meaning an increase in the total number of elements present in the culture and a rise in the average standard of living, without major shifts in values or direction. This distinction is in many cases partly a matter of degree but is nonetheless useful for that reason. To illustrate: when an agricultural society becomes industrialized, culture change takes place. In order to adapt to their new way of life, the people must reorganize themselves and adopt new goals and methods of attaining them. However, when industry already established becomes stronger and takes on greater scope and variety, it becomes a case of cultural development. It is therefore a most important and complex empirical problem to discover at what precise point a change in degree becomes a change in kind. We find that within the area we studied, there were wide variations in degree of industrialization and that these variations obtained even before the beginning of this century—that is, before the beginning of the present stage of development.

These are the concepts we use to explain and interpret the data we obtained from the Soviet sources. It must be kept in mind that they differ in some cases from the explanatory concepts used by the authors of the sources themselves. In setting out to deal with Soviet data, we step into a maze; there are, inevitably, many unknown quantities and gaps in our information, and many matters which would be obvious in other contexts become extremely puzzling.

If we take the Russian case as an instance of national development, we are confronted with specific and unique circumstances in the realms of economics, ideology, and culture itself. These circumstances limit the choices open to the regime and help to determine in each case how the choice will go and what the result will be. Furthermore, the Russian peasant as he is today—what he wears, what he eats, the implements he uses and works with, the way he behaves, and even what he thinks—is obviously the product of the interplay of these factors. We have tried to demonstrate that when certain choices are made in terms of economic development, certain results (making allowances for the peculiarities of the cultural and historical context) may be safely predicted. In order to make this demonstration, we have had to deal in some detail with the economics of Soviet collective farming, the procedures for setting goals and assessing results on individual farms, and other matters not usually discussed in anthropological texts. This is because the conditions under which the interplay of economic factors, ideology, and original peasant culture takes place are set by an overarching politicoeconomic structure, with its own assumptions and requirements, of which the Russian peasant himself is only one component part. Finally, though it may seem hardly worth emphasizing, international events—in the form of two world wars and a continuing climate of tension and competition—have not left the Russian peasant untouched either, since they set the conditions under which the over-all structure operates. Our study attempts to weigh all these factors and work them into an understandable equation, although, by virtue of the nature of the data and the present stage of development of social science, it can only be an approximate one.

Russia as an Underdeveloped Country

Prerevolutionary Russia was a classical example of what we would today call an underdeveloped country. The population in 1913 was 82 percent rural, and only 9 percent of those gainfully employed were working in industry (large- or small-scale) or in construction. Industry had been developing at a rapid rate, particularly since the abolition of serfdom in 1861, but it was still very unevenly distributed and primitively equipped. This fact applied particularly to heavy industry. More important, the changes in social structure which usually accompany industrialization had not kept pace with the process itself, and indeed were being artificially held back in many cases. Political power was largely in the hands of a landowning aristocracy, and the rising middle class had not attained recognition or political influence in proportion to its economic capabilities.

Furthermore, mechanization in agriculture was almost nonexistent (except on a few estates owned by wealthy nobles and on a few peasant holdings). There was some attempt to purchase machines collectively by groups of peasants, but in general the system of landholding (in small strips which were redistributed every few years) precluded their efficient use, and productivity per man-hour was generally low. If we bear in mind, in addition to this, the fact that a large part of the land area of Russia is located above 60 degrees N, and that there is a correspondingly short growing season, we can easily see the reason for the chronic shortages and periodic famines that plagued the economy.

The situation we have just sketched presented the Soviet government, at its accession to power in 1917, with several urgent problems—besides the more familiar one of retaining control of the country. An industrial base had to be set up within a relatively short time and, simultaneously, agricultural productivity had to increase sufficiently to provide food for the workers who were to staff the new industry. It is in terms of these objectives—and their accompanying necessities—that we must interpret most of the changes that have taken place since 1917.

The Marxist Ideology: Worker and Peasant

These objectives and necessities are common to many or most underdeveloped countries now and in the past. The Russian case, however, presents certain special features. For one thing, the development program was undertaken in the name of a specifically revolutionary ideology, which included doctrines relating to the proper locus of political power and to the course of past and future history. Secondly, the program was implemented in an area with a strongly centralist political tradition, which the Revolution did not alter, although for a time it appeared that it might do so. The ideology had important effects both on what actually took place and on the way these events were later reported. The aspect of the ideology which concerns us most at this point in both of these respects is its doctrine relating to the nature and mechanisms of social progress. In particular, the doctrine of Marx as elaborated by Lenin holds that revolutionary movements are brought about by the proletariat, which is the spearhead of progressive social change, and whose interests the Revolution mainly serves. In contrast to the proletariat, the peasantry plays an ambivalent role. The peasant is at one and the same time a laboring man exploited by the capitalists, and (usually and to some degree) an owner of property. Characteristically, his interests are divided, and he must go through a process of re-education before he can become a true revolutionary. The industrial worker, on the other hand, occupies this position from the very beginning by virtue of his personal experience.

This ambivalent approach to the peasant was reflected in the classical ideological statements of Soviet communism, which nearly always spoke in terms of two allied or cooperating classes—workers and peasants—but at the same time always gave primacy to the workers.[2] This may be a reflection of the presence in prerevolutionary Russia of a well-developed populist ideology, the proponents of which (*Narodniks,* from Russian *narod,* "people") held that the revolutionary movement

---

[2] The terminology of the Revolution in the early period also defined the organs of government as belonging to workers and peasants, although more recently this pairing has been superceded by the term "laboring people" (Russian: *trudiashchiesia*), which covers the whole population.

which would transform Russian society would come from the peasantry. The Russian Marxists, including Lenin in his early writings, engaged in sharp and prolonged debate with the *Narodniks,* and their own views were partially formed in this process. Here we have an example of the effect of a unique historical circumstance on a general or widespread process.

The ideological insistence on the primacy of the proletariat has had its effect on Soviet writing in the social sciences. Until a short time ago it was mandatory, in discussing culture change among the peasantry, to emphasize the role of the worker and the effect on the culture of the seasonal migrant laborer (usually in mines or factories), which is still common for peasants in many parts of the Soviet Union. By the same token, it might be dangerous to call attention to the converse—the effect of peasant culture on the lives of workers who until recently were peasants. Even though the primacy of the proletariat is no longer insisted upon as a point of doctrine at every available opportunity, Soviet studies of culture change still tend to be written from this point of view. For most of the Soviet social scientists now active, this is one of those biases which have become almost unconscious—just as it is natural for many Western anthropologists to consider the isolated primitive tribe as the fundamental human group and to describe all other groups in terms of their departure from this ideal type.

It can be justifiably contended that the ideological point we have been discussing is only a pretext for a policy which had to be adopted for other reasons— that of sacrificing agriculture and the standard of living of the population, particularly the rural population, to the development of heavy industry. Nevertheless, ideological insistence on the primacy of the proletariat had two important results. One of these, in the field of social-science theory, we have already dealt with. The other, in the practical world, was to create an order of prestige or status in which the urban worker ranked consistently above the peasant. This in turn created a selective drain of population toward the cities which is being felt today as intensely as ever. This is one of the most prominent features of the Russian rural scene, and currently one of those most disturbing to the regime.

The goal, in ideological terms, toward which the Soviet regime describes itself as working, is that of industrializing agriculture and wiping out all differences between city and countryside. This goal is consonant with a worldwide process to which all peasant societies are subject to degrees and in forms that depend on the policy of the central government: on the population pressure, on the climate, on the presence or absence of foreign intervention, and on the peculiarities of the original peasant culture.

In the Russian case, as we have indicated and will describe later in more detail, some of the measures adopted by the regime are contrary to the stated goal. In other words, the process of culture change within the countryside is being held back. This introduces yet a futher complication into our discussion, and at the same time points up its relevance for other parts of the world.

We can now pass to a detailed exposition of Great Russian peasant culture as it has developed historically and as it now exists.

$$\boxed{1}$$

Geography and History

I N BROAD GEOGRAPHICAL TERMS, the area with which this study will deal [see frontispiece map] constitutes a portion of the Russian or East European Plain, which occupies the greater part of eastern Europe to an extent of about 4 million square kilometers. The plain is bounded in the south by the Carpathian Mountains, the Crimean peninsula, the Black Sea, the Caucasus Mountains, and the Caspian Sea; in the east by the Ural River valley and the Ural Mountains. Geologically, the plain is a fairly even platform, broken in places by mountain ranges and upland areas, generally running north and south. Of these, one of the most prominent is the Central Russian upland, which covers much of the region with which we are directly concerned. This upland is a heavily dissected loess-covered plateau, cut through by numerous ravines, some still in the process of development. Its average elevation is 230–250 meters above sea level, but at some points, particularly near Tula, it reaches 290 meters. The northern part of the region is dotted with many lakes and is heavily glacial in structure, marked by moraines or piles of rocks pushed aside by glaciers in their progress.

The climate is continental, with a long and relatively cold winter and a hot summer. Mean temperature in January varies between −20° and 0° C, and in July between 15° and 20° C. Winter precipitation is 150–200 millimeters from November to March, and summer precipitation averages 300–500 millimeters from April to October. These average figures do not reflect the actual situation as the peasant faces it, however, because both temperature and rainfall are subject to wide fluctuations from place to place and from year to year.

The dominant soils in the area are of the relatively infertile, turf-podzol type; gray in color and clayey or sandy. At a few points in the south—particularly near Tambov—there are pockets of the much more fertile *chernozen* or black-earth soils, which make the Ukraine the main granary of the Soviet Union. Prehistorically and until fairly recent times, most of the area was forested, and remnants of this virgin forest persist in some places. Other districts are swampy or poorly drained, and require extensive reclamation to make them agriculturally productive.

7

Prehistoric and Early Historic Times

During the Neolithic era (2500–1000 B.C. depending on the spot being considered) the area with which we are concerned was inhabited by a large group of tribes belonging to what until recently was called the "pit-comb ware culture," from the distinctive decoration of its pottery. In the past few years, a number of separate cultures have been distinguished within this general category. Most of the earliest settlements were located on or near lakes and rivers and averaged 20–30 inhabitants. The economy was of the hunting-and-gathering type, and no significant traces of agriculture have been found.

With the development of metal-smelting and agriculture, the economy and the pattern of settlement changed character. The most typical sites of the Early Iron Age are the Dyakovo hill-forts, so named after the one first excavated near Moscow. These were rather extensive settlements, usually located on high ground and surrounded by moats and earthworks for defense against intruders. From within these protective enclosures, the inhabitants went out to tend their fields and flocks. This settlement pattern persisted until early historical times and conditioned the political structure of the area. Each settlement was largely autonomous and the most active political unit was a loose confederation or defensive alliance made up of several settlements within a single area, such as a river valley or part of one. It is possible that this type of settlement influenced the later village pattern, where the houses are clumped together or spread along a relatively short span of a road, while the fields cultivated by the villagers spread out in concentric rings from the village itself.

Land Tenure and Social Organization before the Reform of 1861

As the Russian state became increasingly centralized after throwing off the Tatar yoke (1547–1796), many peasants, who originally had been freeholding farmers, were gradually converted into serfs. As such, they owed various feudal dues in kind and in labor to the landowners and were subject to the juridical authority of the latter in varying degrees. This sometimes extended to the power of life and death. In theory, feudal estates were granted by the Crown in consideration of military or civil service. In practice, however, this requirement was often evaded.

Serfdom prevailed chiefly in the Central Russian provinces. In certain other parts of the empire, it did not take firm hold because (as in the northern forested regions) the land was not suited to agricultural purposes, or because (as in the valley of the Don) the land was settled later, chiefly by runaway serfs themselves. This applies to the huge Siberian territory where, generally speaking, feudal holdings did not exist.

Another widespread category of peasants existed in places where serfdom had not penetrated, and intermingled with the serf populations in the central provinces. This category consisted of so-called state peasants, who were directly dependent on the tsar as their feudal lord. They paid various taxes and fees to the state treasury, and were liable to military service and various forms of compulsory labor —maintenance of roads, and so on. The state peasants did not owe feudal dues to the local landowner, however, and their social position was somewhat different from that of the serfs, or landlord peasants.

Historically, from about 1000 A.D., the basic form of land tenure and social organization among peasants in the central provinces was the *mir* or peasant commune. The *mir* consisted of a group of households, each of which had the right by virtue of its membership to hold plots of land in various categories (crop land, pasture, hay field, forest lot, and so on). Tenure was vested in the *mir* as a whole, however, and the land was subject to periodic redistribution among the constituent households. The *mir* was governed by an assembly composed of all heads of households, usually adult males. The assembly was known as the *skhod,* from the verb *skhodit'*, meaning to come together. Through its agent, the *starosta* (literally "elder"), the *skhod* conducted all transactions with individuals (or other social units) and with the state on behalf of its members. The *skhod* was responsible also for the collection of certain taxes from *mir* members and for their fulfillment of military and other obligations. It is interesting to note that frequently, in villages where both serfs and state peasants lived, or where the land and population of a village were divided between two different landlords, two separate *mirs* functioned side by side. In spite of the fact that their fields often interspersed, the *mirs* often conducted their affairs according to different rules. Intermarriage was infrequent.

In terms of political structure, feudal Russia was a state based on "estates," or formal social categories in which membership was hereditary. A person could pass from one category to another only under exceptional circumstances or by the payment of large fees. The Russian serf was attached to the land that he farmed, as were the serfs in medieval western Europe, and did not have the right to move elsewhere. If a serf disappeared, the *mir* to which he belonged could be held collectively responsible. There was nevertheless considerable population movement; the peasants resorted to various subterfuges in order to achieve change of status without going through the prescribed procedures. State peasants, on the other hand, were not attached to the land, but their movements were controlled by a system of internal passports. The passports were issued by local authorities only with the consent of the *mir,* because the absenting person's obligations had to be assumed either by the *mir* collectively or by some specified individual. If a state peasant wished to change his residence permanently, he usually had to find someone who would buy his house, and his equipment and land allotment, and who would also assume his place and obligations in the *mir*.

In many parts of Central Russia, because of poor soil and rigorous climate, agriculture could not sustain life, and most of the peasants had to combine farming with various other trades and occupations. These included weaving, wood-working, pottery, basketry, metal-work, and such home industries, as well as lumbering, mining, hauling freight with horses or barges, and droving. At a later stage many peasants took migrant-laborer jobs in industry. Peasant women often went into domestic service in nearby cities.

Nonagricultural work away from the peasants' immediate neighborhoods followed in most cases a regular pattern. At the end of the agricultural season in the fall, males from about the age of 17 would set out in groups of eight or ten. They would sometimes go hundreds of miles to factories or mines, work over the winter, and return home in time for the spring sowing. This pattern of seasonal migrant labor is emphasized by most Soviet ethnographers and social historians, who point out its influence on the culture change and on the dissemination of urban ways and new (including revolutionary) ideas in the countryside. There can be no doubt about this, but there are other aspects of the phenomenon. To begin with, it chiefly involved men. Migrant labor by women was neither so widespread nor so strictly seasonal in character. Nor did it usually involve such long journeys. Secondly, male seasonal migrant labor, particularly in mining and the carrying trades, was often carried on through a peculiar social institution called the *artel'*. This was a group made up of a certain number of adult men (often with one or two adolescent boys attached to carry out auxiliary functions) who contracted with each other, and collectively with an employer, to work at a fixed rate in cash and perquisites and to share the proceeds equally. Contracts were concluded by an agent (*artel'shchik*), who acted for the group. All members of the *artel'* performed specific functions; the young boys served as cooks and general helpers. This form of organization was used also in lumbering and fishing operations, although in these cases the *artel'* did not work as a collective employee but as a collective entrepreneur. But the principle of equal division of proceeds still applied.

In this text, the term *artel'* will continue to be used in this narrow sense. During the Soviet period, the same term is applied to the kolkhoz (properly "agricultural *artel'* "), even though it is based on rather different principles, with payment being proportionate to labor performed or degree of skill, rather than equal for all. By and large women were not included in the prerevolutionary *artel'*, although there were special female *artels*. This is another point of difference in the Soviet situation and illustrates the survival of old forms, imbued with new content.

The Emancipation and Its Impact

The immediate and ultimate causes of the emancipation of the serfs, and its direct and indirect effects, constitute a complex topic about which weighty volumes have been written. For our purposes here it will perhaps be enough to remember that the formal change in the serfs' status was not accompanied by any proportionate expropriation of land from the landlords. The latter kept title to portions of their estates, including much of the best land, and rented out agricultural fields as well as pasture and lumbering rights. The collective tenant in many cases was the *mir*, which also purchased outright many lands that had been part of estates. In either event, the charges were assessed by the *mir* to its members on a share basis. This meant that the traditional social structure of the village was left intact, and the *mir* was in fact strengthened by these additional functions.

From a historical point of view, the Emancipation's main impact lay in its removal of some of the formal barriers to population movement and hence to industrialization. Emancipation was followed in many places by a large and rapid increase in seasonal migrant labor and in local industry, and finally, in population. These factors brought about growing social stratification in the countryside and sharply accelerated the pace of culture change in general. The data given by Shingarev (1907) go far toward explaining the inevitability of the revolutionary movement and the form it took. The author describes and compares two villages in Voronezh Uyezd where, for lack of land, the peasants were compelled to engage in seasonal migrant labor, either in Voronezh itself (in which case the migrants did not bother to obtain passports, since they were away only for short periods), or—in the case of the other village—at more distant points. The migrants tried to be home in time for St. Michael's Day (November 8, Old Style, October 25th by our calendar), and this of course influenced the pattern of births. The prolonged absence of males also depressed the rate of natural increase (the number of births minus the number of deaths within a given period) well below that which obtained for the Uyezd, the Gubernia, or European Russia as a whole. Malnutrition was endemic, particularly among landless families and those without male heads of household. The latter category, though small, lacked both cabbage and milk—the presumed staples of the Russian peasant's diet. Shingarev describes "pockets of poverty" in a situation where there were almost more pockets than coat.

Peasant Customary Law and Legislation before and during the Stolypin Land Reforms

Historically, the social unit next below the *mir* or the village in Central Russia was the peasant household. In formal terms, the household was composed of a group of related persons who lived and worked together, held property, and contracted legal obligations as a unit. The details of the household's legal status and structure varied from place to place, but generally the head of the household would contract obligations and attend to other business as agent for the household as a whole. By legal decisions following the 1861 reforms, the principle of family ownership was explicitly applied to both land and movable property. The only conditions under which an individual right of ownership was recognized were those in which the household was divided and two or more new households were set up. In such cases, each member of the family received a proportionate share of the property, either as such or in cash. Property fell into two categories which were handled differently in terms of customary law. The first category included land (either as private property of the household or in the form of rights or shares in land held by the *mir*), livestock, farm and craft equipment, agricultural produce, and cash and produce earned by the male members of the household for nonagricultural work. This category of property was held in common by the household and was not subject to inheritance (the household as a corporate entity survived the death of any of its members), but was apportioned equally when a household divided. The second property category consisted of clothing, bedding, household utensils and cash that the women earned from specifically feminine activities, such as selling eggs and mushrooms and handicrafts. Property of this kind was subject to inheritance in the distaff line, and was not divided when households split up. The conceptual dichotomy implied by these two forms of property inheritance survives in Central Russian peasant practice to this day.

Contrary to what one might expect, the solidarity of the peasant household commune was if anything strengthened by legal development following Emancipation.[1] On March 4, 1906, the tsarist government issued the first of a series of decrees, intended as a frontal attack on the system of communal landholding, in an effort to make over the entire agrarian situation. This legislation is usually referred to as the Stolypin Land Reforms, after Peter Stolypin, the then prime minister.

The ostensible aim of the Stolypin land reforms was to make it easier for needy peasants to buy land on easy terms. This was to be done by allowing the peasant either to sell his share in the *mir* holdings and move elsewhere to a new homestead, or to obtain a single integral plot somewhere on the *mir* lands in exchange for the scattered strips which he held as a member of the *mir*. In practice, almost all of the land was sold to the wealthier peasants. The land reforms were not compulsory; what they actually did was set up a mechanism whereby the peasants could apply for land or resettlement. Actual operations were then carried out by local land commissions on the basis of applications. As a result, the program was characterized in its later stages not so much by the formation of *khutors* (isolated private farmsteads, each containing the owner's dwelling) and *otrubs* (consolidated plots on the outskirts of the villages, with the owner's dwelling remaining in the village), as by the so-called group settlements, in which large villages were broken up into small ones and a large part of the land left in collective ownership. "The reforms had begun as an attempt to hasten what was assumed to be the inevitable dissolution of the peasant communities, but had evolved instead into a means for preserving them by modernizing their economic organization." (Yaney 1964:286)

Another aspect of the Stolypin reforms, as significant as their effect on land tenure, was their modification of the customary law, and in particular, of the relationship between the *mir* and the individual. Specifically, a series of decrees in late 1906 (at the very beginning of the reforms) took away the right of the head of the household to restrict the movements of its members,[2] or to veto any division within the household, and ended family tenure of land not held by virtue of membership in the *mir*. In effect, it finally abolished the household as a property-holding unit by declaring that all household property belonged to its head. The provisions of the Stolypin reforms, with regard to property and the constitution of the household, thus run directly counter to Russian peasant customary law as it had developed historically (Shinn 1961).

Before leaving the prerevolutionary situation, we should note that there were many attempts to bring about social improvements in the fields of agriculture, public education, and public health, by the so-called *zemstvos* and (in the case of agriculture) by peasant societies of the cooperative type. The *zemstvos* were, in principle, representative bodies which were entrusted with local functions—maintaining roads, medical service, schools and libraries, and providing agricultural help —according to a statute of January 1, 1864. In order to finance these activities, the *zemstvos* were empowered to collect a property tax, but otherwise they were not

---

[1] For further details, see the exposition by Shinn (1961), which gives full reference to the original sources.

[2] Previously (by the internal passport statute of 1894), no passport could be issued to anyone without the express consent of the head of his household, and no one could leave the village, even temporarily, without a passport.

directly connected with the central government. The history of the *zemstvos* as described by Vucinich (1960) illustrates the dilemma of the tsarist regime, which wished—or at least some of its representatives did—to grant a degree of local autonomy, and yet prevented this autonomy from operating effectively and achieving the purposes for which it had presumably been set up. A survey carried out by the Council of the All-Russian Congress of Old Believers (*Sovet vserossiiskikh s"ezdov Staroobriadtsev 1910*) is prefaced by remarks indicating that agricultural help by the *zemstvos* was spotty; only in a few localities, such as Penza, did the service operate in a modern, reasonably efficient way. The *zemstvos*, too, opened the first stores in the villages for the sale of agricultural equipment. The store in Penza had sold 185,000 rubles worth of agricultural equipment in 1907 and in 1909 expected the figure to rise to 250,000. A store in Tambov had been established in 1894 with a modest 2000 rubles and by 1900 had sold more than 98,000 rubles worth of equipment (Cheremenskii 1961:163). These figures are interesting when compared with Soviet efforts both early and late. As we will see later, the dilemma of the prerevolutionary *zemstvos* applies in more recent times to the local soviets, to which the Soviet regime is obviously trying to give a more vigorous and autonomous role in government. This effort is retarded, as it was with the *zemstvos*, by a traditional centralizing tendency and an ingrained suspicion of anything that seems to dilute authority.

Besides the *zemstvos*, there were a large number of credit societies and producers' cooperatives which procured agricultural machinery and marketed produce. These are defined by Soviet authors as capitalistic since they required an entrance fee and, in general, were open only to the wealthier peasants. Nevertheless, they enjoyed a steady though not spectacular growth before the Revolution, and were encouraged during the 1920s by the Soviet regime (Anokhina and Shmeleva 1964:26–29).

From Revolution to Collectivization

The Revolution of 1917 supervened after a long war that had left many peasant households without male workers. By the 1917 census, in Morshansk Uyezd of Tambov Gubernia, 38,580 peasant men had been called to the colors, and more than 6000 others had been drafted for work in the Donbas mines. As a result, 24,138 households were left completely without male workers and thus were unable to cultivate their lands, even when they had working livestock (Kushner, ed. 1958:42–43). This situation persisted in varying degrees (depending on the exact period and on the exact part of the country) until the end of the civil war in 1922. A few years later, the Russian countryside was overtaken by the large-scale disturbances attending collectivization, and these were hardly over when World War II broke out. All in all, it might be said that a normal situation (in terms of the availability of labor, capital, and stable social conditions) did not exist in the Russian countryside until the middle 1950s. This must always be kept in mind when considering the cultural changes brought about by the new system and the conditions under which people have lived for the past 50 years.

The regime which ultimately took power as a result of the 1917 Revolution was committed to a radical agrarian reform. The initial decree on land adopted by the second All-Russian Congress of Soviets (November 7, 1917) abolished all private land holdings and, without compensation, turned over to the peasants all private estates, lands allotted to individuals by the tsarist government, and monastery and church lands, with their movable and immovable equipment and buildings. All rentals were cancelled. In general, the principle was established at this time that only laboring tenure of land was to be permitted—that is, a person was allowed to hold land, provided he worked it himself, alone or with the help of his family. We shall see a little later how this radical reform worked out in practice.

The Soviet land reforms were carried out through the agency of so-called *Kombedy*, (Committees of the Poor), which received legal sanction by a decree of June 11, 1918, although they had actually been in operation for some time. During this early period, not all *Kombedy* were under the authority of the central government or acted in accord with its policies. For example, Fenomenov (1925:II,35) cites the case of a chairman of a *Kombed* (by no means a rich man) who, in 1919, swung a decision of the local land commission in favor of one of the wealthy peasants in the village and against the middle peasants who wished to take over the latter's land. The *Kombed* chairman apparently was not penalized for this action. This illustrates the strain to which central government policy was subject on the spot. Formal authority in questions of land belonged to the local land commission, but this body usually was guided by the opinions and desires of the village *skhod*. According to Fenomenov, the opinions were formed with little reference to ideology or formal policy—family connections and personal interests were much more important.

The three main tasks of the regime in the countryside at this period were (1) to establish and maintain political control, (2) to feed the cities and supply sufficient labor to restore and expand industrial production, and (3) to alter the social structure by increasing the proportion of middle peasants (*seredniaks*) at the expense of the wealthy peasants (*kulaks*) and the poorest ones (*bedniaks*).[3] To this end, the *kulaks'* land, produce, and equipment were confiscated and turned over to the other two categories. The regime tried to exercise care not to offend the *seredniaks* in any way, although there were individual cases where the distinguishing criteria were disregarded or incorrectly applied. In this early period, there were some attempts to establish collective farms of various types—chiefly the simplest, the so-called "society for joint working of land" (*toz*)—but no concerted drive in comparison to the period of mass collectivization.

Land and Agriculture

Fenomenov's detailed study (1925) yields a fairly concrete conception of the situation between the Soviet land reform and collectivization in one Russian

---

[3] The criteria for distinguishing these categories of peasants varied but, generally speaking, the *kulak* was a person who employed hired labor for his farm work or who owned, besides the farm, an enterprise such as a mill or a lumberyard which employed hired labor. The *seredniak,* typically, owned his farm and worked it without hired labor, supporting his family on what he himself produced. Finally, the *bedniak* was unable to do even this, for lack of land or livestock or both, and in most cases had to hire himself out as a laborer.

village. We will therefore summarize here some aspects of what he has to say, leaving others (chiefly material culture) for later consideration. It must be pointed out at the beginning that the situation which Fenomenov describes is quite specific and in certain ways atypical. For one thing, his village is farther north than any other locality which will be considered in this study. Special conditions—the poor quality of the soil and the impossibility of supporting life by agriculture alone—had created, even before the Revolution, a kind of semi-industrialized peasantry. The same thing is true to a lesser degree in other areas, such as Kalinin Oblast. But in the village of Gadyshi, which Fenomenov studied, wage labor took on a somewhat different character than it had in more southerly locations. Because of the closeness of large lumbering operations, extensive seasonal migrations for work were not necessary, and the men were therefore not removed from the influence of the village environment for long periods of the year.

The village of Gadyshi differed markedly in external appearance from the usual village of the more southerly districts. Instead of one-story huts with thatched roofs, there were one- and two-story timbered houses most of them containing several rooms, with the ground level used for storage. Eighty-two such houses or, more accurately, dwelling complexes (*dvors*), were strung out over more than a *verst* (0.66 mile) in length. Fenomenov's sketch-map shows a typical "line village," with houses on both sides of the main street and colonies or hamlets somewhat removed from the "old village" in the center. The main village street ran east and west, and the houses at the western end of the village go up all the way to the steep, constantly eroded bank of the river. At the eastern end, there is a wooden bridge across the river (which forms an arc, intersected by the main street).

Prior to Emancipation, the inhabitants of the village were serfs belonging to two landed estates, that of the Baranov family and that of the Pestrikov family. During the post-Emancipation period, these families sold off most of their lands to a group of merchants from Moscow, who in turn entrusted them to their manager. These two former estates survived in Fenomenov's time as social units, however, residentially separate and having separate *skhods*. The layout of the village is zoned, with most of the houses standing along the street or facing the entrance to the village from the wooden bridge. All of the threshing-floors and other farm buildings are on the outskirts (behind the houses or across the river); and all the bathhouses are on the river bank. At the same time, the holdings of any particular individual are scattered in various parts of the village. One man, for instance, owned a dwelling in the center of the village, a covered threshing-floor across the river next to barns belonging to other people, a bathhouse alongside the river, and three garden plots in widely separated parts of the village. The reasons for this are historical: before Emancipation, the Baranov and Pestrikov families divided between them all the land which was suitable for household plots, and the serfs therefore had to place their dwellings at the edge of the landlord's property and their farm buildings elsewhere. Once established, this pattern persisted, because of the large supply of land and its relatively low value compared to that of buildings, which represent an investment in labor. Any repartition of the land—redrawing of boundaries between the plots allotted to individual households—would require the removal of some building, whereas land as such can be had for the clearing. Fenomenov (1925:I,21) sums up the situation as follows: "But the land here is considered by the peasants as unsuitable for gardening. The tilled portion of the home-stead plot does not exceed 5–10 percent. Consequently, the chief stimulus for ex-pansion of the homestead—the striving toward intensive cultivation—is lacking here. The homestead plot is a place to put up buildings, to dry hay, and only lastly to grow vegetables." This point is extremely significant, since it represents one of the main differences between the northernmost part of our area and the districts to the south. In south Central Russia, land shortage was endemic before the Revolu-tion and for some time afterwards, but this was not the case in Gadyshi and the surrounding districts. This is confirmed by the details of agricultural practice given by Fenomenov. The area in crops is relatively small compared to the still forested area with which it alternates. Agricultural technology is primitive, varying between the three-field system[4] in the fields close to the village and the slash-and-burn sys-tem in the semiwooded areas farther out. In each landholding, the individual peas-ant allotment consisted of three types of fields: winter (rye), spring (barley, oats, and spring wheat—a combination known by the peasants as *zhito*), and fallow. Not all of the allotments, however, were used at any given time. Some were let go because they were too far from the village, or for other reasons. These soon grew up to forest, and after 10 years were burned over and ploughed up. A few har-vests were taken without the peasants' even bothering to remove the tree stumps, and then they were let go once again.

Besides the fields subject to reallotment, there was a certain amount of pur-chased land which had been bought at various times through the *mir*. This was in general farther from the village, and the proportion of uncultivated land grown up to brush and trees was higher in this category than in that of the regular allot-ments.

Cultivation was carried out as follows: only heavy peat soils were ploughed for winter sowing; fallow land was usually ploughed in June. For rye, manure was put down at the rate of 30–35 loads or 500–1000 *puds* per *desiatin,* a quantity which, according to experts, was about one third of what was needed in this area. Potatoes were also fertilized, sometimes by hand. Spring *zhito* and flax were plant-ed in places manured beforehand for rye; oats were considered hardy, and were planted anywhere, usually without fertilization (in any case, no artificial fertilizer was used). The seed was unselected, and was sown broadside by hand, and hence in spots quite thickly. Under these conditions of small-scale strip-farming, it was extremely difficult to determine exactly where the sown area was, and consequently to determine the exact quantity of seed sown. The yield for barley, except in very good years, however, was usually eightfold, for rye fivefold, and for oats four-fold.

For slash-and-burn planting, trees were chopped down in the spring of the year before the crop was to be sown. Large trunks were sawed up and hauled away; small ones were left lying. In the following spring, on a good dry day, the plot was burned over. Afterwards, the ash-covered earth was lightly scratched with a plough, and *zhito* was sown immediately. In the fall, the *zhito* was reaped, and rye

---

[4] Under this system, which was practiced in most of medieval Europe and in parts of Russia up to the Revolution, one crop was planted in winter, one in spring, and one field was left fallow. With a primitive technology, this was the best way to maintain the fertility of the land.

was sown in its place. This process was repeated for a few seasons. Due to the stumps being left in the ground, the use of any complex equipment or of any but the most superficial cultivation, was out of the question. Even in the fields closer to the village, where the stumps had been cleared away, the peasants did not consider deep ploughing to be worthwhile, and Fenomenov comments that given the scant use of fertilizer and the consequent thinness of the topsoil, this was quite true.

The same picture of rather casual and negligent agriculture that we see in the technology can also be found in the social aspects of north Russian farming. Fenomenov says (1925:I, 77): "Men in Gadyshi pay little attention to working the land. The greater part of the field work is done by women. It will happen that the husband who works all the time in the woods does not know how to sow; the wife does the sowing." Under the traditional division of labor, women ploughed and reaped, but men cut the hay. In Fenomenov's time this distinction was beginning to break down, particularly during the harvest period, when with the exception of a few specialized craftsmen, the entire population worked in the fields.

Fenomenov's general comment on agriculture in Gadyshi is as follows (1925:I, 63): "The peasant pettily calculates all the profits and losses; he fears, in any redivision of the land, to lose or relinquish any of the free gifts of nature, because only he is accustomed to count on them. To make the land more valuable by the application of labor and capital is something which the inhabitants of the Novgorod countryside do not know how to do." A similar picture of a primitive agricultural system emerges from the data given by Anokhina and Shmeleva (1964:10–18), who comment that slash-and-burn agriculture was used in some northern parts of Kalinin Oblast even in the late 1920s.

Animal Husbandry

In the Gadyshi area, animal husbandry was relatively more advanced than agriculture. In 1901, the holdings of large stock (cattle and horses) amounted to 68 head for every 100 inhabitants, male and female. This is close to the average for Novgorod Gubernia, while for European Russia as a whole (including the major stock-breeding districts in the southern steppes), the figure was 48 head per 100 population; in the industrial and agricultural districts, it fell considerably below this. In 1920, Gadyshi had 105 cows and 98 horses for 436 inhabitants, yielding a total of 46 head of large stock per 100 inhabitants. This was far below the average for the gubernia, but it represented a crucial situation that was soon overcome.

Both horses and cows were small, and the cows gave little milk—about half of what would be considered normal in the dairy farms of the Moscow area. Horses were put out to pasture with no supervision at all, except that the fields were carefully fenced to prevent them from getting into the grain. They were pastured in the fallow fields all summer, and let into the grain fields after the crop had been harvested.

Cattle were herded communally by a very ancient system, whereby a herdsman was hired by the *mir* and paid at a fixed rate in kind. This rate was calculated in terms of fractions of a "turn"—one day's keep—for each animal in a particular category of stock. In addition, the herdsman was boarded in rotation by all the families owning stock under his care. The archaic nature of the system is under-lined by the many magicoreligious rites which accompany it. Herdsmen were gener-ally regarded as sorcerers, and were expected to perform magical ceremonies for the protection of the herd. Accordingly, they were treated with a certain deference, al-though Fenomenov drily notes that this was partly the result of a perfectly rational fear of what the herdsman could do if he were displeased. Besides the ceremonies performed by the herdsman, each householder and his wife customarily made a cir-cuit of their animals before driving them out to pasture in the spring. The wife carried an icon of St. George, some eggs, and a bundle containing a small loaf of sweet bread (*kulich*) and a cheesecake made with potatoes (*kokorka*). The loaf was given to the neighbors at the end of the ceremony, and the herdsman got the cheesecake and the eggs. The householder carried with him an axe and a stone. As he made the circuit, he knocked the stone against the butt of the axe so that sparks flew. After the stock were driven out to pasture, the stone and the axe were buried in the manure pile beside the gate. The axe (probably because it was the more valuable item) was dug up again after three days, but the stone remained. In this ceremony, we can see a clear survival of the cult of thunder, which was common to the entire Slavic world, and of which variants can be found in the Caucasus to this day. The pagan ritual bears a thin overlay of Christianity, represented by the icon of St. George and the *kulich,* also used at Easter, which, significantly, were entrust-ed to women.

At the time when Fenomenov studied the village, there was an acute short-age of pastureland, due to a sharp but unexplained rise in population (45 percent since 1901). The population increase, together with the steady deterioration of ex-isting hayfields (many of which were producing almost nothing), had brought about a crisis in the livestock economy. Fenomenov felt that this and the other handicaps from which local agriculture suffered could be cured only through a radi-cal reorganization, in which the old communal system of landholding would be broken up and each family given an integral plot with a dwelling. Livestock could then be pastured in what Fenomenov considered a more rational form—tethered grazing and direct feeding of green fodder in summer. Some families already had moved to outlying farmsteads and adopted these methods. But according to Feno-menov, many others refused to move—out of sheer laziness and force of habit.

Nonagricultural Wage Labor and Crafts

A considerable proportion of the time and efforts of Gadyshi peasants was spent in nonagricultural wage labor, chiefly in the lumbering industry. The busiest period for this was in winter, during the agricultural slack season. The supplying of firewood began in November, and went on for as long as hauling by sled was possible. In areas accessible to large rivers or to the railroad, logs were cut and sawed and hauled to the river or the railroad, whichever was nearer. In April they were floated into Lake Shlino and rafted across by means of poles. Some of the wood was floated to the important railroad junction of Vyshnie Volochki. The rest was unloaded from the river at Gadyshi and piled on the bank before being hauled to the railroad. This went on during May, June, and part of July, stopped during

August for the haying and harvesting season, and was resumed at the end of August when special railroad cars were put on to carry the wood.

Before the advent of the local railroad in 1901, the main method of transporting lumber was by raft. This was done by cooperative groups of the *artel'* type, similar to those described earlier in connection with mining and hauling. In lumber transporting, the extrepreneur supplied the ropes, tackle, and other equipment, and the peasants with whom he contracted built and operated the rafts.

At the time of Fenomenov's study, very little rafting was actually done because it was more profitable to haul the lumber overland from Gadyshi. Taking the logs from the river still had to be done, however, and this was dangerous and unhealthy since the loggers had to stand waist-deep at times in the water. The team for this operation consisted of two men, one standing in the river manipulating the logs, and the other operating the chute on the bank, tying up each bundle of logs and readying it to be taken away by a horse.

Earnings from lumber operations for the average Gadyshi peasant family before World War I varied between 140–210 rubles: this represented the cutting and hauling of 20–30 *sagenes* of lumber and the loading of 20–30 railroad cars. The annual total for the village from the turn of the century until World War I came to more than 10,000 rubles, which broke down as follows: 1500 cubic meters of lumber cut and hauled, at four rubles each; 1500 railroad cars loaded at three rubles each. After the Revolution, when lumbering operations were resumed, the total earnings for the village fell to a little more than 1000 rubles, with a maximum of 1160. This figure broke down as follows: 1000 cubic meters sawed and hauled at 60 kopeks each equals 600 rubles; 1000 railroad cars loaded at 10 kopeks each equals 100 rubles (this work was paid for in salt); 2000 cubic meters unloaded from the river at 23 kopeks each equals 460 rubles. Fenomenov does not mince words: "This period has remained in the memory of the peasants as the period of the second serfdom. Work was obligatory; people were compelled by force to load and unload." (Fenomenov 1925:I,144) During the period of "war communism," payment in kind and in devalued paper currency was the rule. In 1922–1923, wages reached 70 percent of the prewar level. This was apparently due to the effect of the New Economic Policy (NEP), which represented a temporary return to capitalist methods and forms of organization in nonessential industries. Fenomenov points out that NEP had the effect of somewhat mitigating the excesses of the "new serfdom." The rich merchants of Gadyshi and their managers could now exploit the labor of their fellow townsmen only in the capacity of independent entrepreneurs under state control, and not as fully empowered agents of the socialist state.

The significance of the data on lumbering operations in Gadyshi lies in the fact that, as Fenomenov notes later, it was the only field in which the village contributed to the wider market. "All the rest it [the village] produces for itself. It may even be said that Gadyshi as a whole exploits to a certain degree the surrounding country." (Fenomenov 1925:I,146–147) The author foresees a further drain of resources away from agriculture into the more profitable forest occupations.

We have now dealt with the two main branches of the economy of this north Russian community. Subsidiary elements in the economy include the gathering of wild produce—mushrooms and various kinds of berries and herbs—and certain home industries, such as the processing of flax and the production of linseed oil. Also, many peasants were skilled handicraft men, but crafts, as such, were poorly developed because they were not sharply divided from other peasant occupations. Fenomenov's census reveals 25 more or less fulltime craftsmen out of a sample total of 442 individuals. The author lists them thus: (7) carpenters, (3) shoemakers, (3) blacksmiths, (2) seamstresses, (3) coopers, (2) cabinet makers, (1) weaver, (1) tailor, (1) maker of *valenki* (felt boots worn in winter), (1)woman fortuneteller, and (1) beggar. The last two are listed as bonafide craftsmen by parallel with the constitution of the medieval town, where both begging and sorcery were recognized crafts; Fenomenov considers the economic order in Gadyshi to be analogous to the medieval. Fifteen of these craftsmen farmed, in addition to their regular trade; only 10 of them had no farms. Fenomenov's "professional census" reveals no priest, lawyer, doctor, midwife, or medical assistant. These absences are significant—some in themselves and others by contrast with the situation in a Western European, British, or American town of the same size. It is clear from other statements of Fenomenov's that there were no professional medical personnel in the village at this time. The parish was coextensive with the *volost*—the next larger political and territorial unit—which in turn implies that there was no resident priest. This means that the entire ritual life of the village, except for the formal sacraments of baptism, marriage and burial, and the most solemn festivals of the church year, was in the hands of untrained people, and was conducted according to folk tradition. As for a lawyer, he would hardly have been found (at the time of Fenomenov's study or now), even in a considerably larger town than Gadyshi. The social rôle which in a Western European or American town is played by the lawyer—that of intermediary between the internal structure of the community and the larger society—was filled in Gadyshi by a literate peasant of no particular education, who travelled around the vicinity doing business on behalf of the *mir*. Such a person was known locally as a *khodok*, which means walker; the position was quite informal, and not the result of any special appointment.

Socioeconomic Structure

Although there was considerable stratification of the population in economic terms, no single index (such as the possession of land, buildings, or agricultural equipment) would yield a satisfactory account of it. The four criteria which in Fenomenov's opinion can be used to measure economic status are land, livestock, farm buildings, and labor supply. The first criterion is entirely meaningless in this context; the other three all yield considerable degrees of stratification. But Fenomenov's general judgment of the "prosperity" of a given household takes into account other factors as well. "The presence of a large number of livestock and buildings certainly indicates prosperity, but there are households in the village which do not have many animals or buildings, but which are richer than those that do, because they carry on trade, speculate in illegal liquor, or have a profitable craft." (Fenomenov 1925:I,162–163) For this reason, the estimate is based on public consensus as to a given individual's wealth, with account being taken of the labor supply and the amount of capital available to each household.[5] By this criterion, the economic stratification of the population of Gadyshi comes out as follows:

Category	Percent of Total Households	Percent of Total Population	Percent of Total Labor Supply	Percent of Total Capital
Rich	17.5	25	26	30
Prosperous	26	28	29	31
Middle	41	34	32	34
Poor	14.5	13	13	5

The rich and prosperous households together total 42 or 44 percent. These households owned commercial and industrial facilities (sawmills, grain mills, lumbering operations, and prior to the Revolution, shops), carried on crafts (75 percent of all craftsmen were in this category), and hired unskilled labor (70 percent of all nursemaids and domestic servants). In the lower two groups, there was less available labor and less capital. Few of the poorer peasants were engaged in crafts, and many of them hired themselves out as laborers. Half of the households in the middle category were small families recently started, and hence with inadequate labor supply. By Fenomenov's data and the drift of his argument, the expectation would be that such households would become prosperous as the children grew up and became fully capable workers. By the same token, we would expect that a prosperous household, as it divided up, would pass into the middle category, and that old men and old women alone would become poor, even if they had originally come from prosperous households. In fact, the figures reveal a direct straight-line positive correlation between the prosperity of the household and the number of individuals in it. The only point at which this correlation fails to hold is the seven-member level, 20 percent of the households of this size being poor. This reflects the fact that one group in this category consists of households with a large number of young children and few workers. Fenomenov attributes the deterioration in economic status of some peasant households in the middle category either to physical degeneration (alcoholism, chronic disease) or to what he considers incidental causes, such as prolonged absence of the husband and father, or breakup of the household due to internal conflict. A modern anthropologist would not regard either of these causes as incidental, provided the sample were large enough to permit statistical analysis.

It is interesting to note that the correlation between prosperity and the labor supply in peasant households applied as recently as the early 1950s in the kolkhoz described by Kushner's group (Kushner, ed. 1958). Here it is pointed out that the economic status of widowed families (generally a disadvantaged category) im-

[5] Fenomenov calculates the labor supply as follows: any able-bodied person between 16 and 60 years of age constitutes one full worker, regardless of sex. Able-bodied adolescents from 12 to 16 are figured as one-half worker, as are handicapped or sick adults, and old people. The unit of capital is equal to any of the following: one horse; two cows; an *izba* (living-space for one nuclear family); a threshing-floor; a *dvor* (a complete set of outbuildings). A bathhouse, a hay-drying lot, a granary, or an *izba* or *dvor* in poor condition are each worth one-half unit. A share in a threshing-floor (regardless of the size of the share) or in a bathhouse is worth one-quarter unit. The unit of capital is considered equal to one person's share in the communal land holding; that is, a household was entitled to a number of shares in the land equal to the number of its working members.

proves as the children grow up and become able to assume a full work load. Hence, we cannot regard the correlation between the labor supply of a household (the number of individuals of a given age) and its economic status as a result of the rather atypical situation existing in the northern districts during the early 1920s.

The character and extent of economic stratification in Gadyshi and similar places has certain important consequences. Fenomenov states: "Attentive examination of the economic condition of the peasant leads to the conclusion that in general, membership in this or that category of economic status is not a stable index, inasmuch as the accumulated capital is usually small, and is dissipated as the result of divisions. . . . As there is no firm boundary between rich and poor, so there is also none between landed peasants and landless ones. A peasant household which had been weakened would sell its land and become landless." (Fenomenov 1925:I, 165–166) From these conclusions it follows that despite the differential ownership of means of production, such as mills, lumbering operations, and crafts equipment, the village had no stable class structure, and no fixed avenues of social mobility within the community.

When we come to examine social structure in the strict sense—that is, the internal structure of the family and other kin groups, the methods of concluding marriage, and the mechanisms of social control in the community—we find a far more complex and contradictory picture than we do in regard to economic matters. The same is even more true of the values and beliefs of the people. It should be borne in mind that Fenomenov's methods and preoccupations are not precisely those of a modern social anthropologist, and that in many cases he leaves out data which would be of great interest to us.

For example, despite the wealth of detail with which his pages are filled, he does not provide a tabulation on the make-up of family units in Gadyshi, stating just what members are included in the family group which lives together. He states only (1925:I, 165) that 22 out of 88 families in the sample are classifiable as "large" in the structural sense (that is, containing representatives of three or more generations), and that these 22 families account for 152 out of the 426 individuals. In view of the correlation cited above between the number of persons in a household and its prosperity, we should expect that there would be some selection in favor of the structurally large family. Fenomenov carefully points out however, that the correlation applies to numerically large families rather than those which are large in the structural sense. At the time of the study, many families were in process of dividing; in most cases this involved the separation of widows from their children or from their in-laws. Documents printed by Fenomenov in the appendix to Part I (decisions of the village *skhod* and of the *volost* courts dating from the 19th century) make it clear that the tendency of widows to divide off is not new. Such cases usually arise from personal incompatibility rather than from any fixed principle of custom. It is also common practice for married sons to separate from the father's household during his lifetime and for unmarried brothers to live with married ones after the father's death. The separation of married sons, however, was conditional on the availability of sufficient resources to set up a separate household. The modern Soviet ethnographers who studied Kalinin Oblast state that this is still essentially true, but that the period of time required to accumulate the necessary resources has been shortened.

By custom, a brother was expected to arrange his sister's marriage if the father had not been able to do so before his death. However, in Fenomenov's time, this sometimes did not happen. In particular, a girl's property rights were often forfeited if she went away to work. Her trousseau was supposedly left in the brother's keeping, but frequently he would break open the trunk in which it was kept and sell the contents, and this act would go unpunished.

One of the most striking gaps in Fenomenov's account of the social structure is in regard to the wedding cycle, which among most Russian populations was and still is a highly dramatic succession of rituals and dramatic performances. It may be that the difficult economic conditions at the time when Fenomenov studied Gadyshi had suppressed most of the complex, or the apparent absence of an elaborate ritual here may actually be due to local variation. On the other hand, Fenomenov describes a fairly stable courtship pattern in Gadyshi, built around the so-called *posidelka* (or *posidka,* depending on dialect; from *posidet',* to sit for a while). This custom was known in many parts of Russia in varying forms; basically it was a spinning bee, at which the girls gathered, either in the house of one of their number, or in rented premises. The boys then arrived, bringing musical instruments, and sat, squatted, or knelt on the ground. Later they all sang and danced. When the *posidelka* broke up, each boy accompanied home the girl to whom he was paying particular court. In the Novgorod area, the girls were the organizers and hostesses at these affairs, at which no refreshments were served. In some other places, like Riazan, the boys took the initiative, and also provided food, but Fenomenov regards this as a rather recent innovation. Other details of the *posidelka* are known from Kalinin Oblast of approximately the same period (Anokhina and Shmeleva 1964) Here the *posidelka,* as far as the girls were concerned, was divided into age groups—the youngest in some of the larger villages being twelve to thirteen and the oldest thirty. The latter group might include young married couples without children. In large villages, a special *izba* was rented for the winter and a fee of 25–30 *kopeks* was collected from each girl for the purpose; young people not able to pay the fee were assigned the task of chopping wood or hiring the accordionist. If the gathering were large, men from other villages might attend, but only the "masters"—that is, the residents of the village—had the right to sit down. The proceedings were governed by a rather strict etiquette, according to which the girls were addressed as *Baryshnia* ("lady" in a feudal sense) and the men as *Kaval'er* (cavalier.) The entertainment on these occasions began only after the work was completed; it consisted of square-dancing, kissing games, and sometimes card-playing for the men.

The *posidelka* in Gadyshi and at most other northern points was specifically a winter custom. In summer its place was taken by the *gulianie* (walk, stroll, or in another sense, outing). This is so universal that the word *gulianie* has passed into standard Russian as a synonym for courtship. In Gadyshi, several varieties of this custom were recognized: "to walk in the daytime" (*guliat' dnem*) referred to honorable courtship with the intention of marriage; "to walk at night" referred to a clandestine affair which might also end in marriage but often did not. Finally, a popular outing (*narodnoe gulianie*) was a mass expedition to the woods to gather mushrooms or berries, undertaken on certain dates, and was not specifically part of the courtship pattern. Fenomenov leaves the impression, though he never states it in so many words, that the conclusion of marriage in Gadyshi and the surrounding countryside was a matter of individual initiative on the part of the young couple. On the other hand, the study carried out by Kushner's group (1958) states explicitly that in many, if not most, cases in Viriatino village, Tambov Oblast, the marriage was arranged by the parents, and the couple might not even be acquainted before the ceremony. In one cited case, relating to the 1890s, a girl was courted by a young man, and together they agreed that when he returned from the mines they would be married. While the boy was away, however, another man sent matchmakers to the girl's father, and the father, because the man appealed to him as a good

Accordion group, Kalinin Oblast, setting out for a young people's gulianie.
Note Ukrainian balloon pants on boy at left.

worker, decided to give his daughter to him. "I screamed," the girl (now an old woman) told the ethnographers, "I did not want to be married. My fiancé sent me letters from the mine, but I was illiterate and could not answer him. I cried for him—a river flowed, but my father insisted." A fairly common practice in this locality was one of switching brides. One peasant discovered only in church that the bride had been switched, but such was his fear of his father that he said nothing and lived out his life with a woman whom he disliked and constantly beat. (Kushner, ed. 1958:84/note 21.). By contrast, Kushner cites a case (1958:89) in which the prospective bridegroom returned from the mines in the spring of 1911 too late to find a situable bride—the most attractive girls in his village having been married off in the previous autumn wedding season. He was directed by a female relative to a girl in a neighboring village, visited her with his elder sister, liked her appearance and deportment, and thereafter took an active part in the wedding negotiations. This course of action was considered somewhat unusual at the time.

Divorce was possible in Gadyshi, but rare: Fenomenov knew of only three cases, one of which was formalized only after the Revolution. Infidelity was fairly frequent and, unlike marriage, usually took place within the confines of the village, and even within those of the former estate, of which the village contained two. Fenomenov lists a number of cases in which the infidelity was common knowledge; apparently no particular action was taken by anyone.

Before leaving the subject of courtship and marriage, we should mention one more curious fact. Fenomenov cites a custom practiced not in Gadyshi but in one of the neighboring villages, according to which a bridegroom from outside the village had to pay a ransom for the bride to the young men of the village. This ransom was payable in vodka or beer, in accordance with the bridegroom's wealth —two bottles of vodka from a poor man, four from one of moderate means, and a half bucket from one of wealth. Fenomenov suggests, perhaps half jokingly, that this custom may represent a survival of group marriage.

At the time Fenomenov studied Gadyshi, the *skhod* was still in full operation as the major mechanism of social control, although its authority had been undermined by the influence of socio-economic stratification. A wealthy peasant could buck the *skhod* and get away with it, and sometimes even a middle peasant, if he used the right tactics and had powerful friends. It is interesting that in the Novgorod district, the local or village *skhod* was of more recent origin than that of the *volost*. The Novgorod peasant considered the *volost* organization his business and exhibited a good deal of conscientiousness in helping to run it. Any higher organ of government, however, was regarded as an alien body, over which the individual had little or no control. The local *skhod* did not do business according to any fixed procedure. The meetings were disorderly and often interrupted by shouting and fistfights. The chairman, until 1923, was always either a wealthy man or one who was intimate with the wealthy. In 1923, however, a typical "progressive" middle peasant—one quite literate and with some knowledge of law—was elected chairman. This man refused to kowtow to the rich, and even put one wealthy peasant on the list of those guilty of speculating in lumber. Consequently the chairman was subjected to terrorist attacks.

The *sel'sovet*, or local agency of the Soviet government, was at the time of the study coextensive with the *skhod*, and did not operate separately from it, although legally it had the right to do so. If a person were sent out of town on municipal business, he addressed his report to the *skhod*, even though it was the *sel'sovet* (in the person of its chairman) that had signed the order for the trip. Normally the *skhod* decided fiscal matters in accordance with the policy announced by the *volost* executive committee, but it sometimes proved refractory. Thus, in the summer of 1921, the peasants refused to pay the tax in oil. The *skhod* sent its representatives to the *volost* center to notify the executive committee of their refusal to pay, and they were returned under arrest. These emissaries were regarded in the village as men who had "stood and suffered for the *skhod*." Ultimately the tax in oil was commuted into units of grain.

In all matters involving land—such as reclamation, the distribution of allotments, and the hiring of herdsmen—there were two separate *skhods,* one for each of the two communes in the village which had formerly been landed estates. Where it was necessary to give legal force to a decision of one of the two *skhods,* it was certified as the decision of both. But even in such cases it was obvious from the list of those present that the peasants of only one commune had taken part in the decision. (Fenomenov 1925).

Before concluding our discussion of the mechanisms of social control, we should mention several distinct forms of collective labor which were practised in Kalinin Oblast for some time after the Revolution. Relatives undertook to put up buildings in return for an "entertainment." In some cases, the *skhod* undertook to do this in return for an entertainment (a drinking bout for the men), to which the women had to contribute although they did not participate. Again, the same procedure was sometimes followed as a simple business deal, because of lack of machinery or working stock, in order to carry out various agricultural tasks. In these cases there was no entertainment. Finally, also in Kalinin Oblast, there was communal fishing by the whole village, with the owner of the net receiving an extra share of the catch, which was otherwise distributed to everyone, down to the smallest child. (Anokhina and Shmeleva 1964). In short, there were many instances of collectivism, even though these showed important structural differences from the methods which were later applied by the regime.

Values, Religion, Folkways

With regard to values, folk belief, and religion, our sources leave us in something of a quandary. In addition to the usual problem in anthropology—that of putting together an adequate and objective account of a value-system different from one's own—there was in Russia (and this is still true to some extent) a second difficulty. There were actually two Russian cultures—urban and rural. Since ethnographers, at least in Fenomenov's time, were almost by definition city-dwellers, most of them, including Fenomenov, failed in some degree to understand or sympathize with the peasant value-system. Their accounts of it reveal various types of prejudice.

A predominant feature in the value-system of the Russian peasant, by Fenomenov's account, is his belief in the sacredness of labor. This involves a conviction that the right of property is based on the personal physical labor of the owner—for instance, when a house has been received from the *volost* land office and no work has been put into it, the house is not actually the property of the recipient and may be confiscated by collective action, whereas if a roof has been built, or some other work done, it may not be alienated. In this regard, the Soviet legislation of the period was in complete agreement with peasant values. Similarly, when Fenomenov was asked by his informants why he had undertaken the study, he replied quite simply that he was well paid for doing so, and lived by his work. This answer was readily accepted, whereas any other explanation, he thought, would have been incomprehensible.

Fenomenov presents the daily peasant life at this period as being controlled in many respects by pre-Christian superstitions.[6] Most of these, in the form of various omens and methods of divination, are part of the traditional Slavic folk religion (Tokarev 1957). Most of these forms of divination were used during the Christmas season by girls seeking information about their future bridegrooms. Methods of divination fell into three main categories: (1) those based on autohypnosis; (2) those based on the interpretation of supposedly random events—the behavior of animals, and so on; and (3) those based on the interpretation of dreams. The first category is represented by divination with double mirrors, in which a person places one mirror in front of him and another behind him, so as to form an infinite corridor, with a candle on each side to heighten the effect. The future was foretold according to the shape seen in the depth of the corridor. In Gadyshi this method was considered absolutely accurate, but the girls of Viriatino thought it too terrifying and few dared to do it.

The largest single category of methods of divination was that based on the interpretation of random events. For instance, a girl would pluck a sheaf from the field, bring it home, and take out of it the first stem that came to hand. If the stem contained an ear, she would be married in the near future; if the ear was full, the bridegroom would be wealthy; but if the stem contained no ear, she would remain single. Likewise, a rooster would be brought into the house, and grains of corn were scattered, one for each girl taking part in the divination. The first girl whose grain the rooster pecked would be the first married. This method was followed in Gadyshi; in Viriatino, a variation was used to predict the character of the future bridegroom (or the mother-in-law). Certain objects were scattered on the floor—a grain, a mirror, a lump of coal, a dish of water, and so on. If the rooster went to the grain, the bridegroom would be wealthy; if it went to the mirror, he or his mother would be vain; if it went to the coal, the bridegroom would be a miner (or his mother a sloven); if to the water, a drunkard, and so on. Similarly, by running out into the street after supper carrying the unswept tablecloth and performing certain prescribed rituals,[7] one could predict the future according to what one heard, either in the street or in the houses. Songs and laughter presaged good fortune; supper being served meant riches; conversation about the dead, an early death. The first passerby on the street was asked what the bridegroom's name would be, and his reply was considered accurate. Finally, the future was predicted by the shapes appearing when wax, lead, or eggwhite was dropped into a glass of water, or from the shadows cast by crumpled paper.

Dream divinations were always preceded by spells to compel accuracy. Girls believed that in the ensuing dream, the predestined bridegroom (*suzhenyi*—literally, the fated one) would appear. In certain parts of Tambov Gubernia (but not in Viriatino), divination was practiced by men at the new year to foretell the coming crop. On New Year's Eve, ears of various kinds of grain were planted in the snow on the threshing floor; if in the morning any of the grains looked different, that kind would yield a good harvest. Fenomenov makes no mention of this, perhaps because of the secondary importance of agriculture in the area he studied. On the

---

[6] We use the term "superstition" here in a technical sense, to mean something "left over" from an earlier religious system, and at variance with the prevailing one.

[7] Turning three times on one foot, bending down to pick up snow, pronouncing certain words. This form of divination is not mentioned for Viriatino.

other hand, he does describe certain beliefs, which we might call economic, since they mostly have to do with the sale of livestock. For example, if one buys an animal for breeding, one must not bargain; otherwise, the seller will miss the animal, and this may cause it to sicken or attempt to return to its former home. Similarly, when selling an animal, if one carefully mentions all of its defects, they will disappear of themselves.

Kushner and his group describe in some detail the peasant ritual calendar as practiced in Viriatino before the Revolution, but this information is by and large missing from Fenomenov's account. The peasant year is a complex succession of fasts and festivals, whose names and outward forms are ecclesiastical, but whose content in most cases clearly reveals their pagan origin. The peasant calendar determined, broadly speaking, the schedule of agricultural tasks—although, according to the table given by Fenomenov (1925:I, Appendix), the actual dates might vary from year to year. The calendar also regulated, with its succession of fasts, the diet of the peasants, and with its sequence of holidays, their social life. One of the informants of Kushner's group laid out the sequence thus:

> The fair[8] went by, the raising of the cross went by, and all the grain had gone from the fields onto the threshing floors. The nights became quite a bit longer. The young girls begin to hold *posidki,* and from now on spin on new spindles (bought at the fair)—some making puttees, some canvas cartcovers; some knit socks and mittens or spin wool for broadcloth . . . On holidays and Sundays, they go to morning service and to mass. On Sundays in the daytime, they used not to do anything: they prepared themselves for evening in the "street" (young people's outing). Perhaps on that Sunday, someone will have a drinking companion or two. That person will have the "street" gather in his courtyard. This goes on from Mikitev Day (September 15) until St. Michael's Day (November 8). Eight weeks it was this way—*posidki,* drinking bouts, the "street" and mass . . . Then came the eve of the fast, the Advent fast. During the fast, the girls spun and the men hauled, carrying firewood right up to St. Nicholas's Day (December 6). The women retted flax and some of them already began to weave puttees. From St. Nicholas's Day until Christmas, there were no big holidays. Then the Christmas season began. For two whole weeks people were free. Women's work—spinning and weaving—was not done. This continued until New Year. Carnival week[9] is the biggest festival in the year: on Friday, Saturday and Sunday, they had "the street" and fist-fights. Then comes Lent. On Holy Monday, all the women and girls who spin take the distaffs that they use for spinning, and roll down the mountains (snowdrifts) as though cleansing their sins. Then to work again, right up to Easter. Some families had completed their spinning and begun weaving. The bigger girls began to weave, and the smaller ones added a little bit on to what they had already spun . . . (Kushner ed. 1958:98–99).

This account covers the main dates of the fall and winter cycle, and thereby the most important portion of the folk calendar. It is worth noting that many of the purely ecclesiastical holidays—Transfiguration, Assumption, the birthday of the

---

[8] The fair was held in the neighboring village of Sosnovka, on September 14th (Cross-Raising Day). All dates are given according to the Old Style or Gregorian calendar, which lags two weeks behind the Western one.

[9] Here the informant has apparently skipped over the period between the end of the Christmas season and the beginning of Carnival.

Virgin Mary, and the feasts of SS. Peter and Paul and John the Baptist—fell during the peak agricultural season, and were not observed in the peasant cycle at all, although they were officially fast days and the people were obliged to go to church.

On the more than 200 fast days that occurred during the year, "the street" did not gather, and social life was accordingly sharply restricted. On the other hand, the Christmas and Easter seasons created explosions of popular festivity. During the Christmas season, young people divided in groups according to age, and went about the village singing carols of a particular south Great Russian type. The text of these carols consisted mainly of good wishes to the householder and, accordingly, the singers were rewarded with handouts. It was mostly the poorer young people (sometimes including young widows and soldiers' wives as well as the unmarried) who went about singing carols; the more prosperous peasants did not allow their children to take part, since they considered it a form of begging. The carol-singers performed in costume, representing the lord and the lady of the manor, a gypsy woman, and so on. This custom of mumming has survived to the present day, although there have been changes in the personages represented. It is interesting to note, according to old informants, that the mummers at New Year once imitated sheep, goats, and other animals. This custom disappeared some time ago; at the turn of the century there was no New Year's mumming in Viriatino.

Shrovetide or carnival was celebrated in Viriatino with fist-fights in the street, mass outings, and other festivities. In Tver Gubernia (now Kalinin Oblast) there were also large bonfires at which human effigies and towers representing carnival were burned. Special songs with double meanings were also sung on this occasion, and "wrestling with the wheel" was held. On the whole, the pace of social life seems to have been somewhat faster in this northern district, perhaps due to the greater proximity of the cities.

Alcohol occupied a prominent place in Russian peasant ritual life, and this apparently remains true to the present day. Vodka was essential to the celebration of any holiday, christening, wedding, or funeral, and indeed, to the conclusion of any bargain. For this reason, the illegal distilling of liquors was considered a normal occupation, no matter how difficult the economic conditions, or how severe the shortage of grain. Meat was also ritually significant, probably due to its status as a luxury. So strong was this pattern, in fact, that during periods of famine, when livestock for which there was no fodder had to be slaughtered, many weddings were celebrated. (Shingarev 1907).

The whole question of peasant religiosity in Central Russia immediately before the Revolution is complex and our sources are not wholly reliable. The authors of the Viriatino study maintain that a large number of the migrant workers in that village had become atheists as a result of their experiences in the mines and elsewhere. Nevertheless, their picture of village life in general shows it to have been permeated by religious habits if not ideals. At the same time, the official religion administered by the Russian Orthodox Church, and the peasant cycle which centered on festivals of pagan origin, were functionally independent. The priest did not take a prominent part in any of the popular festivals, except at Easter, when he made the rounds collecting a stipulated contribution from each household. It is necessary to bear in mind that by the time of the Revolution, and for some time before, the Orthdox Church had become severely compromised (at least with the more reflective part of the population) by its role as an arm of the state and as a feudal landowner. In many parts of the country, it had ceased to have any significant following, and religious life had passed into the hands of certain sects, either of Western origin (Baptists) or indigenously Russian (Old Believers, *Molokans, Subbotniki,* and the like).[10]

Due to organizational difficulties and shortage of personnel, the Orthodox Church failed to maintain active control over many rural areas which were nominally Orthodox. Therefore, quite apart from the questions of the peasant festival cycle and sectarian influence, peasant religious practice deviated from the official church ceremonial. These deviations sometimes went so far that peasants who considered themselves Orthodox were regarded as schismatics by the Church hierarchy, and were treated accordingly. This is a particularly significant example of the way in which the cultural screen between the peasant and the urban resident operates. The operation of the screen in prerevolutionary Russia produced in effect two cultures in one country, both in point of religion and in other areas of life. It is necessary to bear this in mind when considering any aspect of Russian history, and most especially the role of the Orthodox Church in Russian life.

Immediately after the Revolution, the new regime made a direct frontal attack on the Russian Orthodox Church as an anti-Soviet organization, using for this purpose segments of the church itself which saw in the new conditions an opportunity to revivify the Orthodox Church. These groups, particularly the "Living Church," received some of the landholdings and other wealth confiscated from the Orthodox Church, in a period when agricultural communes (*kommuny*) were being set up by people of diverse persuasions. The decision to collectivize agriculture, which for a period in many parts of the country caused civil war, and World War II, which overtook the Soviet Union soon after, meant that the regime had to make peace with the Orthodox Church. The Church, due to the great inroads of dissident factions within and sectarians and Old Believers without, accepted the situation. Although just a shadow of its former self, the Orthodox Church once more ruled the faithful. But here too, as we shall see later, the Revolution had made its mark. From the vantage point of history we may say that for a generation, religion was used in Russia, both by the regime and by its enemies, in an attempt to bring about changes in a vast peasant society. Yet the peasants, too, were not unaware of the need for change, as is testified by the rapid growth of Western-oriented sects in the first decades of the twentieth century. In the next section of this study we will see how collectivization gave the regime the upper hand in the countryside, which was precisely what it was intended to do. (Dunn and Dunn 1964; Klibanov 1965).

---

[10] The Old Believers (divided into those with and without priests) were the successors of a 17th-century group who had refused to accept the reforms of Patriarch Nikon. The reforms were intended to bring the Russian Orthodox ritual more into line with Greek and hence Western practice, but they also had the practical effect of bringing the Orthodox Church itself under rigid control by the state (Vucinich 1964). Because of the relative lack of control by the Orthodox hierarchy over the population and because of social grievances, a multitude of dissident groups later arose, among them Molokans (milk-drinkers—so-called because, contrary to Orthodox practice, they drank milk during fasts), *Subbotniki* (Sabbatarians, whose practices closely resembled those of Jews, particularly in regard to food), and others. Theological differences do not concern us here—they seem to have been insignificant in any case—but each of these dissident movements arose and developed in a particular social setting and reflected the interests and aspirations of some specific group.

Mass Collectivization and Its Impact

It is worth noting first of all that, according to the British observer Sir John Maynard (1962), 90 percent of the agricultural land in European Russia was still held communally at the time that the resurveying and redistribution of land was stopped in 1927. This stoppage was presumably in preparation for the drive toward mass collectivization which was to follow.

From the beginning the Soviet government had stood for collectivized agriculture, both for ideological and practical reasons. In terms of political tactics, however, Lenin had realized the necessity of distributing land to the peasants before making any attempt at mass collectivization. The way he expressed it was that the peasants had to learn by experience the benefits of collective agriculture and that any attempt to force them into it before they were ready would be counter-productive. As it turned out, force was used anyway in many cases—a fact which is now admitted by Soviet historians of this period. Without going into the rights and wrongs of the matter, let us merely note here the main considerations which led the regime to embark on mass collectivization at this time, the forms which it took, and something of the reactions of the people concerned.

The first and most important consideration which produced the drive toward mass collectivization at the end of the 1920s was probably the inadequate pace of economic and cultural change in the countryside. Although men like Iakovlev (1923) might grumble that sectarians had a fully equipped library while the *volost* library had not functioned for two years due to lack of equipment and sufficiently interesting books, this was hardly the main difficulty. A statistical survey of Tambov Gubernia in 1923 (Noarov, no date) indicated that the relative differences between the various economic categories of the peasantry were slight, and that even among the relatively well-to-do (though their absolute number had increased), malnutrition, underemployment and downright idleness were common. Mokeev (1926), describing a region in northwest Kostroma Uyezd, has basically the same conclusion. We should remember that a well-developed pattern of seasonal migrant labor existed in many of these areas even before the Revolution. But during the 1920s, the situation in the countryside intensified this pattern while on the other hand, jobs for the semiskilled migrants in industry were still lacking. In other words, the regime was caught between a desire for rapid industrialization in order to permit the mechanization of agriculture, and the low productivity of un-mechanized agriculture, which would not support such an effort.

While the application of the Soviet land reforms had reduced the numbers of the absolutely landless and those of the *kulak* households (who presumably held a surplus of land), the holdings of the middle category in large areas of the country were not such as to make their farms economically viable. The process of resurveying and redistributing land was extremely slow and fraught with difficulties of all kinds: not the least of which was that control of the process often passed into the hands of persons not sympathetic to the goals of the regime. By the same token, the definition of a *kulak*—that is, the dividing line between the *kulak* against whom, as a class enemy all methods might be employed, and the middle peasant or *seredniak,* who was definitely not to be treated as a class enemy—was highly variable, and subject to distortion by the people in the rural localities. The process of mass collectivization was preceded and accompanied, in many areas, by measures of "dekulakization," which included confiscation of property and exile to distant parts of the country of those who were considered *kulaks*.[11]

It would be a mistake to think that there were no attempts at collectivization before the beginning of the mass drive in 1928 and 1929. The problem in the earlier period was that collectivization took in largely the poorest section of the population, which had few or no means of production; hence, the economic effect of the change fell far short of what the regime (and probably the people themselves) considered desirable. We must also remember that many of the units were extremely small, composing no more than 20 or 25 individuals (Logunova and Deshalyt 1958). Many also were of an ad hoc or emergency nature, set up for the purpose of tiding the peasant over an immediate crisis, or with a view to obtaining a loan from the state. These collectives tended to disband when the immediate crisis was past, or when the loan had been granted. It is also worth noting that, particularly during the early 1920s, the rate of inflation was such that loans lost most of their value between the spring, when they were authorized, and the fall, when they were actually distributed (Logunova and Deshalyt 1958: Document 19).

The collectivization of agriculture during the 1920s took various forms, depending on the degree to which the means of production became public property. At one extreme were the *kommuny* in which everything except objects of personal use, such as clothing and kitchen utensils, was collectivized. In some areas and at certain periods of time, the *kommuna* was the most viable form of collectivization. Before the Revolution there had been a certain number of *kommuny*—often established by dissident religious groups in outlying areas. There are even indications that some *kommuny* (and other types of agricultural collectives) existed in Tver Gubernia during the very first years of Soviet power before the beginning of collectivization (Logunova and Deshalyt 1958:92). The bylaws of one of the early *kommuny* established in Tver Gubernia contain the following provisions: (1) there is to be no private property, except in articles of personal use; (2) everyone in the *kommuna* is to work according to his strength and to receive according to his needs, depending on the condition of the *kommuna*'s economy; (3) all work is to be done in common; (4) surpluses of produce are to be marketed through the local

---

[11] As examples of the varying use and application of the concept *kulak* we cite the following: Danilov (1958), discussing the lower Volga area, defines a kulak as a farmer owning "means of production" (equipment, livestock, and so on, exclusive of land) worth 1400 rubles or more. On the other hand, Iakovlev (1923) in a monograph describing a village of Kursk Gubernia (on the border between the Russian Federation and the Ukraine) refers to one man as a former *kulak* who had acquired, before the Revolution, eight *desiatins* of land, one horse, 2 cows, 10 sheep and 700 rubles a year as manager for a landlord who planted sugar beets. Before World War I, another man had 40 *desiatins* which he worked with hired labor. In general, Soviet specialists consider the employment of hired labor a more correct and reliable criterion of what is a *kulak* than any arbitrary "means test." Trifonov (1960) cites figures from various areas concerning people subjected to different measures of dekulakization—exile, confiscation of property, relegation to "concentration camps" (the author uses this term) and disenfranchisement. About 15 percent of these people over all, he says, were not *kulaks*, while 15–20 percent of those disenfranchised were subjected illegally to this penalty. In Stalingrad Okrug (on the lower Volga) more than one third of those subjected to dekulakization were really middle peasants, while in 24 *raions* of Moscow Oblast 12,500 out of a total of 18,000 had been illegally disenfranchised as of May 1930.

government purchasing agencies in exchange for needed articles, but produce is not to be sold for cash, except in the case of absolute necessity in order to purchase for cash articles not available by direct exchange;[12] (5) the *kommuna* may not employ hired labor; (6) membership rights are open to all work-capable persons over eighteen; (7) all questions concerning the management of the *kommuna* are to be decided by the general assembly of all active members (Logunova and Deshalyt 1958: Document 9).

A less extreme form of collectivization was represented by the so-called "agricultural *artel'*." Under this form, the major or basic means of production, including the land, were collectivized, but the participating households were left certain specified articles (dwelling house, household plot, outbuildings, minor equipment, and livestock) for their personal use, and retained title to these as long as they continued to be members of the *artel'*. The resulting structure was characterized by division into a private and a public sector, and this later had important consequences for its character as a social unit. The agricultural *artel'* became, during the period of mass collectivization, the approved and almost universal form of agricultural collective. The reasons for this were partly ideological and partly practical. In many cases peasants showed hostility to *kommuny*, even regarding them as hotbeds of immorality and muttering darkly about "socialization of women." Besides this, although the *kommuny* provided for and fed their own members well, they did not supply sufficient produce for the cities, which at this period of strenuous industrialization was regarded as essential by the regime (Dunn and Dunn 1964:467; Wesson 1963:232–233).

The simplest and weakest form of collectivization was the *toz*. This type of organization was based on joint labor and pooling of land, but did not involve the socialization of the other means of production. It was found to be economically ineffective, even though a good many agricultural *artels* (particularly where the collectivization of livestock had to be postponed because of popular unwillingness to give it up) functioned as *tozy*. When the mass collectivization began, there was considerable confusion among the people as to what the regime really wanted, or would accept, and many *kommuny* were set up through an excess of zeal.

In order to give some feeling of what the process of collectivization was actually like in the village, we will summarize here several accounts given in a book published in 1931. Two of these accounts have the advantage of relating to approximately the same geographical area as that discussed by Fenomenov for an earlier period. The *kolkhozy* described by Danilin (1931) were in two *raions*, Valdai and Rozhdestvo, that bordered directly on the *raion* where Fenomenov's study had been made. Danilin's district can be considered average for Leningrad Oblast: of the net production during the years 1927 and 1928, agriculture accounted for 42.9 percent, all forms of industry for 36.9 percent, and handicrafts for 20.2 percent. When mass collectivization started, the agricultural economy was oriented sharply toward milk and animal husbandry. The figures for 1924–1929 show a drop in the proportion of grain sowings from 86.6 percent of the total to 65.21 percent, and a corresponding growth in the proportion of fodder (grass) sowings from 2.52 percent to 21.99 percent.

---

[12] This provision probably reflects the extreme inflation prevailing at the time.

The chief commercial products of the district at this period were flax, milk, and oats.

The number of kolkhozy in the district increased from 26 on October 1, 1927, to 214 on December 1, 1929. Later statements by Danilin imply that these numbers include agricultural collectives of all types. Danilin notes, however, that at this time the process of collectivization was under insufficient governmental control —a frequent complaint in other areas as well. A sharp increase in the number of collectives began especially after the fall sowing campaign of 1929. By March 1930, the collectives, in all the *raions* covered by Danilin's study, took in 20 percent of all the households. This was followed by a sharp drop in the formation of new collectives and the dissolution of some of the ones already in existence, so that by the summer of that year only the most stable and viable remained. The same tendency was noticeable in the total membership of the collectives and in that of individual units. It is characteristic that Danilin attributes these wide swings in the efficacy of the collectivization drive not to changes in the attitude of the peasants, but to shifts and particularly "deviations" in the Communist Party policy as interpreted on the local level. Demands for the total collectivization of certain areas where the necessary conditions for this did not obtain, resulted in the penetration of many collectives by "class hostile" elements—like *kulaks* and their hangers-on. Insufficient preparation led to many misunderstandings. Because of the departure of members between sowing and harvest time, many collectives were forced to resort to the hired labor of non-members—always a sore point.

The most vivid account given by Danilin concerns attempts to form a kolkhoz in the small village of Raevo in Rozhdestvo *raion,* located some distance from the railway line. This is described as a typical agricultural village, where some of the peasants worked permanently as loggers, and in the spring rafted lumber downstream. At the beginning of February 1930, when there was talk in the *raion* about total collectivization, the peasants of Raevo began to talk about forming a kolkhoz. Although the members of the local soviet—on-the-spot representatives of the Soviet regime—conducted agitation "so to speak, in the official order," the actual initiative was with the wealthier members of the community. This group at first said that if a kolkhoz were formed, everyone would have to join, and then all the property would be confiscated. However, after each of them had been taxed 25 *puds* of flax as a measure of dekulakization, they recommended joining the kolkhoz in order to avoid the tax. At this point the village *skhod* was called, the question of collectivization was raised publicly, and there was a great deal of shouting and noise—which seems to be usual at Russian meetings. Most of the women were opposed to the idea of a kolkhoz, asking tearfully how their children would be fed if the cows were confiscated. In the end, this problem was bypassed by the decision to form a *toz,* which would not have then involved the collectivization of livestock and seems to have been favored by most of the peasants on this account. All those present at the meeting, with the exception of one man, put their hands to a document proclaiming the establishment of the *toz.* The man who abstained said that he had sent his wife to consult his relatives. Actually, as it turned out, she had gone to consult a local wisewoman, who recommended not joining the kolkhoz. Danilin does not record the man's final decision. The meeting was already breaking up when the representative of the *raion* executive committee arrived. The peasants informed him that they had decided to form a *toz,* to which he replied that this was not suitable—that there were directives to the effect that all collectives of Rozhdestvo *raion* should take the form of *artels.* The peasants went home depressed and resentful, and met the next day to decide, after another shouting match, that they wanted no part of an *artel'.* The would-be organizers were most disgruntled, considering that the representative's ham-handed intervention had spoiled their chances, and that they would probably have been able to persuade the peasants to convert the *toz* into an *artel'* in the fall.

This setback ended all talk of forming a kolkhoz for several months. When it was revived, with the formation of a collective in the neighboring town of Duple, there was considerable resistance, particularly by the women and young girls, who feared the loss of their reputations if they joined, since collectives supposedly also collectivized women. The next attempt to form a kolkhoz was made on September 7th, when a group of the poorest peasants met at the house of the man who had been instrumental in the earlier attempt. A kolkhoz was formed at a meeting on the following day, but shortly afterwards one of the members dropped out, claiming illness. The chief organizer was later able to determine that the actual cause of his resignation had been the refusal of the midwife to attend his wife at childbirth or to fire up the bathhouse (the couple were too poor to have their own bathhouse). As of the time of writing, the organizers hoped to be able to "reeducate" this man. The success of the newly-established kolkhoz seemed problematical to say the least, given the practical difficulties and the general feeling among the peasants that poverty was disgraceful, and that a kolkhoz formed exclusively by poor peasants was therefore not worth joining.

Most of the kolkhozy described by Danilin encountered great difficulties in formation. These difficulties can be divided into a number of categories according to Danilin's evidence: (1) clumsy interference by representatives of the central government; (2) counteragitation by the *kulaks,* based on the poverty of most of the first kolkhoz members; (3) marital discord among the first members; (4) religious disagreements; and (5) unwillingness of the peasants to work "for others," or "for other people's children." These factors are not listed in order of importance; the source gives no basis for so doing. It is clear, however, that the process of collectivization involved highly complex social changes, and that it was undertaken, in many cases, without accurate conception of its implications.

Whereas Danilin sheds light on the process of formation of kolkhozy in this area (the northern corner of Leningrad Oblast), E. R. Leper, another writer in the same book, (1931), shows us something of what life was like on the existing kolkhozy of a nearby neighborhood. Leper attributes the difficulties of conducting the work of kolkhozy not so much to the errors committed by the leadership or to the "property-owning" psychology of the peasants (in regard to material objects) as to their feelings of insecurity and their peculiar ideas about labor. She notes that although the horses were kept in the courtyards of their former owners and primarily used by them, they were also used by the elected officials. This frequently gave rise to misunderstandings. The old handicapped peasant with whom the ethnographer stayed often told her that if his courtyard, where his horse was kept, had been held in common with other families, he would have considered the horse no longer his own, and would have believed in the kolkhoz to a greater extent. As things were, however, he felt the horse was still his, mistrusted his neighbors, and feared they might do him injury, particularly since he could not work and lived on allotments from kolkhoz supplies. A further example of this man's insecure attitude is the fact that when he and his wife were given a horse in compensation for the sheep they had been forced to sell to the kolkhoz, they still believed that the horse belonged to the chairman and could be taken away from them at any moment. This man was probably an extreme case; nevertheless the things that troubled him are symptomatic of the ambivalence which is part of this form of collectivization. The ethnographer implies strongly that the *kommuna* (which this kolkhoz formerly was) is psychologically a more effective form of organization than the *artel'*, since it does not compromise with private property and does not set up two categories in the minds of the peasants—one which is "ours," and one which is "theirs," "everybody's" and therefore "nobody's." The chief obstacle to be overcome, Leper found, was not attachment to actual physical property but the almost mystical reverence for labor as an agency creating value, which Fenomenov also mentioned. This is illustrated by the following example. A peasant by the name of Polevikov suggested that the kolkhoz fields be divided into individual plots, for each of which one individual would be responsible—he thought this would make for a faster harvest. He suggested also that at threshing time the barn be divided into individual threshing floors, and the grain be parceled out among families, each one being responsible for threshing its quota. Despite possible inequities, (some families might not have sufficient working members and might have to call upon others for help), Polevikov felt that this system would stimulate productivity, since each family would be concerned to do its work as rapidly as possible and to provide firewood for the fire to dry the grain. Polevikov's proposal was rejected solely on economic grounds. No one, not even the chairman, raised the obvious idelogical point that the procedure he suggested would be a retreat from the principle of collectivization itself (Leper 1931:98).[13]

The ethnographer puts the matter with admirable conciseness: "It is characteristic that private property is regarded by the kolkhoz peasants as the product of labor expended: in regretting it, [that is, the loss of it], they regret their labor." (Leper 1931:98) She also comments that many peasants say quite seriously that they would rather go into a *sovkhoz* than into a kolkhoz—that is, they would rather give up their property entirely in the means of production, be provided with everything they need, and receive their wages regardless of the harvest.

In terms of the practical effect of collectivization, Leper's observations are equally revealing—not only for the conditions of her own day but for ours as well. A day nursery functioned on the kolkhoz, but its performance was less than satisfactory. Its main drawback was that it did not free the mother from domestic labor; she still had to cook and clean house. On the other hand, if she hired a nursemaid, the nursemaid was at the same time a houseworker and gave her mistress full freedom to work in the fields. For this reason it was common to keep the children at

---

[13] It is interesting that recently something similar to Polevikov's suggestion has been instituted on many kolkhozy with official approval. The system of the "comprehensive brigade" is clearly a step in this direction, even though the principle of organization is not familial. According to the system a brigade is made responsible for all work on a certain area of land and is entrusted with the necessary supplies and equipment to this end and thus becomes a kolkhoz in miniature.

home even where there were relatively good nurseries. Except in the communes, the women's work was almost what it was before. "If we add to this the greater work-load of the kolkhozniks in the fields [during the summer] compared to the private farmers, it is understandable that the women do not notice the difference in their position." (Leper 1931:102). As we shall see later, part of this rather paradoxical situation survives to this day.

Historical Summary

We have now established the baseline from which the cultural situation to be described in the next section developed. It should be emphasized that the information given in the preceding section does not exhaust what we have to say on the historical background. The history of particular institutions and culture elements will be given when these are treated in detail.

It is clear that the Russian peasantry around the time of the 1917 Revolution was rather atypical. In many places, as we have seen, it was essentially nonagricultural in its occupations. The data given by Fenomenov-show an extreme form of this; yet it does not seem as though the situation in Gadyshi differed in kind from that which existed in the more southerly regions. At the same time, the data make clear that in terms of social structure and world-view, the Russian peasantry retained many of the distinguishing marks which are common to other peasantries—a combination of social control by tacit consent with formal regulation, selective acquisition of elements of urban culture, the prevalence of religious or quasi-religious habits ("superstitions") and so forth. A striking aspect of the Russian peasant community is the absence of stable class structure, despite the differential in ownership of means of production. The data indicate a positive correlation between size of household and prosperity. This situation might be expected to lead psychologically to the situation described by Foster (1965) which he asserts is typical of peasant societies in general. Foster maintains that the peasant proceeds on the assumption that the amount of "goods" available in the society is fixed and that this applies not only to wealth but also to such spiritual "goods" as prestige, honor, friendship and power. The peasant's life experience does not persuade him that he can improve his position by extra labor or by initiative. It follows that the acquisition of wealth by anyone in the community must be due either to what amounts to theft or to supernatural causes (a pact with the powers of darkness, resulting in the finding of buried treasure, or the like). From this there follows, in Foster's view, a whole series of consequences in social structure and daily life—the avoidance of any display of wealth and various mechanisms for restoring the social equilibrium of the community when it has been disturbed by a sudden change in someone's status.

The data of Fenomenov and later Soviet ethnographers, however, do not indicate that Foster's "image of limited good" applies to the Central Russian peasant. Certainly there is no avoidance of conspicuous consumption, such as Foster claims functions to maintain the solidarity of the community. From this we might conclude either that the Central Russian community lacked solidarity to begin with or that its solidarity was not based on economic homogeneity, or finally, that we are here faced with a type of peasantry to which Foster's model simply does not apply. On balance, the third alternative seems the most probable. In the Introduction, we have already described the peasant as a man in transition between face-to-face tribal society and the politically organized society which centered on the pre-industrial city. It seems as though the prerevolutionary Central Russian peasant was in transition in another sense as well, since he was dependent on the larger society outside his village not only from a formal point of view but also economically.

As to the relative conservatism of social structure and world-view which Fenomenov's data indicate, it might be hypothesized that the possibilities for nonagricultural labor close by to the village, with frequent returns to it, led to the preservation of the traditional structure, even when its agricultural base had largely disappeared.

In short, it should not be assumed that the "peasant culture" which we will describe in the next section developed out of a situation even closely approximating the classical model for peasant culture as it has been developed by anthropologists such as Foster and Redfield.

2

Kolkhoz, Village, and Family as Social Units

Kolkhoz and Village

O NE OF THE FIRST and most important questions to be answered in describing any population is: into what sort of units is it organized? In the case of the peasants, this question is particularly urgent, because of their peculiar relationship to the society at large, and because of the fact that the village —a form of organization with distinct attributes of its own—has often been considered diagnostic for peasant societies (see Halpern 1965). In the case of Soviet Russian peasants, we are faced with yet another question—that of the relationship between the kolkhoz (which is the locus of their economic activity and to which they are responsible in a formal political sense) and the village (which is the traditional form of organization and in which their primary emotional loyalties presumably lie).

Soviet agriculture has two main forms, the kolkhoz, which in theory is owned and controlled by the membership, and the *sovkhoz,* owned and controlled by the central government, which takes all profits and assumes all risks. In this chapter, and in the study generally, we will be dealing almost exclusively with kolkhozy for two reasons. First, virtually all the presently available ethnographic and sociological data derive from studies of kolkhozy. Secondly, the status of a worker on a *sovkhoz* is actually different than that of a kolkhoznik, and more closely approximates the status of an industrial worker. The *sovkhoz* worker receives a fixed cash wage independent of the profit or loss of the operation; he can be hired and fired on terms different from those which apply to the kolkhoznik;[1] and finally (and most important), although in many cases he has a household plot and a pri-

---

[1] A kolkhoznik can be expelled only by vote of the membership, whereas a *sovkhoz* worker can be fired by the director or his deputy. The latter may appeal his case however, not to a jury of his peers, but through the grievance mechanism of the trade union to which he belongs.

vate economy, he is not guaranteed these by law. There are also differences between the economic status of kolkhozniks and *sovkhoz* workers and the organizations to which they belong, with sovkhozy, at least in certain areas, getting preferential treatment. It does not automatically follow, however, that it is better at all times to be a *sovkhoz* worker than a kolkhoznik. In fact, the whole complex of problems classified under the rubric of resource allocation often applies with equal force to *sovkhozy*. This is because until recently the state has not demanded of its *sovkhozy* that which Americans would consider sound farm management. More about this later on, but except in a few cases, our remarks will be confined to kolkhozy.

At the beginning of collectivization, when the collectives were small, there might be several of them in one village. As the movement grew and the stronger kolkhozy absorbed the weaker ones, the kolkhoz by and large became coextensive with the village, and this remains true in many cases, including that of Viriatino and the kolkhoz "Path of Lenin." Beginning in the early 1950s, there has been a movement to consolidate kolkhozy and *sovkhozy* which has sometimes resulted in huge operations embracing many thousand people, scattered over ten or a dozen separate villages. For example, Anokhina and Shmeleva (1964) state that kolkhozy in Kalinin Oblast tend to include 15–20 villages, within a radius of 20 kilometers. The largest category of kolkhozy is that uniting 101–200 households, which makes up 30.2 percent of all the kolkhozy in the oblast. Each of these situations has its distinctive character. When it might include more than one kolkhoz, the village played a coordinating role through its soviet. When and where the village is coextensive with the kolkhoz, we find that many of its political and regulatory functions lapse and are taken over by the kolkhoz administration. With the creation of large collectives, the individual village, with its administrative machinery, has begun to regain its former functions and acquire new ones as well. First of all, the kolkhoz or *sovkhoz* is each too large to provide efficiently for the needs of the individual. This is so even if the officials who administer the collective see its function in these terms, which is not often. The collective is first and foremost a means of supplying the state with agricultural goods, and its social rôle, while certainly present, must be secondary. Accordingly, there has recently been considerable effort to find more efficient means of providing for the needs of the population—utilities, educational and cultural facilities, and consumer services (repair and maintenance of clothing and household equipment, public catering, and so on)—on the local level. The local soviet has been increasingly entrusted with these functions, although it does not yet have the authority it needs to carry them out. In Tambov Oblast, local deputies strove to get club houses, public baths and similar facilities built and to improve the water supply. Two large villages had very dirty streets and some households did not observe proper rules of hygiene. The *skhod* was called in to deal with these matters and a group of socially active people was given the responsibility for sanitation in a certain part of the village (*Izvestiia* 25/II/65:3).

We have no firsthand evidence of the people's attitude toward the village and toward the kolkhoz, and must proceed by inference from stories appearing in the press. In some cases it seems that members of a kolkhoz have difficulty in identifying themselves with it as a social unit. For instance, a kolkhoz in Tambov Oblast, composed of 800 households, was terrorized by two brothers who were continually getting drunk and disrupting the kolkhoz's activities. No one undertook to curb the brothers until, finally, one of the brigadiers complained to the local police. As a result, the brothers killed the brigadier—with a pitchfork—and beat up the old man who had served as his witness. The local police had told the complainant only that he could make his complaint in court if he wished. The wife of the dead man had herself advised him to avoid getting involved, no doubt in fear for their four children. After the murder, many people gathered and there were speeches by the kolkhoz chairman, by a woman brigadier from a neighboring *sovkhoz,* and by many others. Everyone demanded that the bandits receive the death-penalty and that the local police officials be punished for dereliction of duty. Punishments and reprimands were distributed liberally. The hooligans were condemned to death by shooting before a crowd of 1500 people. (*Izvestiia* 26/X/62; 15/XI/62:3; 30/XI/62:6). It is significant that it took a capital crime to set the legal apparatus in motion. Not even the kolkhoz chairman took any action until after the crime had been committed.

Organization of the Kolkhoz

As we have indicated, the kolkhoz is a formal organization, a unit in the political structure, and a means whereby people live together. These two aspects cannot actually be separated, but for convenience, we will describe first the formal structure (taking the charter of the kolkhoz "Path of Lenin," village of Viriatino as our model) and then treat such aspects of the informal structure as can be deduced from the data in our sources.

GOALS AND PURPOSES   As presented in the charter, the goals of the kolkhoz are conceived in exclusively ideological terms: "The kolkhoz path, the path of socialism, is the only correct path for the working peasant. The members of the cooperative undertake to strengthen their cooperative, to work honestly, to divide the earnings of the kolkhoz according to work done, to guard public property, and to watch over the good of the kolkhoz . . ." (Kushner, ed. 1958:159).

LAND   The land occupied by the kolkhoz, like all land in the USSR, is the property of the state. It is turned over to the kolkhoz, in accordance with Soviet law, for perpetual use, and cannot be bought, sold, or rented out by the collective. Small parcels of the land in public property are allotted to each kolkhoz household for use as homestead plots. The size of these parcels may vary from 0.15 to 0.4 hectares, depending on the participation of the working members of the kolkhoz family[2] in the collective economy, and on the availability of land suitable by location for the homesteads of kolkhozniks. The norms governing the allotment of private plots to families are as follows: families with three or more working members taking active part in the collective economy and earning the established minimum of labor days, are entitled to receive up to 0.4 hectares as a private plot; if there is only one working member and two or more nonworking dependents, the family is entitled to the same amount of land—provided that the working member earns the

[2] Unless they are medically certified as disabled, men between the ages of 16 and 64, and women between the ages of 16 and 59, are considered working (literary work-capable) kolkhozniks. Individuals above and below these ages may work on a kolkhoz but do so under special conditions, and their pay is calculated on a separate basis.

established minimum labor days. Families whose working members regularly fail without good cause to earn the established minimum of labor days or whose working members voluntarily leave the kolkhoz to seek outside employment, and families with working members excluded from the kolkhoz, may be allotted from 0.15 to 0.25 of a hectare, depending on the participation in the public economy of the other members of the family. Participation of retired or disabled family members who are still able to work also is taken into account. Families consisting of only two members may also be allotted from 0.15 to 0.25 hectares. The size of each household's private plot is established by the administration of the kolkhoz and confirmed by the general meeting. The families of tractor drivers and other workers in tractor brigades living on the kolkhoz (but who are not members of it)[3] are allotted private plots on the same basis as kolkhozniks.

THE MEANS OF PRODUCTION   All farm buildings, agricultural equipment, working livestock, seed, and fodder necessary to carry on the public economy of the cooperative and all subsidiary enterprises, are the property of the kolkhoz as a whole. In case of necessity, the administration may allot some of the working livestock to serve the personal needs of kolkhozniks at an established rate of payment. Transport is provided free of charge for trips to the hospital, and for supplies and fodder received as payment for labor days, and building materials for the repair of houses damaged by fire. For carrying fuel and cultivating the private plot, draft power is to be provided free only to those families whose every working member earns the established minimum of labor days. For families whose working members fail to earn payment for labor days without good cause, draft power for the above purposes is to be provided at a rate of payment established by the administration. Each kolkhoz household may have as its personal property one cow with two calves, one sow with young, ten sheep and goats combined, an unlimited number of fowl, and up to ten beehives.

TASKS OF THE COOPERATIVE AND ITS ADMINISTRATION   The administration and all members of the kolkhoz are obligated to carry on the public economy efficiently, to make provision for the necessary buildings, and so forth. The last two clauses of this section mention raising the cultural level of members, the introduction of newspapers, books, radio and movies, the provision of bathhouses and barbershops, the maintenance of order in the streets, landscaping, and the improvement of homes. Also mentioned in this section are such social objectives as bringing women into the public economy, liberating them as much as possible from housework, establishing nurseries, playgrounds, and so on.

ORGANIZATION OF PAYMENT AND DISCIPLINE OF LABOR   The agricultural work of the cooperative is carried out on a piecework basis. The administration develops, and the general meeting confirms, norms of earning for each type of agricultural work and evaluates each in labor days. The work done by each kolkhoznik is to be written up at least once a week by the brigadier and forwarded to the administration, which in its turn is to post monthly a list of kolkhozniks with the

---

[3] These tractor drivers and subsidiary workers were employed by the Machine Tractor Stations (MTSs), that were officially abolished in 1958. The machinery owned by the MTS was sold to the kolkhozy, and the staffs of the MTS in many cases joined the neighboring kolkhozy. Actually, in many parts of the country, these processes took place considerably earlier.

number of labor days earned by each. Kolkhozniks of retirement age who have worked in the kolkhoz for 25 years uninterruptedly (allowance is made for military service and for training by order of the kolkhoz or in specialized agricultural institutions) and are no longer able to work, are to receive a personal pension amounting to 25–50 percent of the average number of labor days they earned annually over the 25-year period—depending on the condition of the economy and the pensioner's past attitude toward his work. The same arrangement applies to handicapped persons injured in the course of work in the kolkhoz. Men over 70 and women over 65, if they participate in the work of the cooperative, receive a bonus of 25 percent over the rate of payment provided in the present year's norms. Those temporarily disabled receive an allowance of 25–50 percent of the average number of labor days earned monthly on the basis of the last month of work in the public economy. Kolkhozniks who have earned the established minimum of labor days and who have worked a least 300 calendar days in the preceding year, are to receive paid vacations by decision of the administration. Those who have distinguished themselves in work are sent to vacation houses or spas at the expense of the kolkhoz. They are also allotted labor days during the vacation on the basis of their monthly average for the past year, provided that they have worked on the kolkhoz continuously and without fault for at least 10 years. If a work brigade achieves results over and above the plan, its members are allotted a bonus amounting to 25 percent of the overfulfillment, to be divided among them. Special rewards may also be granted by decision of the administration for overfulfillment of plans or for construction in less than the allotted time. Advances in cash may be given to kolkhozniks monthly in amounts up to 50 percent of the sum set aside for wages. Advances in kind may be given from the beginning of threshing in amounts up to four kilograms of grain for each labor day earned.

The provisions of the charter just summarized require various comments. In the first place, the provisions relating to the private plot could be used in theory to penalize kolkhozniks who go away for seasonal migrant labor—as many did, particularly before 1953. There is no indication in the Viriatino study, however, that this was done. Secondly, the fairly generous social-security arrangements are tied to the economic conditions of the kolkhoz, and hence, in many cases, mean very little. Early in 1965, these arrangements were superceded by the adoption of a law making kolkhozniks eligible for state pensions on the same basis as members of other social groups. (The implications of this change will be discussed later.) Finally, the system of payment requires some explanation. Under the system of labor days, an attempt was made to combine differential payments for various types of work with dependence of the whole on the condition of the economy. Those who performed jobs presumably requiring skill and training, such as tractor drivers, operators of other farm machinery, bookkeepers and supervisory personnel are allotted more labor days than unskilled workers for an equal amount of work. Furthermore, the value of the labor day in cash and in kind varies from year to year, from kolkhoz to kolkhoz, and even from brigade to brigade within a kolkhoz, depending on the amount of money and goods available for distribution as wages. Obviously this differential method of payment requires extensive bookkeeping. It has also been found unsatisfactory from the point of view of incentives to the kolkhozniks. Lately, there have been attempts to put wage payments in collective agriculture on a more stable basis by introducing a "guaranteed annual minimum wage," payable monthly, based on the assumption that the kolkhoznik will then know precisely what income he can expect and will be able to budget his own expenditures accordingly. This system is actually in effect in many places, but indications are that the practical result has fallen short of what was expected. The chief difficulty seems to be that since the wage is still tied to the amount of money available—that is, to the sale price of the crop—the wage cannot in fact be guaranteed. It also seems probable that this system could not be made to work properly without the services of many economists and accountants, using highly sophisticated methods. These personnel are not being trained in sufficient numbers and are often unwilling to remain in the countryside—a problem that will be treated in some detail later.

Work in the Public Sector

The organizational unit next below the kolkhoz is the brigade. Brigades are of varying sizes but, in general, each has a particular function—field agriculture, construction, fodder, livestock, chickens, and so forth. The brigadier is directly responsible for seeing that the members of his brigade are available for work when needed, and for keeping track of the time that they work. Recently, on some extremely large kolkhozy, there has been a tendency to make brigades responsible not only for specific phases of agricultural work, but for the entire cycle of jobs on a specific plot of land. Accordingly, the brigade is provided with all working livestock, equipment, and supplies necessary for getting the work done. The effect of this is to turn the brigade into a miniature kolkhoz. In fact, in some areas the brigade becomes coextensive with the village and thence the major social unit above the family (Anokhina and Shmeleva 1964). Furthermore, some kolkhozy which were amalgamated during the 1950s have been left intact and simply incorporated as separate brigades within the enlarged collective.

According to the data of Anokhina and Shmeleva (1964) farm work is planned out in 5-, 10-, or 15-day stretches by the chairman at a meeting with the brigadiers. The brigadiers subsequently give out orders to the members of their brigades, either in the morning or in the evening. The working-day is generally 10 hours, starting at 6 or 7 A.M. and ending at 6 or 7 P.M., with time out for lunch from 12 N. to 2 P.M. Normally, about one-fifth to one-fourth of the population is engaged in animal husbandry, which by general admission is the least mechanized branch of Soviet agriculture. Most of the workers in this field are women, who begin the day at 5 A.M. and finish about 9 P.M.; they must take care of their household affairs as well during this long tour of duty. It is rare to find a man doing anything in connection with animal husbandry except hauling. In kolkhozy where there are enough workers, a day off is arranged, but where there are not, this becomes an individual matter. In some kolkhozy where income is not sufficient, only the workers in animal husbandry receive paid vacations, since they must work all year round.

In other branches of agriculture, the demand for labor varies sharply over the course of a year. The greatest demand is in July and August—when even the old people and children are brought in—and the smallest is from November to March, when only the men and adolescents work. In the past this was the time when most men of working age left the village to seek employment in mines or factories, or in the cities. The seasonal variation of the demand for labor is now recognized as a serious problem by Soviet agricultural specialists and officials, and various nonseasonal or counterseasonal occupations (small manufacturing operations and handicrafts) are being developed to take care of it. This type of small-scale production of articles usually not manufactured in factories, but for which there is still a demand, is one of the many areas of relatively loose organization in the Soviet economy. An article in *Izvestiia* (26/VI/65:3) called for a more systematic approach to this problem.

On the other hand, the demand for labor at peak periods of farming activity is sometimes so great that kolkhozy must hire outside help. Though Anokhina and Shmeleva (1964) mention this problem in passing, a writer by the name of L. Ivanov gives it some prominence. In a trip around Kalinin Oblast in 1962, Ivanov noticed an advertisement in the raion newspaper for mowers to work on a kolkhoz at 60 kopeks per *pud* of hay. The kolkhoz chairman justified this proceeding on the grounds that, having had failures in virtually every other fodder crop, the kolhkoz had to bring in every scrap of hay, whatever the cost, or the livestock would suffer (Ivanov 1963:185–186). The case is significant for two reasons: first, it implies a population deficit on the kolkhoz in question (which is confirmed by data in Ivanov's article on other parts of the oblast); and secondly, it implies the presence of a reservoir of unemployed urban labor—probably female—from which the extra field hands could be recruited. Of course, it is common practice in major grain-growing regions such as the Kuban, the Don area, and Kazakhstan to broadcast appeals for extra hands at harvest time, but what Ivanov describes is a rather different matter. He points out quite forcefully that Kalinin Oblast is an area where people generally are unwilling to stay on the land, because of the lack of assured income.

During haying time on the kolkhozy of Kalinin Oblast, which usually lasts about two weeks, work begins at 3:00 or 4:00 A.M. and lasts until 9:00 or 10:00 A.M., then is resumed at 5:00 or 6:00 P.M. and goes on until 10:00 at night. The purpose of this schedule apparently is to avoid the heat of the day. The division of labor appears to remain traditional, with the men operating the machines in the mechanized enterprises and the women doing the nonmechanical stoop-labor.

The Contemporary Settlement Pattern

The settlement pattern—that is, the general outline of the village and the arrangement of buildings within it—which is characteristic of a given area, tends to show considerable conservatism over the course of time, at least where there are no major disturbances such as those brought about by war. We find this to be true in most parts of Central Russia for which we have appropriate data. The most frequent type of village in the Russian countryside, except in heavily forested districts, has historically been the so-called line village, with houses arranged along both sides of a single street, which may widen at the center to form a square. The public buildings—church, stores, administrative offices—are located at or near this central point, and here also is the traditional meeting place of the *skhod* and the houses of wealthier citizens. The village of Viriatino in Tambov Oblast conformed to this general pattern, with allowance made for the topography of the area. Its houses were located in one row along the river bank, and to this day, several of the streets have houses only along one side. Beginning in the late 19th century, some houses began to be built along subsidiary streets at right angles to the main one, chiefly as a result of the splitting up of extended families. A sketch-map (Kushner, ed. 1958:45) showing the extent of the village at various times reveals no significant changes in layout since 1917, except that a small offshoot or "colony" has been established. This is centered on some of the farm buildings belonging to the "Lenin's Way" kolkhoz. As before, the public facilities—clubhouse, school, headquarters of the village soviet, and the administration building for the kolkhoz—are located in the center of the town.

In Kalinin Oblast, which in the past was also characterized by line villages, we find a somewhat different situation. Here the old villages are small and scattered, and there is now a tendency to grant land for new building not in the confines of the old village but in the new one centered on the kolkhoz. This has brought about the creation of considerably larger villages, with several parallel streets and village squares. However, planning by quarters is very rare, even in villages completely rebuilt after the war. In most cases there is no fixed orientation—that is, the houses do not all face the same direction—but in some villages, the "sunny" or southern end is longer than the northern one. Houses may also be built at an angle to the street, forming a herringbone pattern. Settlement is far less crowded than in the past, when sons would build their houses on the paternal plot and frequent fires would burn everything down. Now there are distances of 10 to 20 meters, or sometimes an entire road, between two houses.

Roads and other service facilities remain a problem in Kalinin Oblast. Most roads are still unpaved. Old wells are still in existence, but some street pumps have been put in, and there is now talk even of bringing water into the houses. The situation in other places is probably far worse. If anything is done about sanitation and other conveniences, it depends on the energy and initiative of the local people, usually working through the local soviet. In general, it is not taken care of by the state, despite constant complaints that it should be. This inherent limitation on investment in utilities and consumer services places a corresponding limitation on resettlement of the small isolated forest villages into the kolkhoz centers. People can only be moved to places where certain minimal utilities and conveniences are available. They might otherwise just as well stay in the roadless forest hamlet alongside a river bank, where they have only to dip a bucket into the water.

Kogan (1964) describes an interesting solution to the problem of resettlement. The "Red October" kolkhoz of Kirov Oblast (northeast of Gorky), after its expansion between 1955 and 1958, takes in 137 populated points—mostly small—3625 individuals, and 46,000 hectares. This is a large operation by any standards, and particularly for this area. The kolkhoz includes 10 brigades, of which two represent the population of the collective before its expansion, and the rest represent the newcomers. The kolkhozniks making up the first brigade have been resettled in the central farmstead (near the village of Vozhgali) from villages which have already been or are soon to be demolished. The second brigade lives in Chekota, which has been rebuilt and where all of the houses, including dwellings, are kolkhoz property. This represents an unusually radical solution to a problem existing in many parts of our area—that of small villages (some comprising only five or ten households) scattered among forests, lakes and swamps, for which it is prohibitively expensive to provide utilities and proper cultural facilities. The problem has been discussed repeatedly in the press, and some writers have stated that radical resettlement is the only solution. But so far very little seems to have been done.

In the "Red October" kolkhoz, there is an interesting organizational difference between the members of the first two brigades and the rest of the population. The household plots of the first group are nominal in size (0.2–0.03 hectares). Kogan (1964) explains this fact by the tradition in the original kolkhoz, which started out as a *kommuna,* and where even in the 1920s the members renounced the right of property in livestock and houses. The kolkhoz administration gives the first two brigades a cash wage plus monthly distribution of goods in accordance with earnings. Goods are distributed through the kolkhoz commissary. Those who so desire, and many do, can receive cooked meals instead. The implications of this situation are startling to anyone familiar with the Soviet peasant scene. On the face of Kogan's data it would appear that the first two brigades of this kolkhoz had given up the usual form of peasant economy and were in fact living communally. This indicates the presence of some previous communal tradition, perhaps of a religious nature, about which Kogan says nothing. The other eight brigades on the "Red October" kolkhoz are organized in a more normal fashion, with the members holding private plots of the usual size, and livestock, and receiving hay, straw, silage, free rights of pasture, and the use of horses and equipment for cultivating their private plots in addition to wages in cash.

Some Soviet writers, including Ivanov (1963), maintain that until recently the Russian heartland was being systematically bypassed in terms of investment in favor of other areas, such as Kazakhstan, the Kuban or Western Siberia, which are presumably more advantageous from an agricultural point of view and better equipped with natural resources. The result of this relative neglect is a heavy loss in population, particularly among the youth out of the rural areas of the northwest, which has recently begun to be recognized as critical.

The Family as Social Unit

There seems to be little doubt that, among the Central Russian peasantry, the family is still the social unit which most powerfully influences the activities and outlook of the individual. This continuing fact has several important consequences. The Russian peasant family, as it now exists, has inherited from prerevolutionary times a specific form and structure, with which the regime has had to deal in undertaking social legislation. On the other hand, this legislation has had the effect of emphasizing certain functions and aspects of the family and downgrading others. In considering the role and status of the family within collectivized agriculture, we must first of all note that while in formal terms membership in the kolkhoz is individual, the right to cultivate a plot of land and to own livestock (which from the individual peasant's standpoint is probably the major privilege of membership in the kolkhoz) is granted not to individuals but to *households.* A single individual may make up a household, as in the case of young unmarried specialists (teachers, agronomists, veterinarians, and so on) who often come from other parts of the country, but live and work in the kolkhoz. Even in these cases, however, the subject of the privilege is not an individual but a living unit.

This feature of Soviet law has the effect of vesting in the family what are still important economic functions. Furthermore, the household is collectively the owner of the buildings, tools, and livestock used in the private economy and of the products of this economy (Kazantsev and others, eds. No date). Thus, the household is made the subject of rights in the context not only of the kolkhoz system, but also in that of the general civil law. The concept of common household property in theory extends even to income received in cash and in kind by members of the household for labor days, and to articles bought with money so received (Kazantsev and others, eds. No date; 328).[4] It is easy to see that these provisions have produced an anomalous situation. On the one hand, we have a regime ideologically committed to revolutionary social change, and on the other, we have an institution so firmly entrenched that the regime itself has had to sanction it and endow it with important functions. The basic tension between these two elements makes itself felt when we examine the economic role of the kolkhoz household.

The household is in the first instance a unit which earns and spends income both in cash and kind. The study of Viriatino contains detailed economic data which throw light on this problem, although the data are by now partly out of date and must be handled with caution in other respects as well. Since the procedure used in carrying out this economic study raises important points of theory and methodology, it may be as well to give here the principles on which it was based. The authors selected the budgets of 24 presumably representative households for detailed analysis. In the study, the amount of income of these households, its sources and nature (whether received in cash or in kind) and the amount and nature of household expenditures are given. The households are divided according to the social status of their heads—rank-and-file kolkhozniks, leading workers and officials, or members of the "kolkhoz intelligentsia" (agronomists, veterinarians, and other technical specialists)—and subdivided according to their occupations within the kolkhoz economy. Households where some members work outside the kolkhoz were placed in a special category. Concurrently, a number of budget classes were set up depending on the relation between the number of breadwinners and the number of dependents within the household. One class included households where the number of breadwinners equals or exceeds the number of dependents; a second, those where the number of dependents exceeds the number of breadwinners; a third, the families of widows, where there are no adult males, and in some cases no working members other than the widowed mother. The total sample studied in regard to the budget amounted to 363 households.

Case. I. Rank-and-file kolkhoznik employed in field agriculture; number of breadwinners equal to or exceeding number of dependents. In 1954–1955, the

---

[4] There was at one time a tendency among Soviet jurists to make the kolkhoz household a juridical "person"; this has been avoided, however, as it would have involved ultimately giving the household legal importance commensurate with that of the kolkhoz. Kazantsev's manual of kolkhoz law states specifically: "The household as the holder of rights may not be considered as either a physical or a juridical person. It is considered a special subject of law, not belonging to either one or the other of these forms." (Kazantsev and others, eds. No date: 318–319)

family consisted of four members: the husband and wife, their widowed daughter-in-law, and her younger daughter, a pupil in the 7th class. Her elder daughter, who finished the 7th class in 1953, went to Moscow to work, and at the end of 1955 returned to the family and began working in the kolkhoz. The members of the household employed in the kolkhoz economy are the head of the family and the daughter-in-law. In 1954, they earned between them 534 labor days (220 earned by the daughter-in-law), for which they received 18.69 *tsentners* of grain and 2937 rubles in cash. In 1955, they earned 517 labor days, receiving 18 *tsentners* of grain (10.34 of these in millet, used chiefly to feed livestock), and 4136 rubles in cash. In addition, the daughter-in-law, because her husband was killed in the war, receives 1320 rubles annually from the state as support for her younger daughter. The family needs at least 11 *tesntners* of grain per year, including the fodder for the animals. Since 1947, the labor day has been worth from 4–6 kilograms of grain, including millet (Kushner, ed. 1958:167)[5] and the family has a grain surplus of approximately 10 *tsentners,* which remains from year to year. No grain is sold. The family has a profitable private economy—0.4 hectares (the maximum) in potatoes and vegetables, including 0.15 hectares in tobacco, which is sold. They have a cow, two sheep with young, and a dozen chickens, and they raise a pig every year to between 110 and 130 kilograms. The produce obtained from the kolkhoz in payment for labor days and from the private economy feeds the family and leaves a surplus. The family is well supplied with meat, fats, and milk products, the bulk of which apparently derive from the private economy. The chief food items purchased are sugar, groats (for making porridge) and fine wheat flour, since the kolkhoz gives only coarse flour for labor days. The parents buy very few clothes—chiefly everyday work clothes. The wardrobe expenses of the daughter-in-law and her younger daughter were formerly paid entirely out of the pension money, which is not included in the family's common fund. In 1955, however, the mother-in-law allotted a considerable sum from her own earnings to buy clothing for her daughter-in-law and granddaughter.

Case II. Rank-and-file kolkhoznik employed in field agriculture; number of breadwinners equal to or exceeding number of dependents. This is a young couple with two young children, living with the old mother. The husband and wife work in the kolkhoz. In 1953, the family's house was burned down during a fire in the village, and almost all their property was destroyed. A new house had to be built during the summer, and the couple's earnings that year were small. A grain surplus of 16 *tsentners* survived the fire, however, and was sold to build the new house. Six sheep were sold also for the same purpose. By 1958 the family was on its feet economically, thanks to aid from the state in the form of a building loan and the provision of free building materials. In 1954 the couple earned 550 labor days, and received 19.25 *tsentners* of grain and 3025 rubles in cash; in 1955, they earned an equal amount of grain and 4560 rubles in cash. Since the family's grain requirement amounts to not more than 10 or 11 *tsentners* annually (including fodder for the animals), there is a year-to-year surplus, as in Case I. During 1955, the family paid off the building loan.

---

[5] On page 158, a table gives the payment for the labor day in cash and in kind between 1952 and 1956 and shows that the grain allotment never during this period exceeded 3.9 kilograms and was usually around 3.5. This is only one of several discrepancies which mar this monograph.

The families in this group, if we take Cases I and II as representative, seem to be fairly self-sufficient, and even, as in Case II, able to stand up to catastrophe. However, the accounts given of these cases contain a number of tantalizing omissions and apparent inconsistencies. For instance, we are not told anything at all about the private economy of the family in Case II, nor are we told where or how they lived while their house was being rebuilt. Likewise, the reader will note that in Case II, there would seem to be three dependents (counting the old mother), and only two wage earners, which is at variance with the classification used by Kushner's group. If this does not represent merely an editorial oversight, it is possible that the authors do not regard the old mother as a dependent, since she looks after the private economy and cares for the children, thus freeing the young wife to work in the kolkhoz. As we will see, this is a common and highly significant pattern in Russian peasant families. Further, the fact that in Case I, the daughter-in-law bought her own and her younger daughter's clothes out of pension money, and that this fact was not reckoned with the family's common resources deserves special note. The same is generally true by Russian peasant custom for the earnings of women, although it apparently does not apply in all cases to cash received for labor days.

The families in the next group, where the number of dependents exceeds the number of wage earners, are in a somewhat different position. Here there are usually no grandparents to take care of the children, and hence the wife is unable to work in the kolkhoz. This leads us into a whole cluster of problems which will be treated in detail when we discuss the position of women. However, we may note here that since, on most kolkhozy, day-care facilities for preschool children either are lacking or operate only part-time or in an unsatisfactory manner, a great many women are confined to their homes and to the daily routine of housework and children. These tasks are more burdensome in the Soviet Union than in the United States because of the far lower level of "domestic mechanization." This, in turn, makes many Soviet women, particularly in the countryside, less accessible than men to the influences of "Soviet reality," which, anthropologically speaking, we would classify under culture change.

Resuming our survey of budget data, we find:

Case III. Rank-and-file kolkhoznik employed in field agriculture and animal husbandry; number of dependents exceeding number of wage earners. The family consists of a husband and wife and four children; the three eldest in school. The wife is in poor health and does not earn the minimum number of labor days. In 1953, the family earned 502 labor days and received only 13.62 *tsentners* of grain because the harvest was poor; five *tsentners* were left over from the previous year. Since the family needed at least 11 *tsentners* of grain (not counting fodder), there was no grain surplus at the end of 1953. The family received 1330 rubles in cash, including 807 rubles in supplementary payments from the MTS, (Machine Tractor Station). The cash expenses of the family are covered out of cash received for labor days, state grants (the father's pension as an injured war veteran and a grant for the fourth child),[6] and the income from the private economy. In 1954, the family earned 540

---

[6] Since 1954, the father's pension as a wounded veteran of World War II has been cut in half: it is not paid from May to October, when he works in the MTS. In May 1955, the grant for the youngest child was cut off when she reached the age of five.

labor day and received 18.9 *tsentners* of grain and 3524 rubles in cash. In 1955, it earned 647 labor days and received 22.46 *tsentners* of grain and 6269 rubles in cash including supplementary pay from the MTS. The wounded veteran's pension (640 rubles) was also part of the family's cash income.

The family has a private plot of 0.4 hectares, planted mainly to potatoes and vegetables, but with some shag tobacco and millet as well. In 1955, they began to put in an orchard (15 apple trees). They have a cow, three sheep with young, and 10 chickens, and every year they raise a pig to 110 kilograms. The private economy gives the family a certain amount of cash income—from the sale of the tobacco, part of the millet, the wool, and the young livestock—but this income does not exceed 2000 rubles in any one year, and in 1955 it fell to 1130 rubles. Whereas in former years, all of the young were sold, in 1955 two sheep were slaughtered for the family's own use, and as a result its consumption of meet and fats rose somewhat by comparison with the previous years. During the summer, the family lives chiefly on milk products and vegetables, with which it is abundantly supplied.

The bulk of the family's cash expenditures goes for the purchase of clothes, of which 87.5 percent in 1953 were for the children. In 1954, the mother went twice to Moscow. A significant proportion of the family's cash expenditures is for the education of the two elder children in the 10–year school at Kulevatovo (300 rubles tuition, 40 rubles a month for room, five rubles each weekly pocket money). The children are provided with food from home in the amounts customary for Viriatino families. The weekly ration per child is: 1–2 kilograms of meat, 1–2 kilograms of wheat (apparently for cereal), 200 grams of lard or clarified butter, 200 grams of sugar, 6–8 kilograms of bread, and 17 measures of potatoes. These are supplied in one batch to last the entire winter.

Case IV. Rank-and-file kolkhoznik employed in animal husbandry; number of dependents exceeding number of wage earners. In 1953, the family consisted of eight persons—the parents and six children. The father worked as a stableman, and the oldest son in a field brigade. Two of the children were in the junior classes of the Viriatino school and three were of preschool age. The mother did not work because of the small children. In 1952, the family had earned 698 labor days and received 27.22 *tsentners* of grain, including 6.28 *tsentners* of millet; five *tsentners* of grain remained from 1951. Since the family needed only 12 *tsentners* annually, including fodder, the supply of grain was not only adequate but left a considerable surplus. In 1952, the family received 1605 rubles in payments for labor days, and 1720 rubles in state grants for large families. The family had a garden of 0.4 hectares, planted to potatoes and vegetables, a cow, two sheep with young, and about 10 chickens. Every year they raised a pig to 110 kilograms. None of the produce of the private economy was sold except for a calf; everything else went to feed the family. The only articles of food bought were sugar and occasionally candy and pastries. The large size of the family made necessary considerable expenditures on clothing. Some money was also spent for entertainment, chiefly for visits to the movies for the elder children. In 1953, during the fire mentioned in Case II, the property of the family and its stores of grain burned, but the stone walls of their house remained. The state granted loans and contributed building materials, and help was also supplied by relatives, so the family was able to make repairs and preserve its livestock intact. The kolkhoz also replaced 6–7 *tsentners* of the grain which had burned. The precise earnings of this family in cash and in kind for 1954 and 1955 are not given. It is merely stated that they were sufficient to permit the family to recover fully from the effects of the fire.

Case V. Rank-and-file kolkhoznik employed in animal husbandry; number of dependents exceeding the number of wage earners. The family consists of seven members—the parents and five children. Two of the children study in the 7–year school; three are of preschool age. In addition, two other children live away from home: a son was called to the colors in 1951, and a daughter is studying at the Teachers' Institute in Tambov and living on a stipend. She is regularly sent food and money by the family. The major wage earner is the father, who works as a stableman. The mother, because of the small children, does not earn the minimum. In 1953, the family earned 531 labor days, and received 13.27 *tsentners* of grain, including about seven *tsentners* of millet. Eight *tsentners* of grain were left over from 1952. The family's cash resources consist of payments for labor days (1035 rubles for 1953), and state grants for the children (1560 rubles). The wife's mother lives with the family in the winter and helps with the housework and the children. As a result, the family is able to use her land allotment (0.22 hectares) as well as its own (0.4 hectares). The private economy is similar to that described for the other cases; nothing is sold.

1954 saw a marked improvement in the material status of this family. Earnings were 18.4 *tsentners* of grain and 2893 rubles in cash, as well as 2040 rubles in state grants. A pig and one sheep were slaughtered, and the family considered slaughtering the calf as well. A large quantity of sugar was bought, which apparently had not been done previously. They sold no grain, and had a year's supply on hand. In 1954, the elder daughter graduated from the Teachers' Institute, found work, and began contributing materially to the support of the family. The improvement in its material condition continued in 1955, when it earned 612 labor days, receiving 21.42 *tsentners* of grain, and 4896 rubles in cash, as well as 2040 rubles in state large-family grants.

From the preceding three cases, one gets the impression that the Viriatino peasant family during the years in question operated to a marked degree on a subsistence basis, at least as far as food was concerned. The grain allotments, of course, constitute an important qualification. It is interesting, however, that until the important changes of 1954 and 1955, the private economies of the "Lenin's Way" kolkhozniks seem to have equalled or exceeded in productiveness their participation in the kolkhoz economy from the individual family's point of view. What money was received from the kolkhoz (or in one of the cases, from the private economy)was spent for capital investment, which under Soviet conditions includes clothing. In Case III, the family had a total cash income of almost 7000 rubles a year. If we take into account that the grain received from the kolkhoz for labor days is part of the family's income, we may conclude that there was an effort at this time to bring the earnings of kolkhozniks into line with those of people in other branches of the economy. According to the most reliable estimates (DeWitt 1961:64n), Soviet blue-collar and white-collar workers in 1955 had an average annual wage of 8500 rubles. It should be borne in mind that both these figures are given in old rubles, of which 10 equal one new ruble. The revaluation of the currency took place in 1960. It was purely a paper transaction and did not affect the prices of goods or services. With regard to the tuition charges paid for the children in the 10–year school in Case III, it should be noted that all tuition charges in secondary schools were abolished in 1956 (DeWitt 1961). Even before this date, tuition charges did not apply in many cases (students from low-income families or families with many children, orphans and half-orphans, children of members of the armed forces, and so on), and most successful students received stipends. It is also worth noting that as far as this account goes, the children in school ate no vegetables—at least there is no mention of vegetables among the foodstuffs provided by the family. Perhaps the problem was one of perishability.

The kolkhoznik in Case V, whose old mother lived with him part of the time and gave the family the use of her land allotment, illustrates a very common problem in the Russian village, and one of great structural importance. The addition of the mother-in-law's allotment increased the land available to the family by more than 50 percent, whereas it would seem that her presence during the winter did not increase its consumption of food by anything like that amount. In view of this fact, the situation looks like a fictitious division—in which a family ostensibly splits up in order to gain an extra allotment but continues to conduct its economy in common. This, needless to say, is highly disapproved of, and kolkhozy have been fighting it almost since the beginning of the system, but no objection appears to be made to it in this case.

Three special categories of kolkhoz families remain to be discussed: those headed by officials, specialists, and skilled workers; those with members working outside the kolkhoz; and widowed families, where often there are no male working members. Each of these groups has its own special characteristics and illustrates particular problems.

Case VI. Brigadier of field brigade; number of dependents exceeding number of wage earners. The family consists of five members—the parents, two preschool children, and the husband's old mother. Until 1955, the father worked from year to year as a stockman on the livestock farm, while the wife worked in a field brigade. The couple earned on the average no less than 550 labor days per year, which at the prevailing rate of pay in grain, not only amply provided for the family but left a surplus. In 1953, their income dropped as a result of the bad harvest: earnings were 589 labor days, 14.72 *tsentners* of grain, and 1148 rubles in cash. In 1954, for 533 labor days, the family received 18.65 *tsentners* of grain and 2931 rubles in cash. In 1955, having been promoted to brigadier, the father earned 540 labor days and his wife 210. They received 26.25 *tsentners* of grain, and 6000 rubles in cash, as well as 650 rubles in bonuses for growing tobacco. The private economy consists of a plot of 0.4 hectares in potatoes and vegetables and some millet; 0.1 hectare is planted to fruit and berries. In 1955, the family had a cow with a calf, a heifer, five sheep with young, and about 20 chickens; and also they fattened a pig to 160 kilograms. As a rule, nothing was sold from the private economy, but in 1955 the family sold the cow for 2300 rubles, but retained the heifer. Their total cash income in 1955 (including the money received for the cow) came to 8950 rubles.

Case VII. Kolkhoz carpenter; number of wage earners exceeding number of dependents. In 1952, the family consisted of eight persons—the old parents, two married sons and their children. There were five working members, three of them highly skilled. Besides the old father, there was a son who was a veterinary assistant and a daughter-in-law who was bookkeeper of the kolkhoz. In 1952, the family earned 1974 labor days and received 77 *tsentners* of grain. The surplus was extremely large, since an equal amount had been received in 1949 and 1950, and the family's need for grain did not exceed 16–20 *tsentners* a year. According to the calculations of one member, the family had on hand at least 55,000–60,000 rubles worth of grain. This considerable resource was entirely controlled by the old father, and the younger generation took no part in conducting the economy or planning expenditures. The cash earnings for labor days (4540 rubles in 1952) also went into the common fund. The only items of income kept separate were the elder daughter-in-law's salary as bookeeper, and the younger son's verteran's pension, which were spent by them as they saw fit. The private economy consisted of a garden plot of 0.4 hectares, planted mainly to potatoes and vegetables, and a cow, a yearling heifer, five sheep with young, 15 chickens, and one or two pigs fattened each year. Nothing was sold from the private economy. The family was well supplied with meat during the winter, and consumed as well a great many dairy products—fresh and sour milk, sweet and sour cream, cottage cheese—and eggs in the spring and summer. The proportion of purchased goods in the diet was insignificant: salt, sugar, fish (fresh in summer, salted in winter), apples, melons preserved for the winter, and candy and pastry, especially for the children.

In recent years, the family had not invested in any home improvements. The house consisted of two rooms—the kitchen where the old parents lived, and the parlor occupied by the young married couples.

In 1954, the family earned 1844 labor days, received 64.5 *tsentners* of grain, and 10,144, rubles in cash. During 1953 and 1954, a child was born to each of the young couples. For this reason, the family broke up in May 1955, and the elder son set up a separate household. Two hundred *puds* of grain (7200 pounds or between 32–33 *tsentners*) were sold from the household grain stores, and a house was bought with the proceeds. The grain remaining after the sale was divided equally, and the separating family received 35 *tsentners* of grain, 17 *tsentners* of millet, a cow with a calf, a pig, a sheep with a lamb, and six chickens. The kolkhoz alloted them a garden plot of 0.4 hectares. The ethnographers comment at this point: "Thus, the young family set up independent housekeeping on a good economic basis, entirely sufficient for the carrying out of the economic plans which it had made (the covering of the roof with iron, the facing of the stone walls with boards, the purchase of furniture, and so on)." (Kushner ed.1958:171) During 1955, the separated family earned 1294 labor days, of which the wife—a bookkeeper for the kolkhoz—earned 1087. For this, they received 45.29 *tsentners* of grain and 13,652 rubles in cash, including bonuses. Translating the payment in kind into cash according to the average market prices, the family's earnings from the kolkhoz in 1955 totalled 25,880 rubles.[7] The young couple's private economy is conducted on a purely subsistence basis: the garden plot is planted to potatoes, vegetables, and the beginnings of a fruit orchard. The young calves

[7] The goods received for the labor day in 1955 were converted into cash on the following basis: one kilogram of wheat at two rubles = two rubles; two kilograms of millet at three rubles = six rubles; 0.5 kilograms of rye at two rubles = one ruble; 0.5 kilograms of potatoes at one ruble = 0.5 rubles; and 2.5 rubles worth of fodder. Together with the cash payment of eight rubles, this totaled 20 rubles per labor day.

and the lambs are not sold but are kept to feed the family, as are the eggs from the chickens. A pig is being fattened. Thus, the cash resources of the family, which are considerable, can be devoted to capital investment—clothing, house furnishings, etc., which the ethnographers classify under "cultural requirements."

Case VIII. Carpenter; number of dependents exceeding number of wage earners; some members working outside the kolkhoz. The family consists of five members—the carpenter, his wife, his son by a former marriage, and his old parents. His father works in a neighboring lumbering operation. In 1953, the family earned 532 labor days, receiving 13.3 *tsentners* of grain and 1037 rubles in cash; 6–7 *tsentners* of grain remained from the previous year. In addition, the head of the family, as a skilled carpenter and cabinetmaker, earns up to 3000 rubles annually outside the kolkhoz by making window frames, furniture, and other items. The old father's pay in the lumbering operation amounts to 300–400 rubles a month, averaging 4200 rubles annually. The private economy is basically subsistence (its proportions are similar to those already described), but some of the produce is sold. For example, in 1953, 1400 rubles were realized from the sale of a yearling bullock and the wool from the five sheep. "Thus, the family has at its disposal rather considerable cash resources; the cash portion in 1953 constituted 61.2 percent of the family's total budget, whereas in the overwhelming majority of Viriatino families the cash portion in 1953 (and in previous years) did not exceed 15–20 percent, and this affected all aspects of the family's way of life." (Kushner ed. 1958:172) This conclusion is presumably reached by calculating the payment in kind for the labor day according to the average market prices in 1953. The ethnographers state that the carpenter and his wife, both veterans of World War II, are widely travelled and rather more sophisticated than most Viriatino people. Hence, their expenditures for cultural purposes (in the Soviet classification) are somewhat greater than might be expected. Their house, one of the best in the village, is furnished in urban style. All male members of the family have bicycles; there is a phonograph and other "cultural" items, and the family spends a considerable amount of money each year on clothing. It is pointed out, however, that expenditures on cultural needs in a narrow sense (tuition for the boy in the 10-year school, visits to the movies, subscriptions to newspapers) are not above the level usual in Viriatino.

The foregoing three cases illustrate a number of highly significant points. Principally, they show that the way to be well off on the kolkhoz (as anywhere else) is to possess skill or training, or to be appointed to a position of authority and responsibility. The availability of special skills in the family is the main explanation for the rather startling prosperity of Case VII. Skilled work is paid for at a rate which often has little to do with the time actually spent. The daughter-in-law who is a bookkeeper may work fewer hours than her rank-and-file kolkhoznik husband and bring home more money. Another explanation for the prosperity of this family is the pooling of resources and expenditures. Just as in the prerevolutionary village described by Fenomenov, the more working hands you have the better off you are. In this connection, the attitude of the ethnographers toward Case VII is extremely interesting. They describe it as the last surviving undivided joint family in the village, and further point out that the family was unable to take full advantage of its favorable economic position because its way of life was "bound by the traditions of the old parents which have not been overcome." (Kushner, ed. 1958:170) Whether this estimate of the state of things would be agreed to by the members of the family is an open question: if any of them were dissatisfied with the way the economy was being conducted, they were presumably at liberty to depart earlier. Case VII represents, as it were, a survival of the ancient Russian peasant joint family that has adapted, apparently with considerable success, to new conditions. As long as the family remained undivided, the salary of the elder daughter-in-law as kolkhoz bookkeeper was not part of the family's general cash fund but was controlled by her independently. The same thing applied before the Revolution to the earnings of women from specifically feminine occupations and enterprises, such as spinning, weaving, mushroom-gathering, or the raising of chickens. On the other hand, women in prerevolutionary Russia were expected to spend money so acquired for household purposes, such as the purchase of soap, salt, and kerosene, and clothing for themselves and their children. The use to which the daughter-in-law's salary was put in the extended family of Case VII is not stated. However, in Case I, the daughter-in-law's pension, which was also handled separately, went to clothe herself and her daughter. In Case VII, when the elder son and his wife separated from the father's family, the wife's salary was contributed toward the economy of the new household. Because of this, the cash earnings of the new family were greater than those of the entire undivided family before the separation. Case VII also illustrates another important point—the peasant habit of using grain as a medium of exchange and regarding it as money in the bank. It is significant that grain is sold, no matter how great the supply, only in order to finance capital improvements or to make repairs. Widowed families as we will see, are an exception to this rule.

If Case VII represents an extreme instance of the continuity of peasant traditions under new circumstances, Case VIII represents a group who in one sense have almost ceased to be peasants at all. We say in one sense, because it is quite possible that if we met these people and talked to them, they would seem not so much different from the other villagers of Viriatino. They conduct their economy in terms of cash to a much greater extent than occurs in any of the other cases, however, and the carpenter himself earns more from outside labor than he does from the kolkhoz. Under the circumstances, it is natural to wonder why he remains a member of the kolkhoz. The answer probably contains a number of elements. As long as he lives in the country and fulfils his obligations to the kolkhoz, his right to hold land is theoretically not open to question. Also, he may feel that he eats better on the land and lives in a less crowded fashion. One of the advantages of rural residence is that it is possible to avoid the problem of the housing shortage.

As a comparison, it is interesting to note that the cash portion of the income of kolkhozniks of Briansk Oblast, when expressed in terms of cash, amounted to 14 percent in 1953 and 63.2 percent in 1963. The average cash income per kolkhoz household for the Soviet Union as a whole was 252 rubles in 1953, 702 rubles in 1958, and 993 rubles in 1963, all of these figures being in new money (Prusakov 1965: 42). This provides us with another index of the relative prosperity of most Viriatino kolkhoz households.

Widowed families—mostly of soldiers killed in the war—are a disadvantaged group, although the degree of disadvantage varies with time and circumstances. Many of these families have no working member other than the widowed mother and therefore are especially sensitive to variations in economic condition and state policy.

Case IX. Rank-and-file kolkhoznik employed in field agriculture; one wage earner, one dependent. The head of the household is a widow whose husband was killed in 1942. Left with two small children, the widow was unable to earn more than 130–140 labor days in the kolkhoz annually. She received for the children annual state grants totalling 570 rubles. In 1951, the daughter completed the 7–year school and went to Moscow to work. Previous to this, as both children were growing up, they had begun to work in the kolkhoz, earning 30–40 labor days each summer. After the daughter's departure, the mother was left with the son, a pupil in the 7–year school. In 1953, the family earned 170 labor days (the son earned 30 of these), and received 4.25 *tsentners* of grain (including 2.21 *tsentners* of millet), and 331.50 rubles in cash. In addition, the widow received 480 rubles in state grants for the son. The household plot (0.35 hectares) was planted to potatoes and vegetables and in part to millet and tobacco. The family had two goats, a sheep with young, and chickens. Nutrition was on a low level. Some of the grain had to be sold to cover taxes and current expenses. In 1954 and 1955, with the general increase in earnings, the family's budget was considerably strengthened. In 1954, having completed the 7–year school, the son began to work; he and the mother between them earned 220 labor days and received 7.7 *tsentners* of grain and 1200 rubles in cash. In 1955, they earned 419 labor days and received 14.66 *tsentners* of grain and 3352 rubles in cash. They bought a cow, sharing its cost with a neighbor, and also began raising a piglet. They also made a number of large expenditures on clothing. As of 1958, they intended to remodel the house. A combined stove and range—for both heating and cooking, in place of the traditional Russian stove—had already been put in.

Case X. Rank-and-file kolkhoznik employed in field agriculture; one wage earner and one dependent. At the death of her husband in 1943, this widow was left with a small son. In 1945, she separated from her mother-in-law's family. Working in the field brigade, she earned an average of 140–150 labor days annually. Her earnings from the kolkhoz between 1947 and 1952 consisted of from 5–9 *tsentners* of grain and not more than 300 or 400 rubles in cash. The grain supply was sufficient, except in 1948 and 1953, which were bad harvest years. (In 1953, when the labor day was worth only 2.5 kilograms of grain, most families in this category had to borrow grain against the coming year's earnings.) Even with sufficient grain, however, they were unable to keep the cow, because the house needed immediate repairs. They bought a goat and sheep instead, and beginning in 1953, raised a piglet every year. The garden of 0.23 hectares is planted to potatoes and vegetables, with some millet and tobacco. The vegetable supply is sufficient. In addition to this, the widow received 480 rubles a year in state aid for the son.

In 1954, the son went to work and, together with his mother, earned 283 labor days, receiving 9.9 *tsentners* of grain and 1556 rubles in cash. In 1955, the mother and son earned 375 labor days and received 13.12 *tsentners* of grain, including 7.5 *tsentners* of millet, and 3000 rubles in cash. The family bought a cow, going shares with a widowed neighbor. Their nutrition improved and they were able to buy some things, including a bicycle for the son.

It is clear from the cases just summarized that widowed families are handicapped by a shortage of working hands, and by the inability of many widowed mothers to earn more than the bare minimum of labor days (150 per year according to the Charter as amended in 1956, but only before 120 before 1954). It should be pointed out that wages in cash and in kind earned by dependent adolescents are paid to the adults, since minors are technically not full members of the kolkhoz. For this reason, they are not subject to the minimum, and any work they do is paid for at the established rate. Widowed families are especially susceptible to the influence of changes in the wage scale, and the sharp rise in payments during 1954 and 1955 affected them with special force. Their vulnerability is increased by the lack of working hands and they are not able to maintain the private economy at the level which allows other kolkhoz families to operate on a virtually subsistence basis from year to year (making allowance for wages in kind), and devote their cash resources to capital expenditures. By the same token, where there is no man available to make routine repairs on the house, or to cut and transport turf for fuel, the widow is compelled either to hire specialists to do these chores or to ask the help of relatives. Only in the widowed-family category is it mentioned that grain was sold to pay taxes and current expenses, or that it was necessary to borrow grain in advance during years of bad harvest. The improvement in material status of widowed families, which was noticeable over the years covered by Kushner's study, was due on the one hand to rising wage scales, and on the other merely to the passage of time, during which the widows' children grew up and bagan to work. The most disadvantaged group of families—that in which there were no working members other than the mothers—numbered 41 in July 1953, but only 26 on January 1, 1956. We see here the same process observed in Gadyshi in the 1920s and earlier, by which families rose and fell in the economic scale through the influence of biological factors.

The Public versus the Private Economy

It has been implicit throughout the foregoing discussion that the kolkhoz system contains two elements which are in effect in competition with each other, although the intensity of this competition and the forms it takes vary with circumstances. The kolkhoznik, or perhaps more accurately, the kolkhoz family, is constantly faced with the choice of whether to devote its main effort to the public economy and attempt to live on what it earns from that, or to perform the minimum of work in the public economy (only that needed to keep itself in good standing), and emphasize its private operations. Soviet ethnographers and agricultural specialists frequently point out that on weak kolkhozy, as would be expected, there is a tendency to expand the private operations, and ·on strong kolkhozy to contract them. The situation also varies from time to time in the same kolkhoz, with variations in the labor day or (particularly recently) with the introduction of other modes of payment. It is worth noting that the competition between the public and private economies takes place on the level of the family rather than on that of the individual, because in most cases it is the wife and mother (and the grandmother if there is one) who looks after the private economy. A division of labor is thus established—with the men doing the heavy work of preparing the plot for sowing, sometimes with the help of kolkhoz machinery or working stock.

In summarizing the data on the private economy, the authors of the Viriatino study (Kushner ed. 1958:177) state that the kolkhoz families "are not only fully provided with food but also have significant surpluses of grain, the sale of which allows the family to raise its standard of living from year to year." They attribute this situation to high and stable rates of pay in kind and in cash for work on the kolkhoz. Tables in other sections of the study indicate that these rates varied rather widely within the period in question, but by comparison there can be no doubt of the relative prosperity of the "Lenin's Way" kolkhoz.

Khrushchev, in a speech before a meeting of Communist Party governmental and agricultural officials on February 28, 1964 (*Izvestiia* 7/III/64:1–7), stated that in 1952 the labor day was worth one kopek in cash in Kaluga and Tula Oblasts, two kopeks in Riazan and Lipetsk Oblasts, three kopeks in Briansk and Pskov Oblasts, and four kopeks in Kostroma and Kursk Oblasts—while in other places there was no cash payment whatever. These rates contrast with a payment of 2.30 rubles per labor day reported for the "Lenin's Way" kolkhoz in 1952, expressed in old money. This marks the "Lenin's Way" as a relatively stable and prosperous kolkhoz. It seems obvious that in most parts of the Soviet Union, up to the early 1950s, the cash wage for work on the kolkhoz was nominal and the kolkhoz was regarded by its members almost exclusively as a source of grain. The basic importance of the private economy from the family's point of view is that it liberates the cash resources obtained from work in the public economy to permit a rise in the level of consumption, since very little money need be spent for food.

The Standard of Living: the Role of the Family and the Level of Consumer Services

In most Western countries, the standard of living is usually measured according to the per capita expenditures for various categories of goods, such as food, housing, clothing, and household equipment, and for services such as utilities, maintenance of goods, and entertainment. Such a method of determining the standard of living is not easily applicable to the Soviet Union. This is because much of the necessary information is not readily available and, in a socialist economy, certain categories of expenditure such as those for housing or medical care, become nominal or disappear entirely. A further complication in dealing with peasant populations results from the fact that they themselves produce a significant part of what they consume, so that a mere statement of cash income and expenditures does not adequately reflect the level at which they live. Accordingly, in the following section, we interpret "standard of living" as referring to the actual distribution of available goods. This interpretation has the further advantage under Soviet conditions in that it takes into account not only the financial resources present—that is, what a given family or population group would be able to "afford"—but the vagaries of the distribution system. Quite often we find that an item which the rural population could easily afford and would be glad to buy simply does not reach the village store, for any one of a variety of reasons. The limitation on consumption here is not an economic one from the point of view of the individual or of the family; nevertheless, it does affect the individual and the way in which the family lives.

Utilities

In this most basic category of services to the population, the regime faces severe and stubborn problems. In view of the persistent emphasis on rural electrification since the Revolution, it is rather startling to learn (*Izvestiia* 6/IV/65:1) that only 4 percent of the total electricity consumed goes to rural users, and only 2 percent is used for productive purposes in the countryside. This is in spite of the fact that two-thirds of the agricultural operations (including both kolkhozy and sovkhozy) are connected with the power network. *Izvestiia's* writer, like most Soviet writers on this topic, seems to attribute the difficulty to divided responsibility and the various bureaucratic tangles which result therefrom. He states that from now on, the Department of the State Power System (recently made over from a State Production Committee into the USSR Ministry of Power and Electrification [*Izvestiia* 3/X/65:1]) should be responsible for interruptions in service and for any consequent damage to agricultural operations. A more basic difficulty, however, would seem to be that of keeping the electrical facilities in operation with inadequate supplies and personnel. The Ministry of Agriculture is supposed to be in charge of this kind of maintenance, but it has no workers and no organization in the countryside capable of doing the work. For 11 years, the rates charged for electricity had been the same—prohibitively high for use on most kolkhozy. As of January 1, 1966, the rate was to be one kopek per kilowatt hour (*Izvestiia* 26/XII/65: 2).

This situation is reflected not only in conditions inside the kolkhozniks' homes—most of which, it seems certain, do not have electricity—but in the public facilities available to the rural population. It is very difficult to set up, for example, permanent and smooth-running child care facilities or large scale public catering without an adequate power supply. We know that even in the relatively advanced "Lenin's Way" kolkhoz, the power supply in summer up to 1956 was insufficient to provide the radio service that almost always receives first priority. In fact, it seems that Soviet authorities regard the provision of radio service as a category separate from electrification in general. Radio service is usually provided by a small loud-speaker in the home. This speaker is connected with a radio relay station (there are more than 236,000 of these in Tambov Oblast) which receives and rebroadcasts the programs from the center. Such a system involves minimal expenditures of power and minimal installation costs. Some very large *sovkhozy* and kolkhozy have their own low-voltage radio stations, which are used by the administration to send out instructions to the personnel (Anokhina and Shmeleva 1964).

In the Soviet context, there are sound social and ideological reasons for regarding "radiofication" as separate from electrification. Where a significant fraction of the population either lacks the time to do much reading, or finds it difficult because of inadequate education, the radio is the only reliable contact with the outside world. In Viriatino, a power station of 50 kilowatts capacity was built in 1947; this made it possible to electrify the basic processes in field agriculture, animal husbandry, and certain subsidiary branches of the economy, such as grain-handling, brick-making, and repairs. The adequacy of this power can be judged by the fact that until 1954–1955, the kolkhoz had 125 working mules, and 89 working horses which were used as sources of power for various processing activities. A subsidiary power station of 10 kilowatts capacity, built in 1948, is used only to run the mill. There are indications that here, as elsewhere, the *sovkhozy* get first call on what-ever resources are available.

We have already mentioned the water supply in connection with the settle-ment pattern. Here we will merely note that in the absence of indoor plumbing in the home (still in the future in most parts of rural Russia), the bathhouse is the only practical solution to problems of personal hygiene—besides having great emo-tional significance for the people. The Russian bath is essentially a steam bath or sauna, heated by a stove with or without a chimney (depending on the owner's economic status at the time of construction) and furnished with benches on which the bathers sit. Steam is produced by pouring water over hot stones at the stove-mouth or on the stove itself. Bathing or steaming has long been one of the major pleasures of the Russian peasant. The bathhouse is also the traditional place for women to give birth, but this custom has now virtually disappeared. In prerevolu-tionary times, every reasonably well-to-do peasant family had its own bathhouse, which was sometimes, as in Gadyshi, located in a special part of the village away from the main farmstead. There are still some private bathhouses, although for most kolkhoz families, space is at a premium. As for public bathhouses, this is one of the most persistent topics for complaint in the press. Bathhouses hardly exist outside of *raion* and *oblast* centers; in 1963 none were being built in Riazan Oblast while in Kaluga Oblast there were only 34. In Moscow Oblast, 622 populated points had 70 baths belonging to local soviets, *sovkhozy* or kolkhozy, and 180 very small ones for private needs. In 20 *raions*, 19,000 people were living without any bathhouses and none were being planned. In other *raions*, nine bathhouses with 108 places had been projected, but only three with 40 places were actually built. These are not modern structures by any means and, in most cases, state money was not used; materials were handed out by the local village soviet executive committee, and such materials (as for any other building) are hard to come by. (*Sovety depu-tatov trudiashchikhsia* 1963, no. 9, 43–48, No. 10, 84–87.)

Under conditions where the nearest source of water is often a considerable distance from the house, where a minimum of 20–30 buckets of water is required for a bath, where the old type of bathhouse is not available, and where the custom of steaming onself on the top of the stove is no longer practicable (due to changed tastes and internal household arrangements), it is not surprising that con-siderations of personal hygiene sometimes get short shrift. These matters may not be too disturbing to the older people, but the younger generation has been led to set different standards for its environment. This is one of the factors which make many young people unwilling to remain in the countryside. Viriatino, however, is relatively fortunate in having one public bathhouse, 80 private ones, and an ade-quate water supply.

In some places, the water problem grows increasingly critical, apparently due to a combination of poor maintenance of wells and a drop in the water table. In a village in Lipetsk Oblast (*Izvestiia* 20/III/64:3), all but two of the 23 springs which ran before the Revolution are now unusable, and the two remaining ones are drying up. In the case cited, this was only one of a multitude of problems—the results of graft, fecklessness and poor leadership—which plagued the population.

Telephones in private houses are not considered essential in rural Russia, and their absence is not even noticed. However, there are places in which even the administration of kolkhozy or the local soviets are not connected by telephone with the outside world. These are often small settlements in the remoter parts of the district, where the only real solution ro problems of communication, transport, and consumer services would be complete resettlement.

Transport

The roads in Russia are generally poor, and unusable for long periods during the spring and fall. This is one of the factors that result in the partial cutting off of the village from the outside world, and in the raising of the cost of agricultural production. It represents a constant drag on the process of development. The presence of seven trucks and various other automotive equipment on the "Lenin's Way" kolkhoz in 1956 is one indication of the relative prosperity of this operation. Of course, this equipment belongs to the kolkhoz, and the individual kolkhoz family must make do with bicycles, a motorcycle (if it is fortunate), or, in some cases, a horse for its personal transporatation. For longer journeys, there are supposedly regular buses which, like buses everywhere, fail to satisfy the commuter. There is also the railroad, but many localities are literally off the track.

Household Goods

According to the Viriatino authors, the records of the local cooperative store show a sharp rise over the years covered by their study in purchases by the kolkhozniks of costly items such as furniture, phonographs, and decorations for the home. At the same time, consumer goods is the sector of the economy with which writers in the Soviet press, and the people in general, are least satisfied. The trade network suffers from the deadening effect of centralized planning, usually done without any knowledge of actual customer demand. Attempts are now being made to correct these deficiencies by the use of merchandizing methods standard in other countries, and by requiring that goods of which samples are shown actually be available for purchase. The Viriatino authors complain that the artistic level of decorations in the village homes is very low. This, they emphasize, is not the fault of the residents, who show fine taste in their embroidery, wood carving, and so on. However, the market is flooded with vulgar painted hangings in farfetched colors produced by means of stencils, which are often the only kind of decoration available.

Housing Construction and Maintenance

The architecture and internal arrangement of the Russian peasant dwelling will be dealt with later in detail under the heading of material culture. Here we will concentrate on the economic aspects of rural housing and the specific procedures for getting a house built.

In Viriatino, and apparently in many other places as well, many prerevolutionary wooden and (particularly) brick houses are still in use. The result is that comparatively little new building is being done in such villages, except when there is a fire or some similar catastrophe. If a new house is necessary, the kolkhoz can make a long-term loan from its capital fund. Alternatively, the head of the household may receive a loan directly from the state, and the local soviet provides building materials (Case II). The labor for building a house is supplied by the construction brigade of the kolkhoz, and in many instances, by members of the family involved. There are many parts of Russia where almost every male peasant has some knowledge of carpentry and can work satisfactorily under supervision. The building of brick houses for private use, which was common before the Revolution and during the 1920s, had ceased in the 1950s. The entire limited brick supply was being devoted to public uses. In fact, brick production in Tambov Oblast has been cut back (*Izvestiia* 26/III/65:3), although plans are being made to remedy the situation (*Izvestiia* 10/VI/65:3). The earlier account notes that on one *sovkhoz* it had been necessary to haul about a million bricks over the previous two years. This meant 900 truck trips in all sorts of weather at a cost of 16,000 rubles. Every year thousands of new homes are built in the Oblast, and many more are repaired, but the work is all done with lumber. Bricks would be cheaper if they were available.[8] The authors of the Viriatino study describe a number of extremely complex maintenance and repair procedures for old houses, such as laying new cement and brick foundations, replacing individual worn-out bricks with new ones, plastering walls inside and outside with special mixtures for fireproofing and against damp, and installing cloth ceilings. These procedures are very laborious but sparing of materials. Their prevalence indicates that labor for repairing an old house is easier to come by than materials for building a new one. Current press reports on construction indicate that the situation has not changed basically since the Viriatino study was written. We must remember that private housing construction must compete with the construction of public facilities and kolkhoz farm buildings for funds and building materials. This is a massive operation, and suffers from all sorts of stresses and strains, not least of which is the fact that construction materials are in short supply, and there is a brisk trade by speculation. (*Izvestiia* 12/III/66:3).

In areas where collectivization or the enlargement of existing kolkhozy involves large-scale resettlement of the population, housing construction is carried out

---

[8] Ethnographically, Tambov Oblast is on the border between a region in which wood is the normal building material for houses (north and central Great Russia) and a region marked by the use of brick (south Great Russia and the Ukraine). In Tambov Oblast, the forests were cut over some time ago, and lumber is scarce, while the supply of brick-clay is adequate, and it is only a question of extracting it.

on a rather different basis. Large appropriations may be made directly by agencies of the government of the USSR or of the Russian Federation. Even here, however, the money appropriated is often not fully utilized. Many agencies carry on construction only in the summer, when it is most difficult to hire workers. (*Izvestiia* 1/V/65:4).

Recently an agency has been established to supervise construction, both public and private, on kolkhozy. But according to a report in *Izvestiia* (30/IX/65:5) reaction is less than enthusiastic, since both workers and materials are supplied by the kolkhozy. The agency only disburses the funds, which are also provided by the kolkhozy.

Cultural Services and Entertainment

The problem of cultural and recreational facilities in the countryside is more important than it might appear at first glance, for a number of reasons. First of all, the regime is committed to making over the Soviet citizen in a new image, and to this end must use every means of ideological influence—the arts, popularization of scientific discoveries, and the direction of social activities. Secondly, it has become increasingly clear that an adequate recreation program in the countryside is one of the pre-conditions for halting the departure of the young people to the cities, which in some cases has reached disastrous proportions. The chief problems encountered in trying to set up recreation programs in the countryside are capital investment and personnel. In the fierce competition among various branches of the economy for funds, cultural services are frequently shortchanged. Ideally, every kolkhoz village should have a clubhouse equipped to present films, concerts, plays, lectures, and so on. In practice, for example, there are 90 places in Tambov Oblast with populations of 500–3000 which have no clubs at all. (*Izvestiia* 3/VI/65:3). In many other places where clubs do exist, they function intermittently, and do not present a balanced program. Trained personnel are wanting in most cases. There are 530 people leading clubs in Tambov Oblast, but only 40 of them have special education. The kind of training the ethnographers seem to favor is choreography, choral music, and folk instrumental music (Anokhina and Shmeleva, 1964).

The problems of maintaining these services are compounded by the fact that there is no separate provision in the state budget for the repair of clubhouses and cultural facilities. The local soviets are expected to handle this matter from their own already limited funds, sometimes with the aid of a general subsidy. Thus, the clubs and cultural institutions of Tambov Oblast receive only about 15–20 percent of the plaster and other materials needed for repairs. At the same time, the clubs are not allowed to rent out their premises or to keep more than a small fraction of what they receive in admissions to films.[9]

A writer in *Izvestiia* (1/X/64:3) points out that the over-all state plan of investment for the building of clubs, libraries, movie installations, and so on is

---

[9] In the cities of Smolensk Oblast, 25 percent of net collections for movies is retained; in *raion* centers, it is 13 percent, and in the villages, only 3 percent. (*Izvestiia*, 4/XII/64:5).

set up in terms of totals for the whole country and does not specify the distribution of these facilities. The result is that they are built by economically strong kolkhozy and *sovkhozy,* but not by the weaker ones, thus intensifying both the difference between the two groups and the drain of young people from the countryside. The writer suggests that long-term loans be granted to kolkhozy and *sovkhozy* for the building of clubs and cultural facilities, and the loan policy of the State Bank be changed to permit it to finance the construction of small movie houses (150–200 seats). Subsequently (*Izvestiia* 10/XI/64:5), an official of the State Planning Commission explained that movie houses were usually built through loans from the State Bank made to motion picture administrations under Republican Councils of Ministers and Krai and Oblast Executive Committees. Thus, yet another class of agencies was interposed between the state which made the original investment and the people for whom the facilities were ultimately intended.

The general inadequacy of cultural and entertainment facilities in the Russian countryside (there are exceptions, but they are strongly pointed out as such) has two further significant consequences—one chiefly from the regime's point of view, the other chiefly from the observer's. In the first place, where cultural and entertainment facilities break down, religious groups step in to fill the vacuum. This may mean the Orthodox Church, but more frequently it is one of the more aggressive Protestant denominations. The point is that where, as is usually the case, religion is the refuge of the elderly and uneducated, the regime is not overly concerned. Antireligious propaganda, though still part of the ideological program, receives a low priority. Where religion begins to attract the young people for esthetic and social reasons, however, energetic measures are likely to be taken. The result is that whatever cultural facilities and entertainment are available are oriented toward the youth, and the middle-aged and elderly tend to be left to their own devices. (Iankova 1963; Kryvelev 1963). But where an appreciable portion of child-raising is done by grandparents, in order to permit the mothers to work, the older generation is not without social influence. Thus, the common Soviet attitude which tends to dismiss the older section of the population from consideration in matters of policy is at least open to question.

Secondly, as Anokhina and Shmeleva point out (1964), in the absence of satisfactory clubhouses and other facilities for organized social activity, the traditional social and courtship patterns (the *posidelka* and so forth) reassert themselves. They are abandoned immediately, however, when a club is established.

Izvestiia (8/IV/65:3, 10/IV/65:5) undertook an analysis of cultural services in Tambov, which they considered an average oblast center. Television comes from Moscow, but Tambov is not on the route for road shows. A population sample of 540 people were given questionnaires, and it was found that 60 of them were engaged in some form of study. Of the four individuals whose recreational interests were studied in detail, the oldest, a housewife, was also the most cut off from any cultural interests. She had no books, no television, attended no meetings or social evenings at the factory, and had no specific plans for the future. Of the three younger people mentioned in detail, two are studying. Only one does any appreciable amount of reading apart from study. They attend meetings and the like about four to six times a month, and enjoy other forms of outside recreation (dances, movies, concerts, the theater) with about the same frequency. The people surveyed spent 10–15 percent of their evenings "in the collective"—that is, with large groups, usually at their places of work. The writers imply that time spent in the collective is insufficient. The ambitions of the people studied in detail are to buy a motorcycle, to live in a big city, to enter a teacher's college in the foreign language department. These are the usual terms in which social mobility is conceived in the Soviet context. The essential problem as the authors of this survey see it—and this applies in the countryside perhaps even more than in towns—is that the campaign to "reach everyone," to put everyone in contact with public life in some form, applies only to people who are in trouble. If a man fulfils his work norms, does not drink to excess, or beat his wife (or if she fails to complain), what is the reason to reach him? The authors also note the lack of an adequate cafe as a meeting place for young people. A restaurant is used for this purpose once a month, but they consider this insufficient, and in any case, the premises are not properly outfitted. Another restaurant could be used in the afternoon for this purpose, or various enterprises in the town could be moved to make room for it. Finally, the baby-sitting problem hampers educational and cultural work: young married people cannot attend the meetings. The organizer would like to see a nursery established at the club house, staffed by adolescent girls, but funds for this are lacking.

In summary, we see no indication that peasants in any age group would not take advantage of "socialist forms" of leisure-time activity. Where these are available, they closely approximate urban forms—movies, plays, symphony concerts, choral performances, and art exhibits. The point is that in most places, they are not available.

Consumer Services

Under this heading, we will discuss such matters as the repair and maintenance of clothing and household equipment, public catering, and miscellaneous service facilities such as barbershops. The social importance of this class of services lies in the fact that if facilities for them are not provided, the services must either be done without or obtained within the family. Their presence or absence therefore reflects directly on the scope and importance of the functions which the family has to perform.

Complaints about consumer services are plentiful both in the lay press and in specialized ethnographic literature. It is readily admitted that in large sections of Russia such services hardly exist outside of oblast or *raion* centers. Experiments have been made with mobile service facilities in other parts of the Soviet Union (Siberia, Kazakhstan, the Baltic Republics), but these have not yet been extended to the area with which we are concerned. Almost everywhere service agencies lack their own means of transport. Hence, one must go considerable distances for such simple projects as having a suit cleaned, a pair of shoes resoled, or one's hair cut.

The problem is only partially one of investment. Indeed, in this matter we encounter an absence of the centralized planning that might provide the only answer. In an article in *Izvestiia* (7/VIII/65:4) dealing with the city of Lipetsk, the problem is discussed in some detail. The writer states that the principle of organizing consumer services by industry—that is, one set for railroad workers, another for metal workers, a third for textile workers, and so on, (each presided over by the Union Ministry having jurisdiction over that particular branch of industry) —leads to a great deal of duplication and waste of resources. In most cases, this is not justified by the specific character of the people for whom the facilities are intended. The point here is that kolkhozniks apparently form an exception to this rule: no single central agency concerns itself with providing consumer services for them. This is once more left to the kolkhozy, which are overburdened as it is, and whose main functions lie elsewhere. Part of the job is also left to the local soviets, which do not have the resources to cope with it—particularly in areas of widely scattered population and poor communications. Where consumer-service facilities do exist in the countryside, they are usually totally inadequate to meet the demands placed upon them. Blame for this unsatisfactory condition is usually laid on the building agencies for their failure to complete the construction of such facilities within the allotted time; or on bureaucrats who may allocate to other agencies existing buildings or parts of them which were supposed to be used for consumer services. As usual, such attributions of responsibility are half-truths—half-truths which ignore the fact that the builders spend much of their time waiting for supplies, and that the bureaucrats, besides being only human, have to strike a balance with a dozen other quite legitimate demands for every square meter of space.

There is yet another problem connected with the consumer-service network in Russia: the fact that the Soviet people pride themselves most of all on having provided basic necessities (primarily education and medical service) and a few luxuries to enormous numbers of small communities. Thus the Minister for Communal Services of the Russian Soviet Federative Socialist Republic (RSFSR) noted that as of January 1, 1963, there were 640 million square meters of new housing in the RSFSR—a 29 percent increase over 1958—which benefited 35 million people. The number of boarding schools had increased 3.6 times over the same five-year period, and in the RSFSR as a whole there were 89 hospital beds and more than three doctors for every 1000 people (*Izvestiia* 5/IV/63:1–2). Pravye Lampki, within visiting distance of Viriatino, is a small cluster of villages which has four clubs with movie projectors, four libraries, four medical points, and four primary, one middle, and one eight-year school. The latter has electricity and central heating. There are also two electrical stations, about 50 automobiles, many combines and tractors and an inter-kolkhoz brick plant with a 4-million-brick capacity—no doubt responsible for the many new brick homes—and, so the writer claims, even television. (*Izvestiia* 6/XI/63:3) There were more than 5000 television sets in Tambov Oblast in 1961, most of them in clubs, and "red corners" or recreation centers.

Child Care

The providing of day-care and preschool facilities for small children is perhaps the most important aspect of the cultural and consumer services problem. This is so for a number of reasons which are in themselves socially significant. Obviously, the admission of married women into the labor force is contingent on their children being cared for during working hours—either by grandparents or babysitters, or at centers maintained by public agencies. Many women in Viriatino and in other places (the exact percentage cannot be determined) do not work at all in the kol-khoz or do not earn the minimum of labor days, because they are burdened with small children and no grandparents are available. This has the further effect of lim-iting the exposure of women to "Soviet reality." Their cultural and social handi-caps are thus compounded.

In most kolkhozy of central Russia, day-care and preschool facilities either do not function at all or operate only during the peak agricultural season. In some places in Kalinin Oblast, very small children are looked after by somewhat older ones, especially during the summer—this pattern is traditional for many peas-ant societies. The lack of satisfactory day-care facilities is recognized by the leader-ship as a serious problem, and from time to time, efforts are made to correct it. However, this is but one of many problems which do not particularly lend them-selves to centralized planning. In this respect, child care differs from other types of cultural and consumer services. Entertainment, education, shops, and so on can be provided by investing money, putting up buildings and, if necessary, importing spe-cialized personnel from the outside. A day-care facility, however, is essentially not just a physical plant, but a matter of social organization. A director for a club-house, a storekeeper, or even a teacher can be brought in from the outside with a fair chance of success, but when it comes to caring for children of preschool age, people are not likely to appreciate the services of strangers. A nursery, to be effec-tive must be organized on the spot with local personnel, and, to run smoothly it must become part of the informal structure of the local community.

In the matter of day-care facilities, we see again the familiar competition for funds, not only between different categories of enterprise (cultural and consum-er services, education in the narrow sense, public health, economic development, and so on) but between enterprises. According to an account in *Izvestiia* (25/IX /65:4), the State Planning Commission had promised to build a day nursery for the workers of a chemical plant near Moscow, but the funds were then re-allocated to a day nursery for another enterprise. Although an oral promise had been given to the deputy representing the chemical workers,[10] the planning procedure did not as-sure the final destination of the funds. The plan specified that the money would be used to build a nursery, but did not say where it would be located. In her original appeal to the Supreme Soviet, the deputy pointed out that it would be cheaper to build day nurseries so that wives of the workers could be recruited for work in the plant, than to build new housing to accommodate workers recruited from the out-side. The context here is industrial, not agricultural, but the same point applies with even greater force to the countryside, because rural areas are usually the last to receive funds and the first to suffer when there is a cutback.

Wages and Social Security

The labor day has long been recognized as a higly imperfect instrument for distributing income among kolkhozniks. Its chief drawback from the point of view of the kolkhoz family is that its yield is not predictable from month to month,

---

[10] Deputies to the Supreme Soviet, and also to soviets of more limited jurisdiction are often elected not on a residential basis but by the staffs of particular enterprises in which they work.

and intelligent fiscal planning at the family level is therefore impossible. This reduces the kolkhoznik's personal incentive and hinders the expansion of the public sector, since the kolkhoz family must provide for its needs as far as possible out of its private economy. Furthermore, the labor day leaves something to be desired on the score of fairness, inasmuch as its yield varies for reasons which are completely beyond the kolkhoznik's control.

In 1957, four kolkhozy were allowed to introduce, as an experiment, a guaranteed annual wage paid on a regular monthly basis. About 9000 out of 37,618 kolkhozy now use this method of payment (Prusakov 1965:41). Soviet writers usually describe the guaranteed annual wage as a much more progressive method of payment than the labor day and stress its incentive effect. At the same time, however, they warn that the transfer to guaranteed cash payments should not be attempted until the operations of the kolkhoz have reached a certain economic level. In particular, there must be a sufficient backlog of cash to cover wages until the crop is sold, since the State Bank will not lend money on a regular short-term basis for this purpose. All accounting must therefore be postponed until the entire crop has been sold. The kolkhoznik cannot know how much he will be paid, or when (*Izvestiia* 7/X/64:3). An official of the State Bank maintains that, on the contrary, 75–80 kopeks of each ruble paid out by kolkhozy and *sovkhozy* (including wages) were covered by bank loans during the first half of 1964 (*Izvestiia* 21/III/65:5). The catch is that wages have traditionally been paid last. The guaranteed cash wage therefore falls short of its main objective—the provision of a stable predictable income for the kolkhoz family.

The importance of the guaranteed cash wage, should it become universal or even predominant, is hard to overestimate. Leaving aside the question of incentive and the effect of the guaranteed wage on productivity, its introduction would eliminate at one stroke most of the elements which have historically characterized the peasant, and which are responsible for the Central Russian kolkhoznik remaining in that category up to the present time. That is, it would eliminate the peasant's basically subsistence approach to his land—his attempt to make it provide him and his family with food, and with money only to the extent that he needs things he cannot personally produce. Certainly this is the effect which Soviet ethnographers expect from the guaranteed cash wage (Dunn and Dunn 1965a).

The Soviet regime is committed to the ultimate goal of providing complete social security for all citizens. This has been extended to workers for some time, but unfortunately the kolkhozniks came under the provisions of the program only in July 1964—effective at the close of 1965. The terms of the pension are: 50 percent of earnings up to 50 rubles a month, and 25 percent thereafter, to a monthly maximum of 102 rubles. Those eligible are men 65 years of age or older, after at least 25 years of work; women 60 years of age or over, after at least 20 years of work; and mothers who have raised five or more children to the age of 18 are eligible at age 55 after at least 15 years work. A pension is to be given for job-connected disability or disease without regard to length of service. In other cases, the disability pension follows the norms established for blue-collar and white-collar workers.[11] The pension is to be financed through a rotating central fund, into

---

[11] As follows: length of service for men, from one year (if disability occurs before age 20) to 20 years if disability occurs after age 61; length of service for women, from one to 15 years, according to the same scale.

which all kolkhozy pay assessments (to be determined by the Councils of Ministers of the various Union republics). The funds subject to assessment for this purpose are deductible for tax on kolkhoz income. Those entitled to pension for the loss of a wage earner are children under 16 (18 if they are students) or older if they were disabled before reaching the age of 16; brothers, sisters, and grandchildren (subject to the same criteria of age) provided their parents are unable to work; and grandparents, if there is no one legally obliged to provide for them (*Izvestiia* 16/VII/64:2).

This does not represent the first social security for kolkhozniks. Both old-age and disability pensions have existed in some places and for some people since the beginning of collectivization (see Chapter 1). In Viriatino, pensions were written into the kolkhoz charter. Previously, however, social-security benefits for kolkhozniks were financed by each kolkhoz individually, and hence depended on the economic strength of the operation. The significance of the new pension laws lies in the fact that they eliminate another of the juridical distinctions between kolkhozniks and workers; this is in accord with the regime's general program, which envisages the eventual disappearance of all such distinctions.

Internal Structure of the Family

The data under this head will be presented in tabular form, with some brief explanatory remarks. We have two outstanding examples that show the predominant structure of the Central Russian kolkhoz peasant family—one from Viriatino dating from 1953 and the other from Kalinin Oblast, dating from 1956 to 1962. The two examples are not strictly comparable, in that one of them comes from a single village, while the other is gathered from 19 villages in three different *raions*. However, the basic data do not show any striking differences.

Certain aspects of the data from Kalinin Oblast are not reflected in Table 4. We are told (Anokhina and Shmeleva 1964:189) that 317 of the 541 families in the sample are headed by men and 224 by women, but there is no breakdown of these figures into the categories provided by the table. Rather, the heads of families are broken down as follows: of the men, 306 are married, 7 are widowed, 2 are divorced, and 2 are single; of the women, 20 are married, 178 are widowed, 11 are divorced or separated, and 15 are unmarried. Secondly, Table 4 does not list the 102 persons living alone, including some young specialists from outside the locality who have no private economies and live in apartments. Thirdly, the tables do not detail the actual make-up of families. A two-generation family, for instance, may either be constituted "normally" of parents and their children, or may consist of a childless couple making a home for an aged parent. Finally, a word of caution is in order concerning the tables generally: many of the units listed may not be economically independent, and may have been divided in order to derive the benefits (chiefly household plots) which can be had by this method under the kolkhoz system.

Both the authors of the Viriatino study and Anokhina and Shmeleva state that the dominant form of the family is the "small" (in English social-science terminology "conjugal" or "nuclear") family, consisting of parents and their chil-

TABLE 1

DISTRIBUTION OF VIRIATINO INHABITANTS BY GROUPS OF FAMILIES
(by number of members)

Family members	Families with male heads	Families with female heads	Total	Number of persons	
				Total	Percent of population
1	6	39	45	45	2.9
2	40	67	107	214	13.8
3	53	50	103	309	20.0
4	66	30	96	384	24.8
5	43	17	60	300	19.4
6	22	4	26	156	10.1
7	14	1	15	105	6.8
8	2	0	2	16	1.0
9	2	0	2	18	1.2
Total	248	208	456	1547*	100

* 358 persons are away from the village for long periods (at work, in the armed forces, and so on)

TABLE 2

DISTRIBUTION OF FAMILIES IN VIRIATINO BY NUMBER OF GENERATIONS

Family members	With one generation	With two generations	With three generations	With four generations	Total
1	45	0	0	0	45
2	41	66	0	0	107
3	1*	87	15	0	103
4	1**	67	28	0	96
5	0	31	29	0	60
6	0	14	11	1	26
7	0	8	6	1	15
8	0	2	0	0	2
9	0	0	2	0	2
Total	88	275	91	2	456
As Percent of Total Population	19.3	60.3	20.0	0.4	100

* Sisters.
** Brothers and sisters—orphans.

TABLE 3

VIRIATINO FAMILIES BY FORM AND NUMBER OF MEMBERS

Number	Form			Total		
Family members	Undivided (joint)	Divided, complete, (heads of both sexes)	Divided, incomplete	With sons-in-law	With daughters-in-law	
1	0	0	45	0	0	45
2	0	38	69	0	1	107
3	0	53	50	0	10	103
4	0	65	31	2	20	96
5	0	42	18	1	26	60
6	0	22	4	0	12	26
7	0	14	1	0	7	15
8	0	2	0	0	0	2
9	1	1	0	1	1*	2
Total	1	237	218	4	77	456

* Two daughters-in-law.

(Source for Tables 1–3: Kushner, ed. 1958: 207–209)

TABLE 4

FORM AND NUMERICAL MAKE-UP OF FAMILIES, KALININ OBLAST

Number of family members	Number of families	Percent of total	One-generation families	Two-generation families			Three-generation families		
				complete	incomplete	total	complete	incomplete	total
2	128	23.6	61	0	67	67	0	0	0
3	107 ⎫		3	60	33	93	0	11	11
4	152 ⎭	48.0	0	77	23	100	38	14	52
5	81 ⎫		0	44	4	48	30	3	33
6	45 ⎪		0	20	4	24	20	1	21
7	23 ⎬	28.4	0	17	0	17	6	0	6
8	4 ⎪		0	3	0	3	1	0	1
9	1 ⎭		0	1	0	1	0	0	0
Total	541	100	64	222	131	353	95	29	124

Source: Anokhina and Shmeleva 1964: 184)

dren. This is the same pattern which is regarded as standard in Western Europe and the United States. The major deviations from the pattern found in the Soviet data are attributed by Soviet authors either to the effects of World War II (the large numer of widows) or to survivals of earlier peasant tradition. However, there is evidence, at least in the Kalinin Oblast study, that the nuclear family is not considered ideal by the people themselves, whatever ethnographers or officials may think. Anokhina and Shmeleva state specifically that it is not considered proper to leave the old parents alone, and that, furthermore, when one or both parents are still living and are domiciled with the children, the grandfather (or in his absence the grandmother) is usually considered the head of the family. Exceptions to this may occur if he or she is extremely old or incapacitated. The significance of this point lies in the fact that a structural dichotomy exists between the concepts of "head of family" and that of "head of kolkhoz household." The first is part of the informal

TABLE 5

Make-up of family	Head of family	Number of cases
Male		
1. Single people; married couples with or without children	husband and father	191
2. Married sons with old parents	old father	32
3. Widowed father with old mother	father	1
4. Married couple with wife's old mother	father	5
5. Married son with widowed father	married son	2
6. Married son with old mother	married son	17
	Subtotal	248
Female		
7. Women living alone; widows with children and sisters	widow	156
8. Widows with married sons	widowed mother	23
9. Widows with widowed daughters-in-law, children and grandchildren	widowed mother	3
10. Widows with sons-in-law or widowed daughers	widowed mother	8
11. Widows with married daughters and their children; old mother in house	widow	4
12. Widows with children and mother-in-law	widowed mother	5
13. Women who have taken husbands into their homes*	wife	9
	Subtotal	208
	Grand total	456

* This would occur on a second marriage, the woman being the owner of the house.

(Source: Kushner, ed. 1958: 212)

structure of the community (although it is registered in the books of the local soviet) and applies to a representative of the oldest surviving generation (male if present, otherwise female). The "head of kolkhoz household" concept applies to the formal political structure (the kolkhoz) and attaches to the chief wage earner in the family. The two positions may and often do coincide, but they are nonetheless functionally separate. The Viriatino authors take care to explain that the status of "head of family," when held by an old man or woman no longer working, is largely formal, and that the actual control of the family's affairs is in the hands of an active worker, but the facts of Case VII are enough to cast doubt on this as a generalization. Anokhina and Shmeleva (1964:195;198) cite cases similar to this, where all expenditures are controlled by the old father; in one of these cases, the young married kolkhoznik, who is an only son, hesitates to break away from the family for this reason.

Comparing the situation described in recent Soviet ethnographic studies with the traditional Russian peasant order, we find at least one major change in kind, not to speak of the changes in degree. Traditionally in the Russian village, a woman could not be the head of a family, having no right to represent it in the skhod. Fenomenov (1925) and earlier writers whom he cites, mention cases in which the family was represented in the skhod by adolescent sons in the absence of adult males. In the modern Soviet village, however, there are a number of instances in which women are considered the heads of families. Perhaps the best illustration of this state of affairs is Table 5, supplied in the Viriatino study, which shows the locus of power in relation to the structure of the family.

It will be noted that some of the categories in Table 5 describe essentially the same structure of family from different points of view—for example, categories 6 and 8 or 4 and 11. In these cases, the family may be headed by either a man or a woman, and it is in these cases also that factors of personal character or coincidence presumably come into play. For instance, in one case (probably Case II above), the husband's old mother was head of the family until the fire of 1953 and the subsequent rebuilding. This circumstance required complex and time-consuming arrangements which were beyond the mother's ability; therefore leadership in the family passed to the son.

In the Russian peasant family, where there were no sons, a son-in-law traditionally was taken into the home and became the heir. In such cases, the entire order of the wedding ceremony was changed, the bride's side taking the initiative in arranging the marriage. This kind of son-in-law is called a *primak;* orphans or farm laborers were usually chosen for the role. The relationship between the father-in-law and the *primak* was regulated by written contract. The *primak's* position was unenviable: he could not become true head of the household even after the father-in-law's death, since he remained under the influence of the surviving women. It was proverbially said of a tailless dog that he must once have lived as a *primak* and lost his tail (Aleksandrov and others, eds. 1964: 467). It is interesting that Kushner's group describe no case of true *primachestvo,* although categories 10 and 11 of Table 5 would seem to indicate that it still exists. Anokhina and Shmeleva (1964) distinguish specifically between *primachestvo* and various situations in the modern kolkhoz family which superficially resemble it, such as a man making a home for his mother-in-law.

Fictitious Divisions; Extension of Kin Ties
beyond Nuclear Family

Since each separate kolkhoz household is normally entitled to a full-sized household plot, it would seem to follow that a premium be placed on the establishment of separate households. We would also expect that some families would ostensibly divide their operations in order to gain access to more land, while in fact maintaining unified budgets. Soviet authors tell us that this did happen on a large scale at the beginning of collectivization and during periods of slack discipline, such as World War II. They even admit, in general terms, that it still happens today. They are markedly cautious, however, in handling this matter, and the reason is quite obvious: it goes to the very root of the social structure—relationships between kin. For example, in Case V above, the old mother-in-law lives with the family in the winter, maintaining her own household in the summer, but the family has the use of her household plot both winter and summer. Likewise, Kushner's group (Kushner ed. 1958:208) stresses the extremely close ties in the areas of economy and daily life between old parents and the families of their married daughters. One of the Viriatino war widows receives grain for labor days in common with her father, who lives separately, and this grain is shared equally between them, regardless of who earned it. Anokhina and Shmeleva state (1964:187) that an only son will separate from his widowed mother only if she and his wife find each other absolutely incompatible, and that even in such cases, he continues to provide for her personal economy. Traditionally, the youngest son was expected to provide a home for the old parents and to "nourish" them. Now any one of the children may undertake this function by general agreement within the family. However, the responsibility falls on the daughter only if the sons are scattered or there were none in the first place. If this occurs, a son-in-law is generally taken into the home. None of the cases mentioned above are described by the Soviet authors as constituting fictitious divisions, yet it seems clear that such is their effect.

Anokhina and Shmeleva note that in the Russian countryside, the circle of kin continues to be relatively wide. The kin group includes not only relatives in the direct line, but also many collateral kinfolk (uncles, aunts, and their descendants) and a considerable array of relatives by marriage. Family festivities are attended by as many as 40 or 50 persons, the majority of whom are consanguine and affinal relations. Mutual aid between relatives—in the cultivation of the household plot, the provision of lumber and turf, the building and repair of houses, the lending of money—is an ordinary phenomenon. However, the extension of the kin group reveals a clear emphasis on the paternal line at the expense of the maternal one. Paternal relatives are the first to be invited to family festivities and are given (at the insistent demand of the older generation) the places of honor on such occasions. The following account given by Anokhina and Shmeleva (1964:200) is typical:

A vivid example of the vitality of this tradition is provided by the instance which we encountered on the kolkhoz "Russia" of Ves'egonsk *raion*. The young married couple N, arriving from the city on vacation, had to set out directly from the station for the house of the husband's mother, with whom they were to stay. The wife's mother, impatiently awaiting her daughter, was able to see her only after three days' time, although the couple could have dropped in on her on their way. She did not consider it possible to go to see her daughter at her son-in-law's father's house in the neighboring village, and waited until the daughter and son-in-law paid her a visit themselves.

Social Control: the Family as Mediator

The modern Soviet kolkhoz household appears in sociological terms as a communally operating collective, intervening between the kolkhoz—in its political and administrative aspects—and the individual. The household (which here we equate with the family) is a body upon which the regime has only limited means of direct influence—and it may be reluctant to use these means for fear of compromising social stability and productivity. The family therefore has the effect of more or less insulating the individual.

The corporate nature of the modern Soviet peasant family is obvious on a number of counts. A glance at the budget data will show clearly that the family operates on a communal basis, with money being lumped together and spent in common (with such exceptions as wages earned by women, state grants, and pensions). Payment in kind received for labor also goes to feed the household regardless of who originally earned it. The produce of the garden plot is likewise devoted to common use, and the plot itself is held by the family by virtue of one or more of its members belonging to the kolkhoz. The family's corporate character, which is so clearly expressed in its productive function, extends to consumption as well. In places where for reasons of over-all policy the state is unable to assume certain necessary functions (providing adequate day-care facilities for preschool children, supplying labor-saving devices in large quantities, or making public catering available either directly or through the kolkhoz), these tasks must devolve on the family. The general argument of this chapter has been to show the over-all conservative tendency in the Russian countryside which this situation produces. At the same time, we must not exaggerate this aspect. The kolkhoz system, with its peculiar combination and interweaving of public and private operations, has produced certain striking changes in the structure of the Central Russian peasant family. In particular, the provisions with regard to the use of land have encouraged the establishment of a large number of smaller family collectives in place of a small number of larger ones. This process has been also influenced by what Soviet ethnographers refer to as the spread of urban tastes, the details of which we will consider in a later chapter. It seems clear that the direction of development of the Central Russian peasant family is toward the small independent unit, with relatively limited functions, that characteristic of Western European and American society as a whole. This development, however, is held back by a number of factors arising both from the over-all policy of the state and from the peculiarities of the traditional Russian peasant household which was its raw material.

3

Education and Social Mobility

Social Mobility in the Peasant Context

IN OUR INTRODUCTION we said that one of the important criteria which distinguish the peasant from the primitive tribesman is that the peasant is structurally related to a larger society, which includes workers, professionals, and (in some countries) merchants and entrepreneurs. The fact that the peasant is part of such a structure implies, at least in principle, that he can move out of the peasant category and join one of the other categories. Every society has distinctive avenues and methods which make this possible. One way to describe a given society is to characterize these avenues and methods of social mobility and note precisely how they work and for whom, both in theory and in fact (as this can be checked statistically). In this analysis, we must also discover how the people themselves measure social mobility—that is, what are their criteria for social status. For instance, if a peasant becomes a worker, is he generally considered to have risen in the social scale because, let us assume, he lives better? Or, is he considered to have fallen because he has to some extent lost control of his own standard of living? Or finally, does judgment on this question depend on some other factor entirely?

Social mobility in the modern Russian countryside has certain special characteristics. Whereas in a capitalist society (for example, Tsarist Russia in the last decades before the Revolution) a peasant may have the opportunity to become a merchant or manufacturer—thus amassing wealth and achieving social mobility through purely economic means—in the Soviet Union this cannot be. The economic form of social mobility which is possible in capitalist society has the characteristic that it does not depend directly on formal training. The forms of social mobility which in the Soviet context would correspond to the capitalist idea of "making good in business"—becoming, let us say, a doctor, an engineer, the manager of a factory, or a high government official—all depend on formal education, among other factors. (This is true nowadays: it was much less true earlier when a likely youth—for example Khrushchev—might be noticed and given secondary schooling or professional training by the Communist Party.) Therefore we find that both Soviet writers and foreign observers unanimously emphasize the tremendous drive for education among all sections of the Soviet population. Ambition expressed in this form is explicitly sanctioned and praised in the Soviet system of values, except where it leads to behavior (for instance, the forging of academic credentials) that is clearly antisocial.

When the Soviet rural youth completes his primary education, there are, in effect, three choices open to him: to drop out of school and go to work on a kolkhoz (and probably remain for the rest of his life a rank-and-file kolkhoznik); to acquire technical skills which will fit him for a higher status occupation on the land —equipment operator, brigadier, agronomist, or perhaps eventually chairman of a kolkhoz; or to leave the land entirely and seek his fortune in the city. These choices are not necessarily clear-cut at any given moment, but in fact we find that everyone eventually makes the choice of one or the other of them. We find further that, at present, the balance is heavily weighted in favor of the third choice. Since it is obvious that qualified people are needed to run agriculture, this is a matter of great concern to the government. Recently, the government has begun to make intensive efforts to keep people on the land—with generally indifferent and spotty success so far. The great difficulties which attend these efforts have profound sociological and political causes which we will examine in the course of this chapter.

Educational Opportunity in the Countryside

The proudest boast of the Soviet regime is that in less than 50 years it has turned a largely illiterate nation into an overwhelmingly literate one. Put in these simple terms, the contention is unarguable. Eight-year education is now compulsory for all Soviet children, and though we occasionally read in the press of instances where children were taken out of class—often under the guise of "practical work experience"—and made to do manual labor in the fields, this does not alter the over-all effect of the requirement. The Viriatino study (Kushner, ed. 1958:255) contains a table showing literacy in relation to age and sex (see Table 6). The nine men and 16 women studying in technical and higher educational institutions are treated separately, presumably because they were not actually present in the village at the time of the study, and hence are not part of the population to which the table applies.

The over-all literacy rate for Viriatino in 1953 was 79 percent, school-children being included in the population; 21 percent were illiterate or functionally so. In view of the age distribution of literacy, we can assume that the literacy rate will have risen between the time of the study and now, even though we have no later data on this particular area.

Beginning in 1934, all children of school age were in fact in school. During the war, however, some young people were unable to acquire the seven-year education regarded by the regime as minimal. In 1955, an evening school was set up which embraced all individuals between the ages of 15 and 25 lacking seven-year education. Out of a total of 34 pupils, however, there were only four females— a fact which may indicate that the education of girls is generally regarded as less important than that of boys. The authors state that this is only just now being over-come (Kushner, ed. 1958:254–255).

The data on relative literacy and level of education from Kalinin Oblast, though far less complete, present something of a contrast to the situation in Viriatino. In order to allow the reader to draw his own conclusions on this somewhat obscure matter, we quote the relevant passage in full (Anokhina and Shmeleva 1964:327–328):

> We can judge to some degree concerning the considerable rise in the level of education of the Kalinin Oblast kolkhozniks by our questionnaire data. Analysis of them shows that the percentage of illiterates in the kolkhozy studied is very small; almost all the illiterates (except for a few persons) are elderly women, born in the period 1870–1900. The overwhelming majority of the population born before the Revolution has elementary education to the extent of two or three or more rarely four grades [normally, such people could be considered functionally illiterate, it would seem]. Within this group, the level of education among men is somewhat higher than among women. Kolkhozniks of more advanced age with education in excess of four grades are few.
>
> Among kolkhozniks between 50 and 55 years of age, there are almost no illiterates.
>
> Those with elementary education [four grades or less] make up approximately 40–45 percent. These are people of different generations, but those between 50 and 55 years of age predominate. The majority of the population which went to school after the Revolution (55–60 percent) has education in excess of four grades. If the population of this group is taken as 100 percent, then persons with seven grades of education will be about 48 percent, with 5 or 6 grades 30–31 percent, with 8 to 10 grades, about 10 percent, and with specialized secondary and higher education, 10–11 percent. Consequently, in the kolkhoz countryside, 68 percent of the population of the middle and

TABLE 6

LITERACY IN VIRIATINO POPULATION IN RELATION TO SEX AND AGE

Age	Total Population			Men			Women		
	Total	Literate	Percent	Total	Literate	Percent	Total	Literate	Percent
7–30	444	444	100	186	186*	100	233*	233	100
31–40	160	149	93	59	57	97	101	92	91
41–50	235	190	81	73	71	97	162	119	73
51–60	180	112	62	68	63	93	112	49	44
Over 61	236	102	43	83	67	81	153	35	23
Total	1255	997	79	469 +9**	444 +9**	95	761 +16**	528 +16**	70

* Not counting those studying in technical secondary schools and higher educational institutions.

** Studying in technical secondary schools and higher educational institutions.

younger generation has seven grades or more of education. . . . The relatively low percentage of persons with complete secondary, specialized secondary, and higher education is to be explained by a definite drain of the intelligentsia[1] after completing school into the *raion* centers, settlements, and cities.

This passage presents a number of difficulties, not all of which can be resolved from the information at our disposal. The first has to do with the definition of incomplete secondary education. Before the educational reform of 1958 this meant, in effect, seven grades; since then it has meant eight (DeWitt 1961: Chart I). However, neither the Kalinin Oblast study nor the Soviet statistical sources which we use for comparison tells us whether they are defining incomplete secondary education as of the time of publication or as of the time the people went to school. Thus, when we find in a statistical handbook (*TsSU RSFSR,* 1964:12) that 33 percent of the population of the RSFSR, (estimated as of January 1, 1964) has incomplete secondary education or higher, we do not know exactly how this compares with the 20–21 percent of the Kalinin Oblast sample who have completed eight grades or more. It would seem that both Kalinin Oblast and Viriatino in Tambov Oblast are somewhat backward educationally in relation to the country as a whole. But we must remember that education in rural areas lags generally. According to the 1959 census, only 19.4 percent of the Soviet Union's rural population had incomplete secondary education or higher, compared with 28.1 percent of the population as a whole (*TsSU SSSR,* 1962:81). In most parts of the Soviet Union, the level of education for women is noticeably lower than that for men; the difference is especially marked in the rural areas. In the RSFSR as a whole, as of 1959, 28.9 percent of the men had incomplete secondary education and higher as against 27.7 percent of the women (*TsSU SSSR,* 1962:86). This would seem to confirm the backwardness of the two areas for which we have detailed data, but we must remember that there is a surplus of women and a surplus of elderly people in the countryside that would tend to lower the level of general education.

Anokhina and Shmeleva (1964:328) profess to be satisfied with the present availability of schools. An elementary school in the area they studied usually serves four or five small villages located at distances of one–and–a–half to three kilometers from each other. If the school is farther away, the kolkhoz organizes transport by truck or bus. The radius served by the seven-year schools (which, as we have noted, should have been eight-year by the time of the Kalinin Oblast study) is considerably wider, but these schools usually provide boarding facilities. For instance, in Ves'egonsk *raion,* there were 230 school boarders in 1959, and 576 in 1960.

A recent study by Shubkin (1965) indicates that rural young people suffer from an educational handicap and are less likely than urban youth to acquire higher education, even given equal capacities. While Shubkin's data come from Novosibirsk Oblast in Siberia, he stresses that there is no reason to assume that they reflect a special situation and implies strongly that the phenomenon is Union-wide.

Stories carried in the current press indicate that construction of boarding facilities is slow and falls far short of demand in most areas. In some schools children are studying in shifts for lack of space. Quite frequently we hear of school

---

[1] Intelligentsia (which should not be identified with the concept of "intellectual") refers in Soviet usage to that class of people whose occupations require some degree of formal training. Thus it applies equally to professors and to tractor-drivers and mechanics.

buildings being built or repaired by the population on a volunteer basis. While ordinarily such accounts must be taken with a grain of salt, the extreme importance
of education in terms of social mobility makes it quite probable that when it comes
to schools, people actually do pitch in.

The regime makes an effort to raise the cultural level of the adult population
as well, through such devices as the "universities of culture." These are maintained
in towns and at the clubhouses on some of the larger kolkhozy. We quote the program of the "university of culture" at one kolkhoz: "(1) Our goal—communism;
(2) a new era in the conquest of space; (3) the origin of religion and Christianity;
(4) the image of the Soviet person in creative literature; "Let us talk heart to
heart"; (5) young housewives' evening; (6) "on the spiritual beauty of man."
Other subjects range from the 100th birthday of the writer Anton Chekhov, to the
latest achievements of agricultural science. It sounds dull, and the propaganda content is obviously high. Anokhina and Shmeleva admit that competent lecturers and
suitable audio-visual materials are hard to find. They maintain nonetheless that
when properly set up, the lectures arouse great interest, particularly those on literary and humanistic topics (Anokhina and Shmeleva 1964:298–299). The point is
elaborated by Iankova (1963) for Riazan Oblast; she says that the poor condition
of the clubhouses is not the only thing that keeps people away. When there is an
interesting topic, they come, even to a poor building. Iankova's remarks are especially significant because they are made in the context of a discussion of the new
tactics of the churches. In an effort to attract more worshippers, especially young
people, the churches are beautifying their buildings and improving the artistic
quality of their services, as well as trying to improve the intellectual content of the
sermons. The ideological competition between the church and the state which is
revealed by Iankova's data explains much of the adult education program listed
above. In places where the church appears to be having some success, a crash program may be initiated to improve the level of adult education, or to provide better
facilities.

Social Mobility

Social mobility in the present-day Central Russian countryside means, in
most cases, mobility out of the countryside. There are only a limited number of
ways in which this can be achieved, and these fall, broadly, into two groups. The
first, as we have just seen, is educational; the second is occupational. We do not
mean to imply that there is a hard and fast line between the two, which obviously
go together. However, if one wishes to leave the countryside, or to increase one's
earnings while remaining a kolkhoznik, one has, in effect, two choices. Either one
can acquire a marketable skill, through education, or one can leave the kolkhoz and
search for unskilled work, which is usually seasonal.

Modern Otkhodnichestvo

A tradition in the Russian countryside dating back at least a hundred years
is *otkhodnichestvo,* seasonal migrant labor by peasants. Soviet ethnographers and

historians attribute great cultural importance to this pattern as it existed in Tsarist times, in terms of the spread of urban habits and, particularly, of revolutionary ideas. At the same time, most Soviet writers, for obvious reasons, deny that *otkhod-nichestvo* exists at present. Our evidence indicates that whether it exists or not at any given time depends on the conditions in the countryside. The Viriatino study contains detailed data which show the existence of a considerable body of migrant laborers on the "Lenin's Way" kolkhoz before the major agricultural reforms of 1953.

> *Case IX.* Tractor-driver. Number of dependents exceeding number of wage earners. The family consists of the tractor-driver, his wife, and three small children. Only the father works. In 1952, the family earned 250 labor days and received about 10 *tsentners* of grain and 1200 rubles in cash. Since the family required at least six *tsentners* of grain a year, there was no surplus. The family had a garden of 0.4 hectares in potatoes and vegetables. There was no livestock except a few chickens and a cow maintained in common with another family. Low earnings prompted the father to go south in the winter of 1952–53 to the Donbas coalfields where, working on the coal-face, he earned 1200 rubles a month. During four months' work, he was able to send home only 400 rubles which, of course, had almost no effect on the family's standard of living.
>
> The following year the family's position improved considerably. Working as a brigadier of the tractor brigade, in 1954 the father earned 600 labor days, and received 21 *tsentners* of grain and 6900 rubles in cash. For repairing machinery he was paid, according to the new wage scale, 800 rubles in addition to his earnings from the kolkhoz. Furthermore, the MTS supplied him with four cubic meters of firewood free of charge and the transport to bring it home. This, together with the turf which he was permitted to cut on the kolkhoz land, took care of the family's fuel needs for the winter. The family's economic position improved further in 1955. They acquired a cow and were raising a pig to 110–120 kilograms. Considerable capital investments (purchase of clothes, re-tiling of the roof of the house) were made during this period.
>
> *Case X.* "Semiworker" family. The father until 1955 lived in the Donbas, where he worked as a rank-and-file miner. The wife, daughter, and younger son lived on the kolkhoz. The wife and daughter worked on the kolkhoz; the son was a pupil in the 9th grade in the school in the neighboring town. The elder son lived with his father at the mine from 1953, when he was demobilized, married, and began working at the mine with his wife. Some years the mother of the family went to visit her husband during the two or three winter months. In 1952, when the budget was studied, the family earned 274 labor days, and received 11 *tsentners* of grain—an adequate supply. However, they had no saleable surplus. Their cash income consisted essentially of the money sent home by the father. In 1952, he sent 5000 rubles, as well as 2000 rubles' worth of clothes. The cash was sent primarily to support the private economy (particularly to buy fodder for the livestock), for food, for cultural needs, and for the younger son's education. The money sent in 1952 made up 60.9 percent of the total budget of the family, while the income from participation in the kolkhoz accounted for only 28.2 percent, and the private economy for 10.9 percent. In 1953 and 1954, because of the daughter's marriage and departure

for her husband's home, the remaining members of the family earned only 63 and 43 labor days respectively for the two years. In 1955, the father retired from the mine on a pension and returned to Viriatino where, as of 1958, he works in the kolkhoz.

Case XI. Rank-and-file kolkhoznik. Number of dependents equals or exceeds number of wage earners (parents and three children). During the winters from 1927 until World War II the father of the family had worked in the Donbas mines. After the war, he returned to the mines from 1951 through 1953. The grain supply was sufficient; lack of money for clothes, shoes, and so on had prompted him to go out for seasonal labor. In 1952, he worked in the Donbas for four months, earning a total of 7839 rubles,[2] of which he sent 4000 to his family. In the summer he earned 2085 rubles in the kolkhoz (including payment in kind evaluated at current market prices). In 1953, the family (father, daughter, and son working) earned 680 labor days and received 23.8 *tsentners* of grain, including 13.6 *tsentners* in millet, and 5440 rubles in cash. There was a considerable grain surplus for the year in question, mostly in millet. The family has a garden of 0.4 hectares, planted to potatoes and vegetables and some millet; there is a cow, three sheep with young, about 10 chickens, and a pig. The adequate food supply permitted considerable capital expenditures—2000 rubles for clothes for the daughter and the son in 1955, as well as a sewing machine and two bicycles. Money was also spent for the education of the younger son at the 10–year school.

From one angle, these three cases seem to illustrate three rather different phenomena, which it would be stretching a point to include in the same category. In Case IX there is no indication that the tractor driver was a miner by either previous experience or tradition. He simply went in cold and applied for a job. As the result shows, he was not particularly successful in supporting his family, although his pay amounted to almost as much per month as he made in a year on the kolkhoz. Furthermore, the motives for his seeking work, and its social significance, approximated those of prerevolutionary *otkhodnichestvo*—the sheer inability to make ends meet otherwise. This man's experience after the agricultural reforms of 1953 illustrates vividly the direct influence of state policy on the lives of individuals.

Case X is essentially a worker returned to the kolkhoz by the fact of retirement. The data provide no direct answer and the question remains: why did he leave his family on the kolkhoz while he himself worked outside it? One explanation might be the effort to lower the cost of living; another might be the difficult housing conditions at the mine. We still find complaints in the press from mining districts about poor food, lack of amenities, and delays in housing construction, so we can presume that 13 years ago the situation was considerably worse. Furthermore, by retiring to the kolkhoz, this man placed himself in a more advantageous position than he would have had by living in the city or worker's settlement: he was entitled to a private plot and had the right to grow food and sell the surplus as long as he was able to do so. For any work that he did on the kolkhoz he would be

---

[2] This was a skilled, experienced miner, and he earned considerably more than a "chance miner" or unskilled person, such as the man in Case IX.

paid at a 25 percent premium if he were more than 70, or on the same basis as anyone else if he were younger.

Case XI is in some ways the most interesting of all, because it illustrates a traditional and long-standing pattern of *otkhodnichestvo* under Soviet conditions. Soviet authors deny the existence of *otkhodnichestvo* after the Revolution, except for some remnants during the early 1920s. They claim that industrial labor was recruited by government agencies specifically set up for this purpose. The authors of the Viriatino study state that at the time the book went to press (1958), no one in the village any longer went out for migrant labor, and two of the participants in the Viriatino study personally told us the same thing in more general terms. It is a fair presumption that this reflects an improvement of conditions in the countryside at the time of this study, and conversely, that if this trend should be reversed, *otkhodnichestvo* would reappear. Of the 14 recorded cases in which the father of the family worked outside the village (usually in the Donbas), two families completely severed connections with the village and with the kolkhoz; three moved to the father's place of employment but retained title to their houses in the village; four others split up and the fathers founded new families outside. In four other cases, the fathers quit work and returned to the village, where three of them are now working on the kolkhoz. In only one case was the father still working outside in 1953 while his family continued to live and work in the village. The sample is too small for us to make any firm judgments about the mobility between agriculture and industry, but we can safely say that the situation is unstable. Personal reasons and the operation of chance in various ways probably play an important role. The departure of five of the 14 families either permanently or provisionally, to be sure, puts an end to this unstable situation, but it does not argue for the improvement of conditions in the countryside to the extent where *otkhodnichestvo* was no longer necessary—which is clearly the impression the authors wish to make.

Prerevolutionary *otkhodnichestvo* was of two types, depending on the class of people it engaged. The poorer peasants went out for migrant labor because they had no choice. The richer ones went out because the family had a surplus of working hands, and used this means to accumulate cash and thereby achieve social mobility. In the Soviet context, the extremes of wealth and poverty have been eliminated, although variations are still considerable. Probably *otkhodnichestvo* now is called forth chiefly by the desire for material signs of social mobility—better clothes, new furniture, a motorcycle, remodeling of the house—or for such prerequisites as education for the children.

There is evidence in the press that whatever may be true at Viriatino, *otkhodnichestvo* still exists in other parts of the country. In Kurlovo *raion*, Vladimir Oblast (*Izvestiia* 30/III/63:4), there is a local industry of rug painting, traditional for the area. These rugs, used as wallhangings, are painted by means of a few simple cardboard stencils and a shoebrush, with patterns derived from folk tales and traditional historical ballads—reindeer, swans, wolves, Red Riding Hood, folk heroes, and so on. The craftsmen work by *otkhodnichestvo*, and even in 1963 made a great deal of money. However, most of the kolkhozy in the district were operating at a loss, partly because many of their able-bodied population were away. One of the local inhabitants explained to the correspondent that the rug-painters were not interested in seeing the kolkhoz prosper, because if the labor day were paid for at a decent rate, there would be no excuse for going out for migrant labor. On one kolkhoz there were 540 able-bodied members, but only 140 of them worked there; the rest were all itinerant rug-painters who nevertheless enjoyed all the rights and privileges of kolkhozniks in good standing.

A more recent example (*Izvestiia* 21/X/65:3) comes from Lipetsk Oblast, where a carpenter in a sovkhoz had only 12 days work for the first nine-and-a-half months of 1965. The rest of the time, he was working as a *shabashnik* (itinerant house builder) in the neighboring districts. For this work he was paid not only in money but in lumber. The cost of building a house includes 40 cubic meters of lumber—enough to build three house frames, each of which is worth 1200 rubles. *Sovkhozy* in various neighboring oblasts, and a lumbering operation in Tambov Oblast, send trucks to this village to recruit personnel. People go out for a month or for the whole summer without registering with the personnel department of their own *sovkhoz,* or taking their documents along, and are received by the other enterprises without questions. Both of these procedures are illegal.

These current instances fall into a pattern which we might call craft rather than industrial *otkhodnichestvo,* and which apparently existed before the growth of industry. In its present form, it is one of the many institutions which fill the interstices left by the Soviet system—in particular the periodic extreme local shortages of housing and consumer goods.

Contemporary Population Movement

We should remember that the peasant population of most parts of Central Russia has traditionally been more mobile geographically than other peasant populations. The British observer, Sir John Maynard describes the Russian peasant by temperament as a kind of land sailor. A number of Russian proverbs stress preference for a wandering life and contempt for the ignorant stay-at-home (Mel'nikov 1963: IV, 11). It should not surprise us, therefore, that the populations with which we deal remain highly mobile. In fact, the population of Viriatino is so mobile that widely varying estimates are given at different points of the study without any particular attempt to reconcile them. It is said that as of January 1, 1955, there were 1442 persons in Viriatino, plus 323 regular residents who were temporarily absent. On the other hand, as of January 1, 1957, the population of the "Lenin's Way" kolkhoz is put at 428 households, including 1128 persons. This should not be identified with the *membership* of the kolkhoz, since it includes a number of individuals who work elsewhere. By the basic "household census" taken in 1953 and used for the tables, there are 456 households in the village, including 1547 individuals, with 358 persons absent for long periods. However, the figure of 421 is also given for those temporarily absent in 1953 (perhaps representing a different time of year). This figure breaks down as follows: 44 percent of the total number were women;[3] 25 were students in technical secondary schools and specialized higher in-

---

[3] Taken by itself, this figure would be quite high, but bear in mind that there are 312 women of working age in the kolkhoz, as against only 172 men; these totals refer to the membership of the kolkhoz, not to the population of the village, but there is no reason to assume any significant difference in these proportions.

stitutions preparing for the professions; 69 were serving in the military; 161 (including 64 women) were working in transport and construction, and 47 in other branches of industry; 38 were employed in commercial enterprises, in the administrative apparatus, and as civilians at military installations. Finally, 28 persons were working in the professions, and the remaining 53 were listed as working in the home. The age distribution of the non-student portion of those absent is as follows: from 15–28, 243 persons; from 29–38, 97 persons; from 39–43, 29 persons, and from 44–68, 27 persons. Of those who had left the village but retained contact with it, 44 percent had education to the extent of seven grades and beyond (including higher), and 55 percent had between four and seven grades.

The data on population movement supplied by Anokhina and Shmeleva (1964:63–67) for Kalinin Oblast present certain difficulties and are not strictly comparable with the Viriatino data, due to the difference in the form of the study. The Kalinin Oblast figures indicate that about half the persons permanently absent (but retaining connections with their home community) are workers; 20 percent (chiefly women) are employed in government agencies (organs of economic administration, vital-statistics bureaus, and so on), and 15 percent are housewives who do not work. The remainder presumably are working in agriculture elsewhere (including skilled occupations—brigadiers, equipment operators, agronomists, livestock specialists, and even kolkhoz chairmen). Of those temporarily absent from villages in Kalinin Oblast during 1957–1958, the majority were in the armed forces or studying, with only a few persons employed as nursemaids, carpenters, or the like (occupations traditional in prerevolutionary *otkhodnichestvo* from this area). This situation, compared to the one obtaining immediately after World War II and in the early 1950s, reflects a marked improvement. Previously, many girls went out during the summer months to work on the turf fields in order to earn their *pridanoe* (marriage portion). And some men, just as in Fenomenov's time (1925), left the kolkhoz in the winter to fetch timber form the woods.

During the early 1950s, there was apparently a great deal of unorganized population flow within the oblast—the more prosperous kolkhozy gaining members while the weaker ones suffered a net deficit. For instance, Anokhina and Shmeleva give figures for the inflow and outflow on three kolkhozy (Table 7). This table would seem to indicate that intra-oblast—or, so to speak, intra-agricultural—mobility was greater for women than for men. This is especially true if we consider that, by the conditions of the study, the persons listed here were moving without their families. That is, the women included in the table are not housewives and mothers moving with their families, but independent workers. The differences between the dynamics of population on these three kolkhozy are to be explained by their economic status and geographical location. Both Il'ich and Aktiv are large operations, with fairly well established cultural and consumer services. They received a net gain in population, mostly female. The kolkhoz "Russia," while numerically larger than either of the others, is also more isolated and has a lower income, and cannot provide the same amenities.

Anokhina and Shmeleva (1964) mention the return of about 70 persons to the "Victor" kolkhoz of Ves'egonsk *raion* during 1955 and 1956; these were people who had left the kolkhoz at various times. Similar cases were mentioned to us personally by participants in the Viriatino study. Doubtless others occurred as well, but in all these cases, three questions must be posed: (1) what kind of people are these—rank-and-file kolkhozniks, agricultural specialists, former industrial workers, or miners? (2) How old are they? (3) Will they stay put? So far, answers to these questions are not forthcoming.

Between 75–80 percent of the persons moving away permanently from kol-khozy in Kalinin Oblast are 35 years of age or younger. This illustrates what is certainly one of the most significant and (from the Soviet point of view) disturbing phenomena in the Russian rural scene. It is becoming increasingly difficult to keep young people on the farm, particularly those who have skills and education and whose presence therefore would be the most valuable. The predicament which this situation represents is vividly illustrated by the results of a study published in *Izvestiia* (22/XI/64:2). Four hundred and thirty secondary school graduates in Smolensk Oblast were interviewed as to their future plans and intentions. Of the total number, 27 would remain at work on their kolkhozy; 56 planned to attend an agricultural technical school or higher institution (and presumably return to work in agriculture in some skilled capacity); 31 intended to seek jobs in industry; 102 to enter a higher technical institution in some field other than agriculture; 124 were planning to go on for professional training (engineering, medicine, teaching, and so on), while 90 intended to continue their education, but had not yet decided where or with what aim. "Thus, only 83 persons—less than 20 percent—intended

TABLE 7

POPULATION CHANGES BY SEX IN THREE KOLKHOZY, KALININ OBLAST

	Il'ich kolkhoz Bezhetsk *raion*	"Russia" kolkhoz Ves'egonsk *raion*	Aktiv kolkhoz Krasnokholmsk *raion*
Total adult population	559 228 331 Males Females	689 268 421 Males Females	386 156 230 Males Females
Newly arrived	192 79 113 Males Females	56 20 36 Males Females	143 61 82 Males Females
Left during post-war period*	148 63 85 Males Females	266 98 168 Males Females	119 60 59 Males Females
Net change**	+44 +16 +28 Males Females	−210 −78 −122 Males Females	+24 +1 +23 Male Females

* This category includes only those who left while retaining lively connections with their families. Families all of whose members moved out of the village are not indicated, since they would not show up on the cards.

** The net change is calculated as from some unspecified date, before the beginning of the post-war population movements.

(Source: Anokhina and Shmeleva, 1964: 64)

to devote themselves to agriculture. Let us add the 48 graduates who chose nonagricultural professions but intended to return to the village as physicians, teachers, or engineers. Of the 90 who have not yet chosen their profession, some will probably remain in agriculture, but even so, a clear majority is going to the city." We have already noted that the rural schools in this area (and many others) must serve a large and widely scattered population, and that cultural and consumer services are poorly developed. The authors of the article state specifically that the movement away from the land is normal in principle: it is its intensity at the present time that disturbs them. They also exonerate the school system from any blame for the situation; in fact, they maintain that the better the rural schools do their job, the more intense the movement to the cities will be. The reasons, given by those interviewed, for moving out of the countryside fall into six categories: (1) a choice of career (hardly a satisfactory explanation, being conditioned by other factors); (2) generalized boredom; (3) dissatisfaction with the level of pay; (4) dissatisfaction with working conditions; (5) dissatisfaction with standard of living (which in the Soviet context is not directly dependent on financial status); and (6) dissatisfaction with cultural opportunities (clubhouses, movies, theaters, concerts, sports facilities). In terms of the number of responses giving these reasons, categories (5) and (6) are by far the most frequent. Category (1) comes next. Dissatisfaction with rates of pay, as such, is far down the list. It is notable that certain kolkhozy in the area have less trouble than others recruiting young personnel, and this seems to be directly dependent on the level of expenditure for cultural services.

Recruitment of Leading Personnel

A major and continuing problem in Soviet agriculture is that of supplying trained personnel for administrative and supervisory positions (kolkhoz chairmen, brigadiers, and so on) and for the professional specialties—equipment operators, veterinarians and their assistants, agronomists, and assorted technicians. This problem appears under a number of aspects. First, facilities must be set up to train the personnel; then, the right type of people must be persuaded to go in for training, and finally, the trained personnel must be properly allocated and kept on the job. Higher educational institutions, including agricultural ones, not unnaturally tend to be concentrated in or near the cities, and the population from which they draw their students is therefore predominantly urban. It is worth noting that in 1961, only one-third of those admitted to higher agricultural schools were peasants. The Moscow Land-Use Engineering Institute, for example, admitted only 27 people from villages, as against 248 from cities. This compounds the difficulty of maintaining adequate personnel on the land since, as some Soviet writers themselves point out, city people can hardly be expected to exile themselves voluntarily to the provinces. In 1962, a group of professors at Leningrad State University suggested that particular faculties be assigned parts of the country with which they would maintain liaison. These faculties would prepare cadres of specialists, assign entering students to a particular area, and psychologically prepare them for such service. To our knowledge, nothing concrete has come of this proposal, but the problem is still being discussed. The difficulty of retaining farm personnel may be judged from the data of Morozov (1961), which derive from various points in the European USSR, some of which fall outside the area with which we are concerned. There is no indication, however, that the situation in the central and northern districts differs significantly from that found elsewhere. From September 1953 to April 1957, in Saratov Oblast on the lower Volga, 334 engineers and technicians were sent to do agricultural work, but 195 of them quit, for one reason or another. In some other places, the turnover was still higher (1961:37.) After the September Plenum of the Communist Party Central Committee in 1953, agronomists were placed directly on MTS staffs instead of being attached, as before, to Union-wide government agencies. But the expected improvement of service did not materialize, because increased paper work took up most of the agronomists' time. Accordingly, in August 1955, the Council of Ministers decreed that all agronomists should be placed on kolkhoz staffs and made directly responsible to the administration and the chairman. Almost nine years later, nevertheless, agronomists were still apparently not responsible for results in any obvious sense: a writer in *Izvestiia* (28/V/64:3) was proposing that they be placed in direct charge of operations on kolkhozy and *sovkhozy* and he made directly responsible for the work. This was tried out at the village of Dedinovo, in Moscow Oblast (a center for dairying, and the scene of one of the early ethnographic kolkhoz studies), and yields shot up as a result. The editors of *Izvestiia* appended a note to this article stating that according to the Ministry of Agricultural Production and Procurement, RSFSR, 167,000 out of 305,000 specialists under the Ministry's jurisdiction are working directly in kolkhozy and *sovkhozy,* 20,000 of them being section heads, farm chiefs (in charge of particular operations), or brigadiers. The significance of these data lies in the fact that specialists who are not directly attached to *sovkhozy* and kolkhozy cannot be kept in the countryside if they wish to leave—as many eventually do. It is self-evident from the small percentage of rural people with secondary specialized or higher education that properly trained personnel is in short supply. At the same time, Morozov notes substantial gains in the educational status of persons with responsible positions in agriculture. Thus, the percentage of kolkhoz chairmen with higher education rose from 21.1 in 1953 to 63.8 in 1958 and the same figure for chief agronomists increased from 36.8 to 71.4 during the same period. An increase was also recorded in the percentage of heads of repair workshops with higher or secondary specialized education, although the figures are somewhat lower for both dates.

Education alone, of course, is no guarantee of competence or good results. This is especially true in a position where the "human factor" is as important as it is in that of kolkhoz chairman. The press contains accounts of kolkhozy and *sovkhozy* which have had several chairmen or directors in the space of a couple of years—all sent out from the center, though not always with appropriate training. In other cases, described both in the press and in the ethnographic literature, kolkhozy have been run for 20 or 30 years by the same person, who sometimes had started out with practically no formal training. The difficulties of administering agricultural operations, particularly in recent years, have been compounded by the fact that kolkhozy and *sovkhozy* have been expanded, sometimes beyond all reason, and immense efforts are required simply to get from place to place. It should also be recalled that the task of the kolkhoz chairman is in many ways a thankless one, since he must act as a buffer between the members and the state and must endure a

TABLE 8

QUALIFIED LABOR POOL AND RESERVE ON KOLKHOZY

(*Kalinin Oblast: 1956–57*)

	1*	2**	3***
Total employed in kolkhoz economy	387	498	289
A. Including people now working as kolkhoz chairmen, brigadiers, agronomists, livestock specialists, timekeepers	34	30	16
equipment operators	21	20	14
specialists of other technical trades (blacksmiths, builders, and so on)	9	28	17
stockmen	49	65	34
B. People who formerly worked as administrators and supervisors in kolkhozy or in industry	50	45	17
skilled workers and equipment operators in kolkhoz economy	18	19	30
white-collar workers in government agencies	6	3	3
stockmen	85	75	29
C. Specialists, administrative and supervisory personnel, people of specific trades—total	272	285	150
Percent of total employed in kolkhoz economy	68	57	52

* Il'ich kolkhoz, Bezhetsk Raion.
** "Russia" kolkhoz, Ves'egonsk Raion.
*** Aktiv kolkhoz, Krasnokholmsk Raion.

good deal of hectoring and shouting from both sides. For this reason, it is sometimes difficult to get honest and competent people to accept these jobs—not to speak of keeping them honest and competent after they accept the posts. The problem here is that at present the pay of kolkhoz chairmen and officials usually is not geared to results, though suggestions to this effect have been made (*Izvestiia* 6/X/64:4).

The writer of the above-mentioned article describes a case where the chairman of a low-profit kolkhoz received more pay than the chairman of a more profitable one. In the low-profit kolkhoz the situation has been corrected; a brigade with an excessively high cost of production was penalized and the brigadier's pay was docked. This forced the brigade to analyze and improve its work.

Too often, however, incompetence is rewarded, as in the case of a kolkhoz chairman with only seven grades of education, no agricultural training, and no administrative skills. After three years of bungling performance, the man was made chairman of the local soviet (*Izvestiia* 24/VIII/63:1). Reading between the lines of this item, we can discern some of the reasons for the promotion. The public economy was almost bankrupt, but the kolkhozniks' private operations had expanded considerably; they did what they liked, and decided everything according to family interests. It is not hard to imagine that this situation suited them excellently. Here we have an example of the distortion of national goals and centrally established policies by local pressure, of a type not unfamiliar in the "ward politics" of many countries.

Unfortunately, available Soviet sources do not give us detailed data on the provenance and previous training of kolkhoz officials and specialists. The few remarks made on this subject in the Viriatino study are highly anecdotal, and the numbers involved are too small to enable us to form any judgment. About the only solid data on this score are provided by a table (Anokhina and Shmeleva 1964:70–71) showing the pool of experienced and qualified people in three kolkhozy of Kalinin Oblast. (Table 8).

Table 8 calls for some comments. In the first place, the category of "stockman" (most of whom, despite the name, are women) include such occupations as milkers, calf-keepers, and pig-keepers, which in some cases involve skill, but certainly not formal training. A formally trained person in this category would be classified as a livestock specialist. It is clear therefore that the inclusion of the stockmen in Table 8 inflates the percentage of supposedly skilled personnel on the kolkhoz beyond what the facts actually warrant. In the second place, the category of those who previously worked in various skilled or administrative capacities is ambiguous, to say the least. It represents approximately half of the grand total. According to the text, members of this group now work as rank-and-file kolkhozniks. We can only assume that they have been retired. The category of former administrators and supervisors in kolkhozy or in industry may well include returned miners or industrial workers, who have no particular skills applicable to agriculture. If so, this would again inflate the actual number of qualified personnel.

The Position of Women

According to the latest figures, the share of leading positions in the Soviet economy held by women had attained 49 percent by 1964. On the surface this is a remarkable achievement, particularly for a society still about one half rural, and with a deeply ingrained prejudice against women. However, this bare statistic conceals important variations. The highest percentage of women in leading positions is to be found in public health (88 percent) and education (66 percent). Agriculture is at the opposite end of the spectrum, with 21 percent (Dodge and Feshbach, mimeograph).[4]

It is obvious that under these conditions, social mobility, especially for women, means mobility out of the rural environment. Yet we find that women are,

---

[4] It is our impression that even this figure is based on a rather broad interpretation of the concept of "leading positions," perhaps taking in the so-called "link leaders," although the authors' source does not specify.

Girl student from Tambov Teachers' Institute on vacation in Viriatino.

if anything, slightly less mobile than men. This is if we match the proportion of women in the "absent population" (for example), in Viriatino against the known surplus of women in the population as a whole, and particularly in the rural population. All available figures show an educational lag for women throughout the Soviet Union and in most of the republics, including the Russian Federation. This lag is particularly marked in the rural population (Dodge and Feshbach, mimeograph).[5]

It is worth noting that those women who do hold leading positions in agriculture are apparently better educated than their male counterparts (Dodge and Feshbach, mimeograph). This would seem to indicate a situation where a higher level of qualification or ability is required for a woman to attain a given degree of social mobility than for a man. The same situation obtains in many countries, including the United States.

The reasons for the lag in the education of women, particularly in the countryside, are complex and hotly debated, both in the West and in the Soviet Union. Here we can only make a few general guesses. As long as tuition was charged for secondary and higher education, schooling depended on allocation of resources within the family. It would be natural, given the orientation of the value system, for boys to have first call on whatever was available. It would also seem that this is a matter which cannot be very much influenced by state policy. If preference were given to girls in the awarding of scholarships, it might have some effect. However,

[5] The figures compiled by Dodge and Feshbach are not broken down geographically. Totals broken down by levels of education, sex, and republic will be found in *TsSU SSSR* 1962:82–84.

the government is understandably wary of giving explicit preference to any group —among other reasons, it is bad politics.

All this should not lead us to underestimate the importance of what has been done. Definite avenues of social mobility for women, which did not exist before the Revolution, have now been opened. Certain professions such as teaching, medicine, and auxiliary fields are now predominantly feminine. Women are also prominent in the trade network. Finally, a certain number of posts in the Party and the government are held by women, although women are seriously under-represented at the upper levels. The major problem, particularly for rural women, is their continuing insulation to some extent from the influence of social life in general, and the resulting narrowness of their horizons, which reduces their motivation toward social mobility.

In reading the Soviet ethnographic literature, we become aware of the marked difference in the position of women between the formal structure of the society—the kolkhoz, the political hierarchy, and the various ladders by which social mobility is achieved—and the informal structure of the community, which centers on the family. As we attempted to show in Chapter II, the family is the repository of many important functions, and the position of the woman in the family is central, even though the system of values is in many respects male-oriented. The very centrality of the woman's position in the family, however, limits her possible achievements outside it. In the absence of a sharp rise in the level of consumer services, child care, and so forth, this is likely to remain true. This situation is not by any means limited to the Soviet Union, although special factors there of investment and allocation of materials intensify its effect.

It might seem that here we were making a biological point, but a word of caution is in order. Mead and other anthropologists have shown in working with primitive tribes and non-Western peoples that the cultural malleability of the human biological apparatus is almost infinite. Therefore, we cannot maintain, without very grave reservations, that a given situation with regard to the position of women in a given society is biologically determined.

Social Mobility: Summary

What was said above about social mobility for women also applies to the population as a whole: the Soviet regime has created broad avenues and mechanisms of social mobility that did not exist before its advent. However, because these avenues mostly lead out of the countryside, the countryside itself is less affected by the great social changes now occurring than ideally it should be. Soviet scholars, as we have seen, accept the drain of population from the countryside as normal in principle. However, they are disturbed by its present intensity because it aggravates the backwardness of certain areas and threatens to unbalance the economy of the country as a whole. It is in this connection that the distinction between rich and poor kolkhozy takes on particular significance. Rich kolkhozy are able to maintain their populations to a far greater extent than poor ones, by paying an attractive wage and by providing certain cultural amenities—by, so to speak, urbanizing on the spot. The process is self-perpetuating. Poor kolkhozy are constantly losing population, are short of personnel, and hence become poorer all the time.

4

The Folk Institutions

IN THIS CHAPTER we will consider the customs, traditions, and ceremonies which express the values of the local community as such, and make for its integration and solidarity. This applies chiefly to the various rituals and ceremonies which mark turning-points in the life of the individual and of the family—birth, coming-of-age, marriage, and death. In social anthropology these events are called the life crises. To an extent, the ceremonies marking the various stages of the agricultural year, about which something has already been said, are also included in this category. We will also attempt, insofar as sources and available space permit, to describe the status of organized religion in the Russian countryside.

A word of caution: we do not intend to draw a hard and fast distinction between the values of the local community—and the institutions and observances which express these values—and the values and institutions of the society at large. In fact, the process by which these elements converge and coalesce is one of the most important aspects of culture change in peasant and formerly-peasant societies.

Our task is complicated by the fact that there is a marked difference in the Soviet sources' handling of prerevolutionary and postrevolutionary folk institutions. Prerevolutionary peasant customs are described in great detail, often quite colorfully and with relish, and with little of the somber coloration that is given, for example, to descriptions of economic matters. In describing contemporary ritual life in the countryside, however, Soviet authors, with a few significant exceptions (Pushkareva and Shmeleva 1959; Savushkina 1963; and others who deal with outlying districts, such as Shikhareva 1964) tend to confine themselves to generalities. It is interesting that in all cases where a detailed description dating from the Soviet period is available, the ceremonies described are very close, at least externally, to the traditional eighteenth and nineteenth century type.

Life-Crisis Ceremonial

BIRTH   Traditionally, the birth of a child was accompanied by various sorts of rituals, which can be divided roughly into two categories: those performed immediately before and during parturition, to ease labor and to protect the mother, and those performed after the birth itself, to bring good fortune to the child and celebrate the event. The first category of rituals was marked by practices based on sympathetic magic—untying knots, opening boxes, and other symbolic acts—which were almost all of pre-Christian derivation. Soviet authors generally state that these rituals are no longer performed, and it seems probable that (except perhaps in the most remote and benighted areas) this is quite true. The ceremonies performed after the child's birth, although they are called in Russian by the general term christening (*kreshchenie*), contain both Christian and pre-Christian elements. The child was christened according to Russian Orthodox practice obligatorily on the second or third day after birth. This was followed by a secular celebration which, as events have shown, was functionally independent of the religious one. In Viriatino, religious christening at the present time may or may not be held, and if it is held, may be delayed for months or even years; but the secular party is always held immediately after the mother returns from the hospital, or a few days after birth (if she was brought to bed at home), whether or not the child is ever christened.

Certain quasi-religious customs were traditionally connected with the religious act of christening—for example, going to the river for "holy water," which was then sprinkled around the house and the barnyard by old men, and drunk by the family on the morning of the christening; or marking doors, window sills and the front gate with crosses (children formerly did this, but now, if it is done at all, it is by adults). These rituals, while they still sometimes occur, are declared by the authors to be atypical survivals (Kushner, ed. 1958:231–232).

The actual content of the christening feast is described in our sources with some variation. Traditionally, in Kalinin Oblast, the most important figures at this celebration were the godparents and the midwife. An obligatory feature was the special "christening porridge," dished out with a wooden spoon by the midwife to all those present at the end of the dinner. For this the midwife received "thanks" in the form of small change. The infant was presented with gifts "to teethe on." Nowadays the midwife's role is much less significant, and the distribution of porridge to all the guests has disappeared, but the father still must eat a spoonful of oversalted porridge to the accompaniment of considerable laughter and teasing. Nothing specific is said in the Kalinin Oblast study about the rôle of the godparents. According to the Viriatino study, they are always seated at the middle table with the closest relatives of the new parents, while the other guests are arranged in order of relationship. The authors comment (Kushner, ed. 1958:233): "The absence of a number of important features—primarily the participation of the midwife and the taboos on the new mother [who previously was not permitted to be present]—and particularly the fact that the christening feast is held before the child is baptized, deprive the christening feast of its traditional ritual significance. At the present time, it is only a family festival on the occasion of the birth and naming of a child, and is engaged in literally by everyone." This view of the matter shows an extremely narrow interpretation of the concept of ritual. Although it is perhaps a family festival, the number of persons attending may be very large. The dinner is followed by a popular outing, with accordion music, singing, and dancing. In Kalinin Oblast, the entire neighborhood is invited to the party. From indications in the Kushner study, it would seem that Viriatino was not served by a regular priest, even before the Revolution: this fact may have brought about the marked independence of the folk tradition from formal religious observance.

COMING-OF-AGE Among the primitive Slavs, coming-of-age seems to have been marked by some ceremonial observance, as it was among most primitive peoples. To our knowledge, however, no Soviet source mentions any trace of this in the Russian peasant tradition. It is probable that the complex of observances connected with the wedding ceremony absorbed the elements of initiation ritual which had been present, since in the prerevolutionary countryside marriage generally coincided closely with the attainment of biological and social maturity. Under Soviet conditions, a kind of coming-of-age ceremony has been developed, centering either on graduation from secondary school or on the granting of a person's first internal passport. This is not actually a folk institution, as most Soviet writers recognize.

MARRIAGE In the prerevolutionary Russian countryside, marriage was the climax of ritual life and included a highly elaborate set of ceremonies, social occasions, and dramatic performances, which not only served to mark a turning point in the life of the family and the individual, but also provided amusement and artistic outlet for the entire village. Many elements in the Russian wedding ritual are extremely old—so old that their original meaning was long ago forgotten. The terminology and *dramatis personae* of the wedding have become a whole subsidiary field in Russian ethnography, on which substantial monographs and even books have been written.

The traditional wedding ritual was collective in character, involving a large number of participants. Each of the participants had his own particular rôle to play and name by which he was called: *svat* (literally matchmaker, actually an elder male usually related to the groom)[1]; *svakha* (the feminine form of *svat* referring to the *svat's* wife); *druzhka* (the best man, who served as the director of the ceremony, almost in the theatrical sense); *podruzh'ia* (bridesmaids or maids of honor); *tysiatskii* (the leader of the wedding procession, who carried a barrel of beer and various other paraphernalia); *druzhina* (collectively, the male members of the procession who served as deputies to the best man), and so forth. The ceremonial cycle usually began, since most marriages were arranged, with several sessions of hard bargaining. The agents appointed for this purpose—generally elder male relatives of the groom—called on the bride's family. The reverse happened only in cases where a *primak* was sought. The call was always made in the evening, so that the matchmakers would not be seen. It was not considered good form to come to the point immediately, so various allegorical expressions were used at first: something might be said about a merchant and his wares or a hunter and his martens. If the bride's family gave preliminary consent to the match, the prospective groom was given a present. The present was not necessarily returned if the deal fell through, although the bride's family usually made an effort to get it back, especially if more than one initial consent had been given. A preliminary bethrothal ceremony (*malyi zapoi,* literally, small drinking bout or spree) was arranged when the groom had finally been chosen and had given proof of serious intent. On this occasion the time and conditions of the forthcoming marriage were determined. A contribu-

---

[1] The term is also applied to any relation by marriage—even to, for instance, the wife's cousin or the parents of one's son or daughter-in-law, for whom no designation exists in English.

tion from the groom's side toward the expenses of the wedding and the bride's clothes was almost universal in Russia. According to one source (Aleksandrov and others 1964:470) this is to be regarded as a survival of the bride-price, which was prevalent among many Asian peoples of the Soviet Union, but as far as our knowledge goes, this view is atypical. The contribution from the groom's side depended on his family's wealth and the bride's external attributes. The bride's *pridanoe* was also decided on during this ceremony. An inspection of the groom's house was usually held after the preliminary betrothal, particularly if the bride and groom came from different villages. Sometime later, the *rukobit'e* (handclapping) or *bolshoi zapoi* (large drinking bout) was held at the bride's house. This was the final betrothal ceremony. Up to now negotiations could be broken off honorably and without penalities, but anyone who backed out after this was expected to make good all losses and to pay "special damages." Such cases might even be adjudicated by a specially constituted village court. Until the 1920s, in some *raions* of Kalinin Oblast, before holding prayers in front of the icons, the bride sat down to her final *posidelka,* and the groom came to burn her flax-spindle, as a sign that her days as a maiden were over.

When her marriage had been arranged, the girl was released from ordinary tasks in her parents' house and spent her time preparing her *pridanoe,* in which she was assisted by her friends. During this period the girls received guests, including the groom. This was in fact a survival, since in the late nineteenth century most girls had their *pridanoe* made professionally. All those participating in this activity, including the bride herself, wore a special form of mourning dress. In fact, the entire period running from the final betrothal to the wedding itself, was distinctly elegiac in tone. The bride was expected to "lament" in various forms—for example, while bidding farewell to her relatives, including her godmother, or (in the south Russian tradition) while waiting for the dawn of her wedding day. In some places she was assisted by professional lamentors. The songs sung by the girls during the wedding cycle usually contrasted the happy life of a maiden in her parents' house with the hard lot of a married woman.

On the eve of the wedding itself, parties were held in both the bride's and groom's houses; the theme of these celebrations was farewell to youth and to the companions of youth. At the girl's party (*devishnik*), a decorated tree, symbolizing virginity and the freedom that went with it, was dismantled. At the *devishnik,* the couple exchanged "brooms"—small bunches of twigs tied together. These were used in the ritual bath, which took place on the morning of the wedding (or in some places on the day before), and was accompanied by special songs and laments. This ceremony had the function of ensuring good fortune for the bride; water brought from many wells by the bride's friends was used for the bath, which took place at a neighbor's, always on the same side of the street. The south Russian wedding ceremony preserved in great detail the ritual connected with the baking of a loaf of bread, which was accompanied in all its stages (mixing the dough, placing the bread in the oven, taking it out) by special ceremonial acts, songs, and acrobatic turns. In Viriatino, the loaf contained a coin, supposed to bring good luck to the person who found it in his slice. By an innocent fraud, the slice with the coin in it always went to the bride or groom. The north Russian ceremony kept only fragments of this, showing that the "loaf ritual" had at one time been practiced in these areas as well. The historical tradition relating to royal and princely weddings of the sixteenth and seventeenth centuries indicates the same thing.

With the approach of the wedding itself, the entire cycle reached its climax. The bride was dressed by her girl friends in preparation for the wedding ceremony. The final plaiting of the bride's hair was accompanied, like all other features of the ceremony, by special laments and ritual songs. Following this, the bride's parents and godparents gave her their blessing and placed her at a special table with the bridesmaids. Meanwhile, at the groom's house, the groom and his party were preparing to go and bring back the bride. The groom's party set out in strict order with a very large number of functionaries (particularly in the north Russian ritual). Along the way, various obstacles were set up (poles laid across the road, and so on), which the best man had to buy off with gifts of wine and sweetmeats to the bride's party. The same process was repeated before the gates of the bride's house. A scene was played at this point at which the place next to the bride was sold: the buyer was the best man, and the seller was the bride's younger brother. This scene was understood everywhere in a joking sense, but is regarded by Soviet ethnographers as a survival of earlier forms of marriage, in accordance with their general scheme for the evolution of culture. In some places this scene was preceded by the purchase of the bride from the bridesmaids, which included a facetious ceremony of the showing of a false bride (the part being played by one of the bridesmaids). This was followed by a plentiful meal, but the bride and groom were not supposed to eat before the wedding. The departure for the church was always accompanied by the shooting off of guns, three circuits of the wedding train with an icon, cracking of whips, noises and shouts, all to drive away evil spirits. It was for this reason that the best man carried a gun as one of his insignia of office; other insignia were a towel and a flail.

Immediately after the religious ceremony, the bride's hair was replaited into two braids, which was the hairdo characteristic of married women. On coming out of the church, the bride and groom (in north Russia) went together to the groom's house or (in the south), to the bride's house from which they moved to the groom's, in the evening after the wedding feast proper. The *pridanoe* was usually brought on the first day of the wedding, and in some places there was a humorous scene in which it was bought from the bride's party. At the house, the young couple were met by their parents with bread and salt and blessings, and sprinkled with hops or *zhito*. The bride and groom were placed at the head table, and their health was drunk. During the feast, the bride sat wrapped in a kerchief or shawl and did not take part in the general gaiety. At this time also, she was supposed to give gifts of sweetmeats to her new relations, who in return gave her money. Historically, there was a ceremony throughout almost all of Russia, in which the young couple was taken, in the company of the matchmakers and the best man, to a bed in the byre or storehouse at the beginning of the feast, and then were led out at the end of the feast to the ceremony of "gilding," at which there were pelted with money. Later, this particular ritual (taking the couple to bed before the feast) was abandoned, but the custom of putting them to bed after the wedding feast continued almost until the Revolution. The bride was supposed to take off her husband's shoes in sign of submission.

Next day, accompanied by the beating of pots, the matchmaker's wife and the best man got the couple out of bed with rituals such as showing the bride's shift as proof of her virginity. The young couple and the members of their train then went to meet the bride's parents, in whose house the next stage of the festivities was held. The first dish on this occasion was an omelet, which the groom tasted, after which he put money in a glass along with liquor and offered it to his mother-in-law, thereby signifying that his wife had come to him chaste. The party then proceeded to the groom's house, where the festivities continued, and the young couple was pelted with money. In some places (for example, in what is now Kalinin Oblast), young women in costume appeared from the bride's house, dancing and beating pots. An omelet and a special meat pastry were presented and, as before, the groom had to taste them first.

On the third day, the bride was "uncovered"—that is, her kerchief was taken off, after which she could dance and make merry with the other guests. On the same day, she had to undergo various tests of skill, intelligence, and submission, which are reminiscent of fraternity hazing. The post-wedding cycle was characterized by parties held in turn by all the relatives of the couple who had taken part in the wedding itself. During this time, mumming characteristic of the Christmas season was held, and humourous skits of conventional content were performed—a doctor healing the sick, and so forth. The same kind of skit was played at weddings by the Estonian fishermen of Kihnu Island (Kalits 1962).

In the late nineteenth and early twentieth centuries, the entire ritual began to be simplified and shortened; previously, weddings could take as long as six days to complete, and were therefore usually held in the winter—particularly on or around St. Michael's Day (November 8). Certain features of the traditional ceremony were combined or omitted entirely: for example, the formal betrothal was omitted and only the preliminary betrothal was retained, or in some places the formal betrothal was combined with the wedding.[2] In order to see what has become of this complex series of rituals under modern conditions, we shall examine a particular wedding in Kalinin Oblast, as described by Pushkareva and Shmeleva (1959), with comparative data from Viriatino. The authors note that as a rule the whole process of matchmaking has changed content. From a deadly serious economic transaction, it has become a more or less casual conversation between the two sides to iron out the details of the wedding, the number of guests to be expected from each side, and so forth. It is worth noting, however, that according to the Viriatino study, formal matchmaking is still obligatory. The bride, as of the mid-1950s, was still expected to bring with her to the groom's house a certain quantity of grain, calculated according to a set scale—one *pud* per month per consumer. The *pridanoe* continues to be brought, and although according to both the Kalinin Oblast and the Viriatino studies, it is no longer economically crucial or agreed upon in advance, it is still publicly exhibited and is a matter of pride for the young people and their parents. The elements which go into the *pridanoe* are fixed by present-day custom; the Viriatino study (Kushner, ed. 1958:227n) lists them as follows in one fairly typical case dating from 1954: a down puff with three slipcases for it; four "canopies," which are hung one on top of the other from the top of the marriage bed;

---

[2] The foregoing account has been taken from Aleksandrov and others, eds. (1964: 469–472), but we have omitted much of the local variation.

one sheet; four bedspreads (two quilted, one woolen and one cotton or linen) ; two down pillows, with four pillowcases on each one (three colored undercases and one of calico with inserts); one calico bed-curtain; one small wall-rug to be hung above the bed; one colored fine cotton curtain for the storeroom; muslin curtains for the door, the kitchen shelves, the stove and the chimney flue; muslin window shades and tulle window curtains; four towels (two undecorated and two cross-stitched), which are used to clean the icons and photographs hung on the wall; a lace cover for the small table under the icons; a piece of tulle for the shelf that holds the icons; two table cloths; and an oilcloth for the kitchen table. Tradition also dictates that a "bundle" be prepared for the bridegroom (a shirt, drawers, gloves, socks, and soap).

Several things are noteworthy about this "marriage portion." First of all, unlike the traditional Russian peasant *pridanoe,* it includes no clothing, and is therefore functionally quite different. Whereas traditionally, the bride was expected to bring with her the wherewithal to clothe herself and her children, the function of the modern bride's portion is essentially to redecorate the house. Secondly, by peasant tradition, the *pridanoe* was heritable in the female line separately from the other property. However, contemporary sources do not tell us whether this is still the case with the appurtenances of the house, and it should be remembered that the house itself is the joint property of the family as a corporate unit. In Kalinin Oblast, the *pridanoe* presently consists of the bride's clothing and bed linen although, until recently, it had to include articles such as chiffoniers, sewing machines, and bicycles, which were expensive and not easily obtained.

In Kalinin Oblast, the ceremony of viewing the groom's house used to be very serious, involving display of wealth, often carried out with borrowed grain and animals. Now it is only a get-acquainted party for the parents of the couple and is not held if the bride and groom are from the same village. Special ceremonies like the *rukobit'e,* the prayers, and the formal betrothal have gone out, or parts of them have been consolidated into a single family festival, held in the bride's house a few days after formal agreement to the marriage. The bride is not secluded after the arrangement of marriage, and no longer does she lament the end of her maidenhood. Nor is the *devishnik* held in its previous form. Pushkareva and Shmeleva (1959) explain these facts by observing that the sharp moral and customary differences between the single and the married states no longer apply. A remnant of the *devishnik* still exists. In Ves'egonsk and Sandovsk *raions,* decorated trees symbolizing virginity are put up in the houses of the bride and groom, in the corner which looks out on the street and is nearest to the porch. On the Voroshilov kolkhoz, Ves'egonsk *raion,* the trees are decorated to the tune of "Suliko" (a Georgian song now popular throughout the Soviet Union). The marriage feast is considered the most important feature of the whole cycle, and no wedding is complete without it. Therefore, the feast and the registration at the Vital Statistics Office are held on the same day. However, the Viriatino study indicates (Kushner, ed. 1958:228) that the registration and the folk cycle are sometimes separated. In such cases, cohabitation begins immediately after the registration, but the bride continues to live in her parents' house. The traditional ritual is still considered necessary before the bride can move into her husband's house. This situation raises interesting theoretical questions which, unfortunately, the sources do not permit us to answer.

Traditionally, among many peoples of the Caucasus, Southeastern Europe (see Campbell 1964), and elsewhere, the transfer of the bride was conditioned on the payment of the complete bride-price. Therefore, the question of residence was conceptually separate from that of the marriage itself. However, we know of no evidence for any such state of affairs in Central Russia.

Church marriages in Kalinin Oblast are now comparatively rare, although at the time of the Revolution they were almost universal.[3] The wedding itself is now entirely gay and playful in tone, with none of the emotional ambivalence which characterized the prerevolutionary ritual. Many of the old features—for instance, the purchase of the dowry and of the place next to the bride, the blocking of the bride and groom's way, the ceremonial bowing and touching of the earth (traditionally performed by the bride on entering the groom's house, and probably at first signifying homage to the household gods) are retained, but are carried out in a joking and boisterous manner, which in some cases was true even at the beginning of the century.

The number of people invited to the wedding from the bride's and groom's sides are about equal, but whereas in the past only close kinsmen were invited, the guests now include members of the bride's and groom's brigades, the kolkhoz administration, and the village intelligentsia. (This difference is not as great as it might appear, since traditionally, close kinsmen often comprised most of the village.) In a wedding which was observed in detail, the groom came in a passenger car to fetch the bride and take her to the office of the local soviet to register their marriage. The groom and his party were entertained with wine, and a group of elderly women performed some old-fashioned wedding songs, different from those now used. Then the mother of the bride gave her blessing, and the couple went out to the car, accompanied by the young people carrying the tree which had been in the bride's house. The car (or horse) carrying the bride and groom was decorated by the girls with different colored rags or paper flowers or, in the summer, with real flowers and embroidered curtains. This decorating was accompanied by the song "The White Swan" (an old Russian romantic folk tune, but not one of the traditional wedding songs). Some distance away from the office of the soviet, the car was stopped by a barrier of logs that the men had set up. The groom treated them to drinks that he had brought in the car, and then they dragged the logs away and let the car proceed. After the registration, the bride and groom drove around their own and the neighboring villages, "so that people can see how they make [literally, play] weddings in the Voroshilov kolkhoz." They finally arrived at the groom's house, where the bride's relatives and guests were waiting. During this time, the girls made up the bride's "bed" (the same word in Russian is also applied to the *pridanoe*). They dragged the bed and the trunks through the gate, all

---

[3] In the Voroshilov kolkhoz, Ves'egonsk *raion,* between 1946 and 1950, 53 weddings were held, none of them in church, and between 1951 and 1957, two out of 105 weddings were in church. On the Il'ich kolkhoz of Bezhetsk *raion* church weddings were 5 out of 36 between 1946 and 1950, and 5 out of 51 between 1951 and 1957 (Anokhina and Shmeleva 1959:48n.). It is curious to note that the relative frequency of church weddings is somewhat greater in Bezhetsk *raion* where, according to the authors, the folk tradition died out during the nineteenth century, and most of it is not remembered even by old informants, than in Ves'egonsk *raion,* where folk tradition survives almost intact. This suggests that the folk and religious ceremonies may function as alternates.

the while singing "Dubinushka" ("The Oaken Club")—actually a revolutionary marching song associated with the 1905 uprising. The groom's party then "bought" the *pridanoe* from the girls who, in this context, are called *korobeishchiki* ("peddlers"). The newlyweds were greeted at the gate by the groom's parents and pelted with grain, which the young people tried to catch. It is said that the number of children will be according to the amount of grain caught. This account does not mention the pelting of the couple with money, but according to the Viriatino study, it is usually done.

The celebration goes on for two or three nights; beer is brewed, and dances, skits and *chastushki* (four line verses of usually humorous and sometimes romantic content) are performed.

The style and manner of the Russian peasant wedding, both traditional and current, is intensely theatrical. This applies both to the ceremonies themselves and to the incidental entertainments. In fact, this element has, if anything, increased in importance in recent times. Savushkina (1963) describes the performances of semi-professional comedians at weddings in Gorky Oblast. One old man, for instance, appears in the role of a wandering peddler or fisherman, improvising comic turns from familiar elements, more or less in the *commedia dell'arte* tradition. In certain districts, like the Kuban, that lie outside the area of our study, certain elements (particularly types of wedding songs) are preserved which have disappeared in Central Russia (Shikhareva 1964) and in general the ritual is more conservative.

The ethnographers who studied Viriatino claim that the old folk, particularly the women, are chiefly responsible for preserving the folk wedding cycle. It is rather hard to see how this can be taken literally, however, since most of the actual ceremonies are carried out by young people. Occasionally, weddings have been held in "new style"—with festivities only at the groom's house, and without most of the folk ritual. The people involved in these ceremonies are usually, as the authors put it, "the most forward-looking and sophisticated part of the youth, the majority of whom work in industry." (Kushner, ed. 1958:229) Sometimes young people would prefer to be married new style, but are pressured into going through the folk cycle. At the marriage of a career army officer, the couple categorically refused only the ceremony of "gilding" and the beating of pots, but went through all the other rituals.

The usual age at marriage is slightly older than it was before the Revolution —24 or 25 for men and 22 or 23 for women. This is probably due to a number of factors: army service for the men and a higher level of education for both sexes. Divorces are by no means as common as they are in the United States or in the non-Catholic countries of Western Europe, but they do occur. In the kolkhozy of Kalinin Oblast, eight percent of all marriages are second ones, and those who marry again are usually the divorced, rarely the widowed. But as Anokhina and Shmeleva (1964:225–226) comment: "The second marriage is not always registered, since often both sides or one of the parties did not formalize the dissolution of the first marriage." The stringent divorce laws are probably responsible for this situation. It is worth noting that the folk cycle traditionally did not and does not now apply to second marriages.

In summary, we find that the traditional marriage ritual remains current to a great degree. Ethnographic articles and items in the popular press show that modern

Soviet marriage is still in search of appropriate forms. In the cities there have been attempts to dress up the civil wedding by the use of flowers, processions, music, and luxurious surroundings; a beautiful eighteenth-century town house in Moscow has been taken over as the "Palace of Wedding Celebrations." In the country, however, such luxurious accouterments are rarely available, and the music, dancing, processions, and so on are provided by the people themselves. By way of comparison, see Stephen Dunn's paper on Baltic culture (1966).

DEATH   The prerevolutionary burial service among Russian peasants was highly conservative, as it still is. For instance, the burial clothes for elderly people were of the most old-fashioned cut. In the front corner of the house—that is, the one looking out on the street and nearest the porch—the body was laid on a bench with its head toward the icons. In many places, the Psalter was read over the deceased throughout the night by old people or nuns specially hired for the occasion.[4] Often (particularly among the Old Believers), the dead person was carried out feet first, sometimes through the back door or through a window, and the floor was swept and rinsed so the body could not return and harm the living. These ceremonies have close parallels among the native tribes of Northern Siberia. Usually, only the closest relatives followed the funeral cortege to the cemetery. During this journey the women lamented. Particularly in the north, there was a tradition of improvised laments, similar to that known in Ireland, rural Greece, and some other places. Generally the coffin was carried open on the shoulders of pallbearers, but in certain remote areas, such as Olonets and Vologda Gubernias, the custom of transporting the coffin on a sled was retained to the end of the nineteenth century. On returning from the cemetery, the mourners were served a meal featuring pancakes, *kisel'* (jelly) and *kut'ia* (small cakes made from roasted grains of wheat, or later rice, with honey). Vodka was also served, and the meal concluded with wheat porridge, prepared either with milk or (during fast periods) with hempseed oil. It was held that the deceased was present at the banquet (Kushner, ed. 1958:93). Regular memorial services were held on the ninth, 20th, and 40th day after death, and again six months and a year later. These intervals for the memorial cycle are identical with those observed in the pre-Islamic religious ritual of the Central Asian peoples. The dead were also memorialized on certain days of the church calendar with a meal eaten at the cemetery, after which a small portion of the food was left on the grave. On such occasions, prayers were offered by the women, and some of the food was also donated to the poor (Aleksandrov and others, eds. 1964:472–473).

A large part of the funeral and memorial complex is apparently still in operation. According to the Viriatino study, there were only three civil funerals during the period 1952–1956. Those buried in this fashion were an old teacher who had been secretary of the local soviet; a retired miner and Communist Party member; and another Party member who, although born in the community, had lived and worked outside it in industry for many years. In all other cases, the Christian funeral service was performed, with the reading of the Psalter and those ritual forms which are possible in the absence of a priest (Kushner, ed. 1958:233). The

---

[4] These are not nuns in the ordinary Western religious sense, but rather single or widowed women who have adopted the lives of recluses and the somber dress that goes with it. Such recluses were rather common before the Revolution, and in some regions, were the only "teachers" the village had.

regular nine-, 20- and 40-day memorial cycle is still observed in Viriatino, but the memorial cycle tied to the church calendar has almost gone out of use, apparently due to the closing of the village church (Kushner, ed. 1958:233). Anokhina and Shmeleva (1964) note that in Kalinin Oblast, old people (and sometimes younger ones) have prayers read over them. On this occasion, not the priest, but old nuns are invited who make a specialty of this for this pay. Old people also insist on memorial observances (which before the Revolution were called "parents' Sundays"). At one time, this was a regular family festival, but now it is observed only by old ladies. Civil funerals are becoming increasingly common, at least in Kalinin Oblast. A civil funeral generally involves exhibiting the coffin in the club-house, recreation hall, headquarters of the local soviet, or some similar place, followed by a mass meeting with speeches, and a funeral procession accompanied by a band. This order of service is apparently not considered by the people to be appropriate for rank-and-file kolkhozniks, and there seems to be no particular attempt by the authorities make it standard or universal.

Before ending the account of funerary ritual, we should note an interesting point in the domain of Soviet ethnographic theory. In a recent discussion of comparative religion (Tokarev 1964), the author makes an attempt to remove entirely funerary ceremonies from the domain of religion, but sets for them an instinctive origin which antedates that of religion proper in the Marxist evolutionary scheme.[5] He says: "If funerary customs are not indebted for their origin to religious beliefs, . . . it follows from this that our own contemporary funerary practice (cemeteries, crematoria, pantheons, mausoleums and grave monuments) must by no means be considered a survival of a superstitious relationship to the dead, a survival of religious beliefs and rites. It is rooted not in the religious ideology but in universal human motives innate in man himself as a social creature" (Tokarev 1964:212). The author's intent is obvious. By removing the cult of the dead entirely from the sphere of religion, he is trying to take the Marxist curse off a whole range of activities, observances, and emotions which experience has shown to be necessary to man as such, regardless of the social system under which he lives.

Religion

The generally accepted view is that Russian (or Eastern) Orthodoxy constitutes the main form of religious behavior of the Great Russian people both historically and at present. The view which we will take in the following pages departs from this to some extent. First of all, it must be emphasized that what is true of the urban population is not necessarily true of the peasantry. In most cities, the Orthodox church was in fact the dominant religious force, and until secularization became widespread among the working and middle classes, it was one of the leading factors in Russian life. We have indicated, however, that the Orthodox Church's control over the countryside was spotty at best, and at many points completely lacking. Historically, this has had—and continues to have, because the situation is in-

---

[5] According to this scheme, religion is a social phenomenon and therefore cannot be assumed to have existed before the origin of human society in its present form.

tensified under Soviet conditions—two important effects. First, it produced wide deviations—which have already been implied in this chapter—between the official church ritual and the ceremonial attaching to the folk religion. This dichotomy has been noted in many parts of the world, but by virtue of special historical circumstances made itself felt with particular force in Russia. Secondly, the inadequate ccntrol over the countryside by the Orthodox Church gave rise to a proliferation of dissident groups which flowed in to fill up the religious vacuum. This second effect was intensified by the fact that for several centuries the Orthodox Church has been a recognized arm of the Tsarist (and now Soviet) state, and therefore, as in many backward societies, political and social protest has been expressed in religious guise.[6]

The religious situation we have outlined has important implications for a society in process of Westernization and industrialization. Like most established churches, the Orthodox Church is an extremely conservative body. Most of the dissident groups, whatever their actual origin, functioned as bearers of new ideas, including Western ones. Furthermore, as Blackwell (1965) points out, the Old Belief, though it started out as a protest against Westernizing innovations in Orthodox ritual, eventually became the creed of a large part of the rising industrial bourgeoisie (as Calvinism did in Western Europe). The process of social and industrial development brought with it a transition on the part of many in the merchant and industrialist class from the Old Belief into other sectarian groups. This phenomenon occurred in two forms—transition into Western-oriented sects on the part of people who felt the need for social change, and transition into other sects as a result of a personal religious search not directly connected with social factors. The two forms differ in degree and in emphasis, not necessarily in final result. The process has been going on for more than a century and is not over yet, although it has been greatly interfered with by the establishment of a socialist system with its distinctive, secular means of advancement and culture change. What has happened is that socialism has replaced what might be called the social aspect of religion, but those people for whom religion is a personal quest for answers to ultimate problems are in many cases still unsatisfied.

Let us see what this means in Viriatino. As we have already noted, much of the religious life there proceeds without any apparent church intervention. Much of whatever religious ritual remains is centered in the family as a unit. What remains is truly a survival: "Thus, for example, as in the old days, the festive 'dinner' begins with the act of the head of the family at first drinking himself and then pouring vodka for the remaining members of the family by seniority, after which the family begins to eat" (Kushner, ed. 1958:231). Similarly, one man with materialistic views explained the presence of icons in his home by saying that he humored his wife, and she added that she did not want people to come and visit in a home without icons. Other people remarked that a bare corner was a bad thing, therefore, they had icons.

The actual religious beliefs of the villagers of Viriatino are discussed in

---

[6] It may also be worth pointing out that a highly organized, tightly structured body such as the Orthodox Church may be more vulnerable to unfavorable conditions than the looser and hence more flexible religious groups of "Protestant" type which competed with it in the countryside.

vague generalities. We gather only that they are rather strict in some observances, mostly fasts and the decorum to be observed during these: one must not hold a wedding, but one may hold a *"zapoi"* if one does not sing (the singing during a fast is the sin). Also one should not work on holidays. We do not know how serious this is in Viriatino. Elsewhere the refusal to work on religious holidays (which were far more numerous even at the beginning of collectivization than now) is cited as one of the pernicious influences of sectarianism.

We were of the opinion that the Viriatino people were sectarians, basing our opinion on a general knowledge of the growth of the sects—mainly the Baptists. Articles by Koretskii (1961) and Malakhova (1961) on the sects in Tambov Oblast demonstrate that the Baptists are late arrivals in the area, gaining strength primarily after the declaration of religious toleration in 1905 and again with the 1917 Revolution. Their main membership came from Old Russian sects (Molokans, Subbotniki, and the like). A direct question to two participants in the Viriatino study as to whether there were sectarians in Viriatino brought the response that there was one Baptist family, but that sectarianism had little influence. This seemed to imply that Viriatino was an island in a sea of dissent, but given the well-developed *otkhodnichestvo* there, this could hardly have been true. Yet it is quite revealing of the nature and extent of religious dissidence in Russia. As V. D. Bonch-Bruevich (1922) pointed out, in Tsarist Russia many people who might otherwise have been Orthodox, and who did so consider themselves, were forced by the intransigence of the Orthodox Church to become sectarians. In fact, the very term sectarian is applied to those who are not Orthodox. Z. A. Nikol'skaia (1961) reports that the real religious force in the Viriatino area is a group that calls itself True Orthodox Christians (the initials in Russian are IPKh). Historically, this group arose at the time of the disputes between the Orthodox Patriarch Tikhon and certain members of his Church who wanted to reform it. Subsequently, this faction was tarred with a monarchist brush, and driven underground as anti-Soviet. Nikol'skaia says that in the 1940s, 10–15 percent of the population of Tambov Oblast were *edinolichniki* —farmers who refused to join collectives and either moved to cities or settled in the suburbs as artisan-craftsmen. These composed the main membership of the True Orthodox Christians when the churches were reopened; they were fairly strong in the 1945–1947 period and then declined in the 1950–1951 period. There is no clear answer from the Soviet side as to whether they are a sect. We assume that they are not, simply because both historically and in the present, the distribution of the Russian Orthodox Church hierarchy was and is insufficient for full religious control. From these True Orthodox Christians there emerged a splinter group, headed by Liubov Kisliakova, the daughter of a former *kulak*. Kisliakova, born in 1919, declared herself a follower of Nastya Krikova, who lived in Viriatino. According to Kisliakova, Krikova was a saint, and while they were living together in the mid 1950s, a group was formed that called itself *Molchal'niki* (literally, "those who do not speak"). By doctrine, the *Molchal'niki* might be called the puritan wing of the True Orthdox Christians. Its members do not marry. They wall themselves up in their houses and rarely go outside, take vows of silence and, since they refuse to work on religious grounds, are supported by other members of their families. (The vow of silence was traditionally common among both Russian Orthodox and Old Believers as a special "mortification of the flesh.") They also refuse medical assistance, and on this account there have been a number of cases in which the children of *Molchal'niki* have been taken away from them and placed in boarding schools. Of the 71 members, concentrated in villages around Viriatino as well as in Viriatino itself, 30 had never been to school, 36 had finished the first grade of the village school, and five had had 3–7 grades of schooling. Twelve of the members were in the age group 20–25. Unlike the Orthodox, the *Molchal'niki* need no special church but rather pray in holy places and near rivers, practicing immersion, but not as a rite of baptism. In 1957, Kisliakova was declared a schizophrenic and placed in a mental hospital, after which her group suffered a sharp decline.

In recent years Soviet historians and students of the sects have paid some attention to the religious psychology. The remedy for this frame of mind is as striking as it is instructive: the *Molchal'niki* (who were almost exclusively very poor, bereaved women) were given individual attention and material assistance to encourage them to repair their homes and come back into the world.

The extent to which simple isolation is a factor in religious survivals is illustrated by Milovidov (1963) in discussing the decline of the Old Belief in Riazan Oblast. Here there are 800 registered Old Believers in a population of 1,444,800. The 800 Old Believers belong to about six groups, differences among which are small, and though there is a hard core of fanatics which refuses salvation to all but members of its own group, there is growing recognition of a common cause. Milovidov (1963:135) attributes this as much to atheistic propaganda as to the fact that the members of the Old Belief and the sects are much more homogeneous than they were before the Revolution. There are, however, significant exceptions. The village of Aleksandrovskie Vyselki, Putiatinskii *raion,* is composed entirely of Old Believers, who shortly after the Revolution had settled on *khutor* land. The men do not shave or smoke; intermarriage (with other Old Believers or Orthodox, who would have to submit to rebaptism) is rare, and because they do not believe in birth control, their families are very large (in some cases 10 children). Women and children observe all the fasts, though this is rare among youth and even middle-aged men. The village makes up one of the three brigades of the Kirov kolkhoz, and according to the chairman, the Old Believers are excellent workers. Other Old Believers in other villages are mixed in with Russians of other faiths, and consequently preserve the custom of using separate dishes for nonbelievers. Among one group of Old Believers (*Pomortsy*), it is permissible to eat the second course of the meal from a common pot, since a fork—a utensil not found in the Old Russian culture in any case—is generally used. A few Old Believers are still so strict that they will not even wash their clothes with soap (because it contains lard), but these have earned the nickname *"kaluger"* or *"kaloger,"* which Milovidov says comes from the Greek and means "monk." Milovidov specifically attributes the retention of these traits among certain Old Believers to remoteness from industrial centers and even from other rural populations. Yet he observes that there are Old Believers who readily accept all the recent advances of Soviet material culture. The son of one Old Believer is a Communist Party member. The question then arises: to what extent are they really Old Believers? The answer seems to be: in their minds. Milovidov points out that there are no clubs in either of the two most conservative Old Believer settlements. Is this because they are against clubs or because no one has thought to provide them? What would happen if there were? Milovidov has no answers.

And in fact, there are no easy answers. A. E. Katunskii (1964) points out that due to increased efforts on the part of the Old Believers, certain of their communities have even recorded membership gains. Most Soviet students admit that certain periods have seen religious "renascences," but they insist that this is definitely cyclical. People, they say, seek the comfort of religion especially in hard times, which lasted generally until the mid-1950s. This fact does not contradict the steady and inevitable decline of religion in Russia. Yet Soviet writers appear truly baffled by the existence of genuine religious feeling among people who are neither old, poor, sick, nor ignorant. N. S. Zlobin (1963) indignantly rejects the idea that Baptists have, so to speak cornered the market on sobriety and clean living. He ridicules the Baptist belief that Communism is wonderful—but cannot be achieved until the people themselves prepare for it by changing. On the other hand, the present Baptists have, so to speak, cornered the market on sobriety and clean living. He ridicules the Baptist belief that Communism is wonderful—but cannot be achieved until the one factory worker who is consistently among the best, and so on.

His examples are thus cautionary. Religion is bad, but not every believer is bad—an individual approach is necessary. Though Anokhina and Shmeleva (1964) tell us little about the specifics of religion in Kalinin Oblast, they do say (1964:254) that belief in God among men was rather easily weakened, but the woman's position made the loss of faith much more difficult. And again (1964:268) "the family itself" kept women from becoming atheistic. These remarks refer specifically to a situation which is said to have changed with collectivization. It is nevertheless apparent that the family is still a powerful institution in the Soviet Union, and the woman is still largely confined within an environment that can and should demand her best talents but which in fact ranks far down on the scale of valued activities. Thousands of women are given medals each year for having produced many children, but even so the Soviet regime actively encourages female participation in the socialist economy. Almost half of the total labor force is female, but only in a few fields are women skilled laborers. Someone must mind the children. If it is not the mother herself, it is then an old aunt, grandmother, or neighbor, and they, apparently, keep alive religious ideas among the young—or try to.

This explanation, is, perhaps, too simple. We might expect that as the oldest generations pass away, certain universal urges subsumed under the rubric of "religious ideas or habits or feelings" would also disappear, but this has not happened in such a clear-cut way. There are certain survivals, mostly connected with life-crisis ceremonials, but also with certain attitudes toward icons, for instance, which many people feel are a genuinely Russian contribution to art. These are prized as such, irrespective of religious meaning. Some Soviet students profess surprise that even well-educated and otherwise progressive people should not see that icons have an aura of religious significance which makes them impermissible as items of home decor. Likewise, Aptekman (1965) implies that people who allow their children to be baptized—and the majority do, at least in the country (Kushner, ed. 1958; Iankova 1963)—are succumbing to an impermissible feeling that baptism is a part of Russian culture.

Does baptism of infants reflect religious feeling on the part of those who do it? Apparently not; it may be an expression of national feeling, and in some other cases cited by Aptekman, it is a purely magical act, intended to protect the child from illness or other harm. (Aptekman is referring to urban workers in Leningrad, but the same reasons may apply among peasants.) There are several folk ceremonies which serve the purpose of ushering the infant into the world, and he can be married or buried the same way, quite independently of an organized church or of Christian observance. Soviet authors, however, complain that some of these ceremonies have undesirable connotations, and they continually agitate for the introduction and development of specifically Soviet life-crisis ceremonials. Thereby they implicitly recognize people's need for ritual solemnity and spectacle, which appears to be a constant.

Summary: Survivals and Reintegration

"Soviet christenings" at the Vital Statistics Bureau—during which the child's name is inscribed on the books and he is presented with a layette as a gift from the state—do not yet have the solemnity and the festivity of the christening feast we have described. Anokhina and Shmeleva (1964) describe a modern version of the christening feast which lacks only the element of passing porridge around to the guests, as in a form of communion. This was repeated, traditionally, at the wedding and at the funeral. The ceremonial porridge is apparently the only element to which objection is made—whether on ideological or medical grounds, it is hard to determine.

As we have noted, there is the beginning of a Soviet coming-of-age ceremony in the form of graduation from secondary school or university. This hardly differs from the American version, and the ritual is not particularly striking or colorful.

Soviet civil marriages can be very festive, like the marriage of the two cosmonauts Nikolaev and Tereshkova, where former Premier Khrushchev acted the part of the bride's father. This was a dressed-up and expanded version of the typical Russian peasant wedding, and at the same time probably represented the Soviet idea of what was proper and good practice. On a much more modest scale, the wedding described in detail by Pushkareva and Shmeleva (1959) is significant because it presents a fairly satisfactory fusion of the traditional folk elements with elements peculiar to the Soviet period.

Some Soviet civil holidays, such as May Day and the anniversary of the October Revolution, seem to be popular and well established. Certain others, such as harvest festivals and the celebration of Russian Winter, have been deliberately encouraged and made to coincide with festivals in the church and popular calendars —just as the early Christians timed their holiday to coincide with the pagan festivals of the winter solstice and the advent of spring.

Only time will tell how successful the regime will be in establishing new Soviet, nonreligious folk institutions for its people. Probably this is a natural process and only slightly subject to direction or encouragement. But those who wish to create a new folk tradition must first decide what elements they will build on, and this has not yet been done.

With regard to religion specifically, three facts are evident: (1) certain religious survivals could be eliminated entirely if the population had more material goods and intellectual contacts; (2) to a certain extent, woman's role in the family will always be important; and (3) (perhaps most important) two groups of people are bound to ask the ultimate question: what is the meaning of life, and what should we do with it? These groups are the very young—who as yet have nothing to do, but must prepare to do something—and the very old, who have tried, have perhaps not succeeded, and have seen their lives go by.

5

Material Culture
and Its Social Correlates

T HE IMPORTANCE of material culture—the totality of the physical objects
which people actually make and use in their daily lives—as an index of
where people stand is self-evident. A great deal of effort on the part of Soviet ethnographers has gone into the investigation of material culture; the literature
is voluminous and the standard of professional achievement is high. We do not intend to give here a complete account of the traditional material culture of the Central Russian peasant with all its regional and economic variations; this would require a good-sized book by itself. What we will do is consider in detail certain
specific aspects of the current material culture, contrasting them with what is traditional in regard to the same aspect and pointing out, where the data permit, the
differences between the two in terms of culture change.

A further word of caution is in order. In this chapter, we make a distinction between the material culture of the Central Russian peasant, as such, and the
objects which come to him from the consumer-goods industry, and which presumably reflect an urban taste. This distinction is in some degree arbitrary, but we believe that two different traditions still exist, though they are probably in the process
of merging. Finally, in the matter of technology, we will consider the important
question of agricultural machinery, its supply and distribution, and the effect of
this on Central Russian peasant culture as it now exists.

Houses

The prerevolutionary Russian house-type varied regionally, economically,
and historically. Generally speaking, in the northern part of the area with which we
are concerned, the house was built of logs (sometimes faced with planks, in the
case of the more prosperous peasants), while in the south, where wood was scarce,
bricks were the more common building material. The roof was usually two-sided

111

or, in the case of brick houses, four-sided or hipped. It was constructed of small logs, either placed directly on the wall (in the more primitive versions) or laid across projecting rafters, and it was covered either with straw thatch, for the poorer people, or with slate, iron, or tiles for the richer ones. The straw thatch could be made more durable and partially fireproofed by being dipped (each bundle separately) in a suspension of clay.

The classical Central Great Russian cottage is the *izba* (the word is also used for a separate dwelling-unit within a larger house). It consisted of one room with the stove always in the corner opposite the front door. The Russian stove, which originally was, and in many cases still is, the chief appurtenance of the

Nineteenth-century building, Viriatino.

house, took up from a fifth to a third of the total floor space. It was generally made of clay, and was used for cooking, baking, heating, drying clothes and produce, and preparing fodder for the livestock. People slept on the flat stove top and steamed themselves there if they did not have a special bathhouse. Chickens and young livestock were sometimes kept in the space behind the stove, or in a sort of wooden pen attached to it. In the prereform period, most stoves lacked chimneys, the smoke being allowed to escape by the door or through a special hole in the wall. Cooking was done on a special platform in front of the mouth of the stove, and long tongs or shovels were used to move pots and loaves of bread back and forth. Although modern kitchen ranges have gained some popularity, they have not replaced the Russian stove and, in the opinion of Soviet writers, are not likely to do so, since they are less versatile and will not serve the multitude of purposes which the Russian stove does, particularly in animal husbandry.

In Kalinin Oblast, the usual size of the cottage was 7 by 7 or 8 by 9 meters. Occasionally, it covered 10 by 10 meters. In the south, particularly in poor districts and where wood was scarce, it might be considerably smaller. This cottage remained the predominant house-type until the Emanicipation in 1861. However, none remained in Viriatino at the time of the study by Kushner's group; the authors reconstructed the original *izba* from specimens in surrounding villages and from accounts by old informants. The *izba* usually had a yard in front and a built-on shed for the livestock, and sometimes also a lean-to where the cooking was done. (In summer, food was usually prepared in a separate shed.) The external de-

Woman at Russian stove, Viriatino, 1954.

tails of Russian peasant houses—gates, window frames, door frames, eaves, roof trees (crosses)—and sometimes the entire front face, were decorated with elaborate openwork or bas-relief carving, similar to the "gingerbread" with which our grandfathers adorned their houses, but more varied and considerably more artistic. The style was generally abstract and curvilinear, but also included stylized renderings of plants, animals, or motifs from folklore.

The next stage in the evolution of the Central Great Russian house-type is represented by the so-called *piatistenka* (literally "five-waller", that is, four external walls and an internal partition) which was first built by the wealthier peasants and later became standard. This was a two-room house, divided into a "clean" half (parlor, or living-room, where guests were received and the family gathered on formal occasions) and a "dirty" half where cooking and other chores were done and the animals were kept in the winter—similar to the Scottish "but-and-ben." The stove was usually located between the two rooms, so that it could be used from either side, but generally only one room was heated. The Central Russian two-room house might also take the form of two separate house frames (*izby*), connected by an unheated hallway. In Central Russian villages and as far north as Kalinin Oblast, lofts or attics were relatively rare, and used only by craftsmen and traders for the storage of goods and for summer residence; they were always unheated. The development of multi-roomed dwellings in Kalinin Oblast is connected, in the opinion of Anokhina and Shmeleva (1964:103–104) with the development of

Modern but traditional house, Kalinin Oblast, remodeled from old five-walled cottage. Note herringbone pattern on front.

commercial animal husbandry. This required the warming of large quantities of water (or melting of snow), the cooking of fodder, and the heating of a room in which young animals could be cared for.[1] Due to the constant dampness, poor ventilation, and inadequate heating, the structure soon rotted, and it became necessary to separate the living quarters from the part of the house devoted to animal husbandry.

The house-type described by Fenomenov (1925) as typical for the region he studied (Novgorod, Pskov, and part of Leningrad Oblasts) shows certain important differences from the Central Great Russian model and even from that described for Kalinin Oblast. The reasons for these differences are not entirely clear. According to Fenomenov, the typical peasant house of the Novgorod area stands on piles and appears to have two stories. The entrance is usually through a hallway,

---

[1] It is worth noting that by excluding the livestock from the house and thereby presumably taking a step up on the ladder of human culture, the Soviet peasant has at the same time taken a step down in point of animal husbandry. Cattle are now generally kept in unheated barns, except on a few model farms.

the door being let into the rear wall of the *izba* facing the yard. Almost all of the houses have several rooms and all the rooms are heated by the stove's hot air vents. Instead of being separated by hallways, the rooms are connected one with the other, and may occasionally be stacked vertically. Some peasant houses consist of three adjoining frames, and if the upper story rests on the dwelling-rooms or on a storage area, the result can be a fairly imposing structure, with a dozen or more windows. The prevalence of the extended family in north Russia may have had something to do with the generally large size of dwelling-houses. When the family split up, the house was sometimes physically divided, along with the other property, and part transported to a new location. The Gadyshi peasants used the ground level of their houses mainly for the storage of goods and equipment. Livestock were always housed separately. Unfortunately, we lack specific data which would show us what has happened to this rather unusual type of house in recent times.

In the late 19th and early 20th centuries, brick houses began to appear in Viriatino in place of the earlier log structures. They were built usually by families that included a number of migrant workers and which could thus accumulate some capital. The reasons for the transition to brick houses were various: better sanitation, protection against fires (which were a frequent occurrence in the old Russian village and still happen—see pages 49 and 51 above), prestige, and the increasing scarcity of lumber. At the same time, certain changes in internal planning were taking place. The location of the stove was altered—now it often was placed with its mouth toward the rear wall, thus dividing the room into two unequal sections (this plan had been disseminated earlier among the Baltic peoples and certain groups in the so-called Northwestern District—Pskov, Leningrad, and part of Kalinin Oblast). In some late nineteenth-century houses in Viriatino (which were placed lengthwise along the street, in contrast to the traditional oblique or right-angled orientation), the kitchen has two opposite entrances, one from the street and one from the courtyard. In cases like this, the stove stands in the corner opposite the street, with its mouth facing the street entrance. This arrangement required a great deal of heating fuel, and its use was correspondingly limited, but apparently it was regarded as more "cultured" than the traditional plan The brick house was larger than its log predecessor, and there was more floor space per inhabitant. There were some examples, during what the authors of the Viriatino study refer to as "the period of brick building" (from about 1890 until 1917), of row houses in several units being put up along the street. This seems to have been the result of land shortage. These houses were built primarily by the families of former state peasants, whose homestead plots had been dispersed among land belonging to former serfs and therefore could not be expanded in any way.

The Revolution and the civil war brought with them a period of economic decline and hardship in which very little building was done. Eighty new houses were built in Viriatino—60 log and 20 brick—during the early 1920s. In most cases the builders were middle or poor peasants who had not been able to restore their personal economies. Brick building was too expensive for them, and furthermore, there was (and still is) a shortage of bricks. The log houses of this period were not distinguished from the typical nineteenth-century *izba:* they were set on wooden platforms rather than on true foundations, and the roofs were thatched.

Typically, they consisted of one room, and the location of the stove was traditional, facing the door.

During the later 1920s, the housing supply was in general sufficient, and the only building done was the replacement of houses which had fallen into disrepair. Brick houses were popular during this period and were put up cooperatively by two or three households, who bought clay, set up a brickyard, and sold the surplus after construction was complete. According to the statement of an experienced carpenter, the bricks were laid by professionals from the neighboring town of Sosnovka, who knew the urban method, and in general building techniques became more sophisticated. For instance, roofs were not laid directly on the walls, as had been the procedure before, but were placed over projecting rafters. These roofs were in general covered with sheet iron.

After collectivization, the use of bricks for residential purposes was curtailed, and the entire brick supply was devoted to public needs. The log houses built during the early 1930s are not distinguishable externally from those of prerevolutionary date, although the style of furnishings changed somewhat. Marked changes took place in the late 1930s and after World War II. The authors of the Viriatino study point out that there is now no housing shortage in Viriatino, and the only building going on is the replacement of structures that have been destroyed by fire or that have become inadequate through the growth of families.

The data for Kalinin Oblast do not allow such a full and clearly-marked historical sequence as the one just described. Because the district is in a forested zone, timbered construction was always the rule and continues to be so today. Therefore, we do not see such marked changes in building style. The houses have increased in size, and contain more rooms. Economic functions have been relegated to outbuildings or, at the very least, segregated from the living space into other rooms. Porches in various forms have been added. The straw roof which used to be the rule, and which was a mark of poverty, is now relatively rare (14 out of 31 houses, or 10.7 percent of the total on the Aktiv kolkhoz, Krasnokholmsk *raion,* in 1956; none today). The new houses are built on pillar foundations and have double floors and double framed or "storm" windows; such features used to be found only in the houses of the richer peasants. The old *piatistenka* and *izba* (including the double one) are not being repeated, except where they are being used as the nucleus of an essentially new dwelling.

In a long historical perspective, the history of Central Russian peasant housing shows an over-all rise in the standard of living: house-types (and internal arrangements) that were once the privilege of the *kulak* are now standard. The recently-built houses (which are illustrated in Aleksandrov and others, eds. 1964:314–315), of brick or stucco construction, do not have the typical "Russian" appearance created by the luxuriant decorative carving and projecting eaves of the traditional North Russian style. They are square and box-like, with two- or four-sided slate or iron roofs—reminiscent of the typical British or Continental suburban villa of pre-World War I vintage. There is, of course, no way of telling how frequent is this type of house, but the fact that it appears in the illustration in this context indicates that this is what is regarded as up-to-date, cultured, or desirable. In the remoter areas, particularly those with pronounced ethnographic traditions of their own (such as the Meshchera in Vladimir Oblast, and certain parts of Kalinin Oblast), the tradition of decorative carving and the painting of the exterior with oil paints in fanciful colors continues, and even the new houses retain more of their distinctive appearance. Some modern houses in Kalinin Oblast (Anokhina and Shmeleva 1964:Fig. 40) show a curious technique, in which the exterior planking is arranged in a herringbone pattern.

To judge by the interior photographs of the Kalinin Oblast study, most of which show parlors and "front rooms," very little remains of the traditional Russian style of interior furnishings. These somewhat cluttered rooms are decorated in heavy, old-fashioned European bourgeois taste. The one interior illustration given in the Viriatino study (Kushner, ed. 1958:Fig. 38) looks considerably more traditional and is also (from one observer's point of view) in rather better taste. Closets and chests of drawers are rare in the Russian countryside, although closets are coming into use in apartments. Clothes are usually hung directly on hooks let into the wall.

Regardless of one's personal judgment on the style of architecture or interior decoration, it is obvious that the new house is a much better place to live in than the old one. On some large kolkhozy and *sovkhozy,* a few multiple dwellings are being built, but they are not popular except among young unattached persons who live on salaries and have no private economy.

Folk Art

The Russian peasantry has a rich and varied tradition of folk art, exemplified in small-scale realistic sculpture in stone, bone and wood, decorative carving and painting of wooden objects (spoons, pails, dolls, boxes, bowls, and the like), embroidery—both on clothing and on household linens—pottery and, of course, architectural decoration. There was wide variation in these arts during the prerevolutionary period. More important, some of them were true folk arts, whereas others were practiced professionally by the inhabitants of particular villages and regions on the basis of *otkhodnichestvo.*

If we ask what has become of these arts in the modern Soviet context, the answers also vary widely. Some of them, such as pottery, are dying out, and are now practiced only by the older generation of craftsmen (Bobrinskii 1963). In some cases the dying-out of these crafts is taking place while there is still some need for their products in the countryside (Anokhina and Shmelova 1964:53), Others have been industrialized: the craftsmen gathered into fairly large enterprises at certain traditional centers and the product marketed commercially to the urban as well as the rural population. This applies particularly to the tradition of small naturalistic sculpture—carved, painted, and lacquered wood. At the risk of being accused of ethnographic purism, we would maintain that in their present condition these are no longer folk arts.[2] Embroidery in particular finds a ready market among

---

[2] See Aleksandrov and others, eds. (1964:231–235) for illustration showing industrial operation in folk art, and pages 547–557 of the same volume, for illustrations showing modern craft products, including embroidery.

many sections of the population and has been applied to clothing design. Other examples of folk art, such as the considerable assortment of wooden kitchenware and household utensils, are disappearing in favor of aluminum and enamel substitutes (Aleksandrov and others. eds. 1964:405).

Clothes

Peasant costume in Russia is a topic on which an extensive literature already exists. We cannot begin to detail the regional and social variation to which the costume, particularly for women, was subject. The feminine costume in the northern parts of Central Russia was based on the so-called *sarafan,* a long full skirt with a jumper top, made in dark colors for widows and the elderly, and striped or flowered for young women. This was worn over a shift or slip (*rubakha*), usually with long full sleeves, but of widely varying cut. In the south, including Tambov Oblast, married women wore the *poneva,* a moderately long skirt, without jumper top and partly covered by an embroidered linen apron. Single women in these parts wore only the shift or slip.

Male costume was less varied, consisting almost everywhere of the *kosovorotka,* or side-opening shirt (with tight-fitting upright collar and a vent running down the left side, usually fitted with small buttons and sometimes embroidered) and fairly narrow trousers. The shirt was not tucked in, but belted by a special sash. The usual footwear for men was *lapti,* or bast shoes, worn over *onuchi* or linen puttees. These are still worn as work shoes, but instead of being made individually by each family (as they were until the 1930s), they are made for each village by one or two specialists, usually elderly men. *Lapti* were replaced by high boots for dress occasions, and the trousers were tucked into the tops. Headgear for men was commonly a peaked workmen's cap, with earflaps for winter. Women's headdresses were extremely complex and varied, but most of these went out of use sometime before the Revolution, except for ceremonial purposes. The usual headgear for women, now and in recent times, is a kerchief; elderly women are seldom seen without it.

Traditionally, the obligatory hair style for women was braids—one for a single woman, two for a married one—coiled in a bun on top of the head or at the nape of the neck and covered by the kerchief. Men wore their hair somewhat longer than would be regarded as normal in this country or even in Europe, and many grew full beards. At present, no generalization about women's hair styles is possible. Many of the younger generation wear their hair short and waved, while others retain the single braid. Men's hair styles have been modernized as much as the general shortage of barbers allows, and beards are not usual except for the elderly.

The degree to which the traditional folk costume was retained in different areas was subject to economic, geographical, social, and religious factors; the influence of *otkhodnichestvo,* the availability of urban models, and religious beliefs which forbade or discouraged the wearing of "German", that is, Western European clothes. Among the Old Believers particularly, the folk costume was held sacred, and it was considered sinful to appear in anything else. In Kalinin Oblast, because of the prevalence of *otkhodnichestvo* and the nearness of urban centers, the folk costume died out during the 19th century, although some old men apparently still wear a modified *kosovorotka* (Anokhina and Shmeleva 1964:Fig. 52). Even before the Revolution young men liked to wear a citified combination of vest, jacket, and trousers, called a *troika,* and a long-waisted overcoat, which under urban influence was considered "proper." The traditional outer wear for both men and women was the *shuba* or sheepskin coat—rather voluminous and unfitted—for traveling or vis-

Retired kolkhoznik, wearing kosovorotka, *Kalinin Oblast.*

iting, and a short quilted jacket for work. Modern overcoats are not worn except for dress purposes, since they are inconvenient to work in, and the short jacket is retained. The usual male footwear was of bast or rawhide, with or without thongs; felt or leather boots were reserved for special occasions. Most items of clothing were purchased at fairs or in the city even before the Revolution, at least among people who had a money economy. Those who did not often wore clothes which had a patchwork effect because they were made from pieces of cheap fabric bought "by the pound."

In the period immediately after the Revolution, there was a return to home-made clothing out of sheer necessity. But the traditional patterns were not revived; people imitated urban models as well as they could.

A semimilitary type of costume for men (particularly officials and specialists) has been common in many parts of the Soviet Union since the Revolution. This is probably due to the frequent condition of war which has obtained there until quite recently. In the early period it had an ideological significance as well: by wearing something that looked like a uniform, one proclaimed one's commitment to the Revolution.

The wearing of underwear is a new phenomenon in the countryside, and one to which Soviet writers seem to attach a good deal of importance. Probably it is regarded as an index of civilization and as an element of the urban way of life.

As far as our sources indicate, the full folk costume for any particular area is now preserved only for ceremonial or theatrical purposes. The degree of "modernity" in clothing—that is, its closeness to urban or European models—depends of course on the degree of isolation of the particular area being considered, and on the distribution network. In areas where most clothing has to be made either in the home or by local semiprofessional tailors and seamstresses, some folk elements naturally persist. Many women have taken courses in sewing and dressmaking; mass circulation magazines for rural consumption often include patterns. Furthermore, in all except the remotest areas, the peasants can and do occasionally visit a large city and buy clothing in the stores.

Finally two significant factors should be mentioned. First, certain elements of the folk costume are now being commercially produced, including variants of the *kosovorotka* (Aleksandrov and others, eds. 1964:385, illustration), although we have no way of judging their distribution or their popularity. Second, there seems to be a settled ethnic preference for ensemble costume for women (skirt, blouse, and jacket), over the one-piece or shirtwaist dress. Soviet women officials, scientists, and so on, are usually pictured in a type of dress which according to American tastes seems extremely mannish, but which in a Russian context may not produce this impression. The one-piece dress is appearing in the countryside (see Aleksandrov and others. 1964:389, illustration) ;[3] but this is definitely something new, and seems so far to be reserved for special occasions, such as dances. To what extent this is due to the distribution system is not indicated in our data.

Food

The traditional Russian peasant cuisine leaned heavily on starches (bread, various gruels and porridges, pancakes for special occasions and, beginning in the late nineteenth century, potatoes), cabbage, cucumbers, and milk products. Meat was a rarity, except among the well-to-do, and was usually used in small quantities as a flavoring or seasoning. For the devout, a large part of the year was taken up with fasts, during which meat, and sometimes milk as well, were forbidden. Cabbage was usually salted and served in this form, or as a plain cabbage soup (*pustye shchi*), or with a little meat or fish added. During fast periods, vegetable oils (walnut, poppy seed, sunflower seed, or hempseed) were used in place of animal fats. Fish, either fresh or salted, was somewhat more plentiful than meat, particularly in

---

[3] It may be worth noting that this illustration shows young women at a dance in Riazan Oblast, where the wearing, by the unmarried, of the one-piece *rubakha* and nothing else, was traditional.

certain areas, and some large river fish, such as sturgeon or sterlet, were considered the greatest delicacy. Berries, mushrooms, and wild herbs supplemented the diet, and were preserved, either with sugar or salt. Preserved berries were a favorite accompaniment for festive pancakes. A favorite dessert was and still is *kisel'*, a type of natural jelly, made from fruit or groats and served with cream.

Tea, often with lemon, has always been a favorite Russian drink. It is usually served in a tall glass, and sucked through a lump of sugar held between the teeth. Before the Revolution, many peasant families could not afford tea, however, and made do with decoctions of various herbs. Other favorite beverages are vodka, *kvas* (a kind of beer prepared from fermented bread soaked in water), and malt beer approximately equivalent to the European type. Not every family could afford vodka before the Revolution, but the alcoholism rate nonetheless was high. Vodka had a ritual significance, as we have indicated, and was used to celebrate important occasions and to ratify and sanctify all bargains. There is evidence that it still retains this role, which considerably complicates the government's campaign against alcoholism. Tea is probably still regarded as a luxury in the Soviet countryside generally (if we can judge from the budget data), but its distribution, along with coffee and cocoa, has certainly increased.

The peasant diet was subject to various factors—economic, seasonal, and religious. Certain types of food—as was the case almost everywhere before the spread of refrigeration—were available only in summer; eggs and most vegetables fell into this category. Certain items were forbidden, either altogether or on a seasonal basis, among some religious groups; for instance, some Old Believers and sectarians refused to eat pork—on the basis of the Mosaic law, literally interpreted. Some other sectarian groups did not eat potatoes or onions. The potato is, of course, not mentioned in the Bible, and was considered "the devil's root," although Nikol'skii (no date) suggests that there was also an economic reason for the ban. The reason for the prohibition against onions is not clear.

In peasant families, certain rituals were connected with food, for ordinary as well as special occasions. For instance, considerable importance was attached to the father's slicing of bread for the family. This was also a symbolic act, accompanying the splitting-off of a married son from the household. As we have already described, the menu for marriage and funeral feasts was set by custom.

The present-day diet of Central Russian peasants undoubtedly contains a greater variety of foods and is somewhat better balanced, although the general absence of refrigerators to some extent subjects it to seasonal factors. To American tastes, it remains excessively starchy. Table 9 shows the changes in diet that occurred in two villages of Voronezh Oblast between the years 1900–1956. The villages were studied by Shingarev in 1900 and again by Beliavskii and Chernyshov (1958).[4]

---

[4] Fragmentary data from the second edition of Shingarev's work (1907) have been cited in Chapter I. We are indebted to Basile Kerblay, of Paris, for lending us the pamphlet by Beliavskii and Chernyshov. It should be noted that the villages studied by Shingarev constituted an extreme case, and also that the Beliavskii-Chernyshov pamphlet is not scientific in its aim or its execution. However, this is the only case which has come to our attention where a specific village investigated before or around the time of the Revolution has been restudied to any extent in recent times, and where specific and direct comparison are therefore possible.

In Kalinin Oblast, wheat bread is a common food, and the women bake pies several times a week. Tomatoes became an addition to the diet after the Revolution. Meat consumption is now approximately three *tsentners* per year for a family of four or five. This comes out to slightly less than Beliavskii's and Chernyshov's figures. By way of comparison, we can cite a budget study covering 100 families in the cities of Moscow, Ivanovo, and Gorky, which compares the data for 1951 and 1961 (*Izvestiia* 7/I/64:5). Consumption of rye bread is down to 63.2 percent of what it had been in 1951, wheat to 85.9 percent, and potatoes to 90.6 percent. On

TABLE 9

AVERAGE CONSUMPTION (IN GRAMS) PER PERSON IN A 24-HOUR PERIOD

Product	Year 1900	Year 1956
Rye bread	709.50	198.90
Wheat flour	11.10	300.80
Groats and beans	125.10	44.00
Pasta	———	40.00
Potatoes	233.85	576.00
Cabbage	94.06	98.80
Cucumbers	2.74	80.00
Tomatoes	———	102.00
Vegetable Oil	2.49	12.00
Animal fat	0.70	13.00
Sugar	0.78	31.00
Confectionery	———	50.00
Meats	36.62	62.00
Lard	0.34	16.40
All fish	6.37	10.50
Herring	0.28	23.60
Whole milk	220.37	561.40
Eggs	3.13	10.20
Total	1447.43	2230.60

Source: Beliavskii and Chernyshov (1958: 24)

the other hand, consumption of vegetables was 127 percent above the previous level, and consumption of fresh fruits 468.2 percent—this last probably reflecting a very low level. The situation revealed by this study shows a rather nutritionally unbalanced diet, and one somewhat excessive in calories. This is confirmed by an extensive survey done in 1961 by Baranovskii (reported in Fitzpatrick 1963:6–7). From a sampling of Soviet citizens over forty, Baranovskii found that they ate too much and that their diet was monotonous. In particular, they ate too much meat and not enough fish; too much bread and sweets and not enough vegetables and milk products. Although it is possible to grow more than fifty varieties of vegetables in the Moscow area, only a very limited number are extensively used. The underemphasis on milk is attributed to its exclusion in everyday foods; this is apparently not true of peasant groups. Sugar and confectionery were used "in excess of the physiological norm" by 55 percent of those questioned, and three-fourths of this group were women. Almost 100 percent of the sampling reported that they ate to complete satiety.

We see therefore that the workers or the urban population generally do not necessarily enjoy an advantageous position as far as food is concerned. On the other hand, the kolkhoznik, who must use most of his household plot to grow fodder for his private livestock, is sometimes plagued by shortages of certain commodities, especially vegetables, in peak summer periods. A round-table discussion published in *Izvestiia* (14/IV/64:3) indicates that sometimes the plan calls for more lettuce and spinach to be delivered to the state than is possible, and sometimes a farm chairman is told to produce only so many onions and it turns out he could have sold twice that number. It sometimes happens that the chairman must take back his lettuces, because the store with which he has a contract refuses to accept them. The chairman may know that a store on another street or in a nearby city has been suffering a lettuce shortage, but he does not have the right to deal with another store. He can only reurn to his farm and feed the lettuce to the pigs; by this time anyway it is unsuitable for sale. Problems with packing and shipping lead to much spoilage. An agronomist on a *sovkhoz* in Moscow Oblast reported that his *sovkhoz* customarily rejects as unsuitable for sale 6–7 percent of a crop, but the trading organizations (that have to verify the produce on the spot), often discard an additional 12–15 percent, which is explained by the simple delay in inspection. If a *sovkhoz* itself packs tomatoes, spoilage is often as high as 20 percent, whereas tomatoes can be shipped from Bulgaria with only 3–5 percent waste. The problem here is caused partly by the condition of Soviet roads, which often makes a relatively short journey back-breaking and time-consuming. Another factor is the dearth of suitable transport; refrigerated cars are in short supply both on railways and in the trucking industry, and the allocation of transport is subject to severe strain at harvest time. Furthermore, produce is often left to weather for lack of storage facilities. The obvious solution to this whole problem is to can produce as quickly as possible, but even this presents difficulties. Factories will often refuse produce because they have more on hand than they can process. New plants are being built, but slowly, and as far as we can tell, nothing like the inter-kolkhoz canning plants (which in Central Asia deal directly with the farms) are in operation in the central regions of the USSR or are planned.

The effect of such waste and inefficiency on the diet of the Russian peasant is fairly obvious. If he grows vegetables and fruits on his private plot but needs money, he will be tempted to sell his yield (however slight) to the state. Often, however, the state cannot meet the price of produce on the open market, and the peasant will have to take his vegetables and fruits to the city for sale. The Western traveler, accustomed to voluminous baggage, will be amused at the dimensions of this trade. In 1964, when leaving Moscow by plane for the Caucasus and when returning, we saw Soviet citizens with bags and sacks of apples, cabbages, and melons, intended either for sale or in payment for services. In any case, under such conditions, the peasant is unlikely to consume such valuable produce—especially since it seems that what he craves is meat, fat, and sweets.

To enable the peasant to eat more meat, it follows that the whole livestock economy will have to be revamped. On the occasion of presenting an award to Vologda Oblast for success in animal husbandry (*Izvestiia* 4/VIII/63:3–4) G. I.

Voronov pointed out that livestock can gain weight only if they are rationally fed, and even then, the farmer must know when to slaughter his animals for maximum profit. The structure of the herd—the percentage of cows, ewes, and sows—is also important, and on many kolkhozy and *sovkhozy* in 1963 it was far below what is considered desirable. Recent statements (1965) indicate that the situation, though better, still needs improvement.

Another problem is a shortage of pastures and hayfields for private livestock which creates a complex tangle of difficulties. In a sketch from Kirov Oblast, Iarovoi (1965) describes how every day in summer, in the surrounding villages and hamlets, at least 200 people (of whom at least half are of working age) are engaged in pasturing private livestock. This causes a great deal of "down time" for the equipment during the peak harvest period, for lack of working hands. On one large *sovkhoz* there are no pastures or hay fields, although the operation has 700–800 hectares which have been abandoned and allowed to grow up to bushes, and which the *sovkhoz* is not now in a position to use. These areas could be turned over to individuals for their private livestock, and *sovkhoz* equipment could be used to improve them. The same problem exists in Borovichi *raion,* Novgorod Oblast, where on the kolkhoz "Russia" it was discovered that out of a total of 13,800 hectares, 8000 were in forest, swamp, or unarable, and another 2700 hectares had been allowed to grow up to bushes. The new policy is to give these areas to kolkhozniks and white-collar workers who own private livestock. According to a report (*Izvestiia* 26/V/65:3), no more than 15 rubles a season must be charged for this and, where the kolkhoz has no suitable land, state land and forest funds must be made available. Thus, we see that the kolkhoz "Russia" has the opportunity of using private enterprise to do jobs which the public economy is not capable of handling at present. Given the crucial nature of the fodder question, some measure such as the one just described would seem necessary if kolkhozniks and workers are to take advantage of credits extended by the state for the purchase of livestock.[5]

Agricultural Technology, Tools, and Equipment

The traditional agricultural tools of the Russian peasant is a subject on which Soviet scholars have done a great deal of detailed work, but which merits only passing reference in a study of this kind. Much of the equipment, which in form and sometimes in substance antedated the Soviet period—horse-drawn ploughs, harrows, seeders, hayrakes, and so on—was in use until recently on the more remote kolkhozy. Until 1954, the "Lenin's Way" kolkhoz of Viriatino village had 125 working mules, and at the time of the study[6] it had 89 working horses. Among the operations shown in pictures or mentioned in the text as being carried out at least partly by hand during 1954 and 1955, were tobacco cultivation, haying, brickmaking, milking, grain harvesting, and straw stacking. Horses are still used

---

[5] This amounts to a maximum of 300 rubles loaned for five years, with repayment for a cow to start with the second year; for a calf, up to 150 rubles, repayment to start with the third year (*Izvestiia* 2/IV/65:4).

[6] Kushner, ed., 1958.

for drawing harvesters, and the winnowing machine, while electrically driven, had to be fed by hand. The level of mechanization on the "Lenin's Way" kolkhoz, while not particularly impressive by American standards, was fairly high for its time and place. A quite different picture obtains in Kalinin Oblast, according to more recent data (Anokhina and Shmeleva 1964; *Izvestiia* 26/VII/64:2, 29/VII/64:3, 31/VII/64:3, 17/X/64:3). The problems encountered in Kalinin Oblast may be grouped under a number of heads: (1) extremely rapid turn-over of machinery, which applies not only here but generally in the country, to such an extent that the entire tractor supply must be renewed every five years; (2) unsatisfactory technical characteristics of some machines, especially potato-diggers and flax-harvesting equipment; (3) excessive "down time" of machines—for instance, an entire tractor engine must be disassembled in order to replace a piston ring (*Izvestiia* 14/XI/65:2). In addition, spare parts are difficult to get, due to uneven distribution. (4) The nature of the terrain, which is often sloping or stony, or which has small scattered plots of cropland, making it altogether impracticable to use machines; and (5) the agricultural schedule, according to which the flax and potato harvests, for example, coincide and create a major strain on labor resources. All these deterrents mean that many operations such as weeding of flax must be done by hand, even when machines are theoretically available; that flax must be cleaned by spreading it out on the road and running cars over it, which is wasteful. Added to the situation is the fact that the crop structure is in many cases irrational —that is, comparatively little land (and investment) is devoted to the branches of the economy which would be most profitable under the existing conditions. The net effect of this is low crop yields, and profits realized in one branch of the economy are eaten up by losses suffered in others. The theory is that a diversified economy for the individual farm enterprise will permit it to feed its population, market a cash crop, and provide steady, year-round employment—all at the same time. Since in the past, however, crop structure and the distribution of investment has been centrally determined (often by officials with no knowledge of local conditions, and in accordance with plans made on an *oblast,* regional, or even national scale), the results have been something less than encouraging.

A related matter is that of land-reclamation. As we have indicated, the arable land in many parts of North and Central Russia is simply disappearing under bushes and swamps. According to Vishniakov (1965), the amount of arable land per capita over the USSR as a whole was 1.06 hectares in 1958, and is now less than one hectare. In other words, the population is outstripping the supply of arable land, and this situation is particularly acute in certain districts. Vishniakov's solution to the problem, as usual with Soviet writers, is administrative; centralized control over land now scattered among a host of competing agencies. It is safe to suggest, however, that the problem is more complex. To begin with, no complete land survey has been undertaken since the 1920s, (*Izvestiia* 11/II/64:1–4), and there is a tendency to neglect small but possibly significant differences in soil conditions between one farm and another, and to attribute differences in crop yields to mismanagement or laziness on the part of some farm personnel. This is not to say that mismanagement is not at times responsible for low yields, both on the union planning level and on the local one. There has been wide discussion in recent months of increased use of fertilizer, but exact quantities and types are in dispute, even though output has been greatly increased. Fertilization alone is insufficient; the seed used is very important, and until recently Soviet Michurinist science had official sanction over the more orthodox Mendelian plant genetics. Even if the seed were good to begin with—and we must assume that efforts are made to see that it is—seed which has been left exposed to weather, for lack of storage facilities, deteriorates rapidly. If improperly planted (either because of delays in preparing the soil or because of inadequate machinery or knowledge), even good seed will yield a bad harvest. Finally, the supply of fodder is so crucial to the success of animal husbandry, on which many farms depend, that many farm chairmen are forced to jeopardize or sacrifice their seed crops for the sake of fodder.

Nevertheless, it would be incorrect to assume from what has been said above that the agricultural picture in Central Russia is unrelievedly black and hopeless. Many of the factors outlined in this section and elsewhere have never been frankly and openly discussed in the Soviet press until now, with the result that many if not most Western observers have failed to realize that these are problems traditional for Russian agriculture. By this, we mean that they existed under Tsarism, too, and have been only partially met by the Soviet regime. Many of our colleagues prefer to see in this continuity of problems proof that socialism, and the economic planning which is a concomitant of it, is a failure. But we would like to suggest that these cultural continuities illustrate the importance of peaceful conditions. The Soviet Union has had this necessary ingredient only since the death of Stalin in 1953. This marked the end of an era occupied either by continuous war or by its direct economic and social aftermath. The current discussions—some of them on an extremely high technical level—of agronomic practice, and of scales and types of agricultural investment, may indicate at long last the way out of a chronic crisis for Central Russian agriculture.

Summary: Folk Traditions and the Spread of Urban Tastes

In most parts of the world where folk societies still exist, the survival of the folk tradition in material culture is a function of a low standard of living and a faulty distribution system. As regrettable as it may be from an esthetic point of view, most people still in the status of peasants or just climbing out of it, would rather own an ugly factory-made object which they know is used by city people, than a craft product, no matter how artistic, which is connected with their bleak and deprived past. This appears to be true for the Russian peasant. In some instances, house furnishings and house layout form exceptions to this general rule, perhaps because they are connected with ingrained and long-standing ethnic habits and tastes which can to some degree survive economic change. Nonetheless, the use of peasant artifacts by Russian peasants today must be regarded as a survival. Certain forms of work clothing adapted to specific purposes, such as the bast *lapti,* or the headkerchief for women in place of the regular hat, form exceptions to this generalization, because they offer real and obvious advantages. On the whole, the material culture of the Russian peasant is in a state of transition which mirrors the state of transition in which the peasant finds himself as a person, socially, psychologically, and materially.

6

Summary and Conclusions

IN THIS STUDY we have covered, although briefly, a large and diverse body of data. Before stating our interpretations and conclusions, let us refer back to the ideas and concepts suggested in the Introduction. What we have described is basically the process by which a backward agricultural society has been changing into a modern industrial one. Due to the nature of the original data, we have described this change by contrasting the condition of the Russian peasant society at two points in time—first, just before or just after the Revolution, and second, the early (or late) 1950s. The precise location of these points in time is important because, as we have indicated, the condition of the society is sharply affected by specific changes in state policy, by the measures which flow from these changes, by economic circumstances, and by international political events All of the foregoing can be dated within a month or sometimes even within a week. The specific process by which the society of just before or just after the Revolution changed into the one which we find revealed in the study of Viriantino, or that of Kalinin Oblast, remains obscure in many instances, and can only be inferred.

The change from a backward agricultural society to a modern industrial one was subject to the influence of various factors. The first of these, in logical order, though not necessarily in order of importance, was the specific nature of the peasant society which constituted the starting point of the change. The Central Russian peasantry, as available studies have shown us, exhibited a number of differences from the peasant societies that anthropologists have studied in other parts of the world. Land tenure was organized on a communal principle, rather than on the basis of private property. The landholding unit was also the residential unit and, since the commune was in most cases exogamous, a person's membership in it determined whom he would be likely to marry. The commune was also the locus of whatever self-government existed in the face-to-face group. On the other hand, the Russian peasant's participation in the larger society, with its money economy, its established legal norms, and its cultural "great tradition" (which, as we pointed out in the Introduction, is the reverse side of the peasant coin), was largely in terms of nonagricultural migrant labor. The degree to which this was true, however, varied from region to region. Furthermore, the commune was not an egalitarian body, but showed considerable economic stratification—again due chiefly to the differential ownership of nonagricultural enterprises. Our data permit no conclusion as to the extent to which this situation represents a late stage of development of the Central Russian peasantry and, on the contrary, it may be due to longstanding geographical and social factors. Suffice it to say that this was a communally-organized peasantry, stratified on a largely nonagricultural basis, and in process of being transformed into a population of industrial or craft workers. Although this process was well advanced at the historical point described by our sources, the communal structure had not yet been broken down.

At the beginning of World War I, the process of industrialization was going forward with considerable vigor, in spite of being retarded by political and social factors; the changes actually taking place were masked by the apparent continuity of the communal system. There is some evidence indicating that the dislocations caused by the war had a further braking effect on the socio-economic change accompanying industrialization. We can assume that the war, by creating a permanent drain of male population from the countryside, in place of the periodic drain caused by *otkhodnichestvo,* would slow down or stop the process of culture change, which was dependent largely on the new ideas and the capital brought back from migrant labor.

In 1917, there supervened on this situation a revolutionary movement with certain specific characteristics. Those relevant to our study were the ideological commitment to industrialization through state ownership of all means of production, and the identification of the industrial-worker class as the initiator of socioeconomic change. The peasant policy of those who directed the Revolution was complex and was conditioned both by the ideological assumptions we have mentioned and by the requirements of day-to-day (or month-to-month) politics. The peasants were granted land on the basis of private laboring tenure, but Lenin and other leaders always emphasized that this was merely a temporary measure, intended chiefly for didactic purposes. The peasants, it was said, needed a practical demonstration of the advantages of collective ownership, and they needed to be shown that the Revolution was "on their side." We have seen from Fenomenov's data that in the early years of the Soviet period, this policy produced no marked change in the social structure of the peasant community. The communal system, with its specific forms of self-government, continued to operate. It was now not subordinated to a landlord, as before the Emancipation, or to the local Tsarist authorities, but to the local agencies of the Soviet government and the Communist Party.

Our data on the period of collectivization are scanty, and do not permit any very firm conclusions as to the nature and immediate social effects of this process. We are faced instead with current descriptions of the operation of the collective farm system, from which we must infer the functions of the kolkhoz in the community. In the first section of Chapter 2 we concluded that the rôle of the kolkhoz is a dual one—that it functions both as a formal organization and a unit in the political structure, and as a means whereby people live together. On the whole, however, the formal or political aspect predominates. Particularly since the expansion of kolkhozy during the 1950s to the point where they may include ten or a dozen villages (or in some cases even more), they are not perceived as social units by their members.

The social unit next in order above the family in most peasant societies is the village. This is the locus of self-government and of the religious life of the people and determines through either endogamy or exogamy the choice of mates. In the Russian countryside, the social significance of the village is complicated by the fact that many villages had in the past what we call a binary social structure. This means that they contained two self-regulating landholding communes, comprising either serfs belonging to two landed estates or landlord peasants (serfs) on the one hand and state peasants on the other. The groups were residentially separate, and in most cases constituted exogamous units. It will be remembered that in the village studied by Fenomenov, this social structure was still operating, whereas in Viriatino, it was remembered even though it no longer applied.

Perhaps the most important social unit in traditional Central Russian peasant society was the family or household. This functioned as an economic entity, earning and spending income in common, and holding rights in the communal land and real property as a group. The current evidence (early and middle 1950s for the most part), indicates that the family continues to operate as an economic collective, although conditions have changed. This continuity extends even to the separateness of male and female property—that is, the exemption of the women's property from division when the family breaks up, and the inheritance of this property in the female line exclusively. The continuity of the family represents perhaps the most significant element uniting prerevolutionary Russian peasant society with the present-day Soviet countryside. It gives us our most important reason for concluding that these people are still peasants, despite the changes in culture and in their material and intellectual environment. It is worth noting that the continuity of the family represents at present the effect of settled Soviet state policy, even though at first this policy may have been only a concession to circumstances.

To refer again to our Introduction, we find that the peasant is defined both on structural-organizational grounds (in terms of the kind of social unit to which he belonged) and on more narrowly cultural ones. We said that he occupied a marginal position in the nation-state to which he belonged, and participated in its culture through a screen made up of economic, social, and geographical factors. As a result, certain elements of the culture never reached him, while others reached him only in altered form, or after a delay. The cultural screen, however, is a negative mechanism; by itself it creates nothing. What it does is to preserve certain elements of the peasant culture by excluding urban equivalents which would be competitive.

We find therefore that every peasant culture, including the Central Russian, at any point in its history has both positive and negative characteristics. That is, it lacks certain elements present in urban culture, and possesses others created by the peasant—which urban people have lost or abandoned. The positive aspects which reflect the cultural initiative of the peasant community—dances, songs, stories, forms of dress, and decorative and graphic art—cannot be attributed to the operations of the screen. At best, they are only preserved by the screen and may be diffused to the urban population.

During the nineteenth century, the cultural screen between the Central Russian peasant and the urban Russian was so dense that urban intellectuals observing peasant life in the countryside often had the impression that they were in another world. That this remained true despite the effects of *otkhodnichestvo* is a striking fact that should be investigated further. The effect of the screen is, of course, directly related in the modern context to the policy of the state and to the amount of investment for "cultural" purposes—regular and adult education, the popularization of urban art forms, medical service and sanitation, and so on. Without attempting to judge the success with which such measures have been prosecuted in the Soviet Union, we can safely say that the cultural screen still exists, although it now operates rather differently. First of all, a means has been established whereby an individual can escape the effects of the screen entirely by leaving the category of peasant. Education (subject to the limitation set forth below) will permit a person to advance up the social ladder as far as and as fast as his gifts and energy will take him. This, however, brings with it another problem—a mass exodus from the countryside. Some Soviet writers (Shubkin 1965) are now calling for measures—socio-economic rather than administrative—to limit this exodus and keep the population, especially the young people, on the land.

The achievement of almost Union-wide literacy (except for the elderly) has removed the most severe and obvious barrier that separates the peasant from the urban or national culture. But as Shubkin (1965) makes clear, for example, educational handicaps for the rural population continue to exist. Since the avenues of social mobility opened up by the Soviet regime operate almost entirely by means of education, these handicaps are bound to have a structural effect on the society that is out of proportion to the number of people to whom they apply.

In the sections dealing with adult education and cultural facilities, we have made clear the limitations on change in this regard imposed by factors of investment and allocation of resources. It seems that the Central Russian peasant is still cut off, to some degree, from the over-all culture, although the intensity of this isolation varies from time to time and from place to place. The process of change in peasant culture—insofar as this culture in itself can be regarded as a product of the screen—thus becomes a matter of priorities and resource allocation on a nationwide scale. The same is true, as we pointed out in Chapter 5, of the distinctive elements of peasant material culture (apart from some forms of folk art as such) which are replaced by urban industrial items wherever and whenever available.

As for the positive features of peasant culture which are only indirectly or not at all attributable to the screen—folk art, ritual, superstition in the technical sense—we have suggested that in some instances (particularly the peasant wedding) their survival may be connected with the relative lack of other forms of entertainment. Also, since any form of religious observance is specifically discountenanced by the authorities, a need arises for means of ritually marking important events in a way which will fulfill the emotional requirements usually met by religion. We have seen that Soviet social scientists are aware of this problem and have begun to wrestle with it seriously. It seems clear that in many cases these traditional life-crisis rituals, even (or perhaps especially) where they contain elements not approved of by the regime, continue to express the values and solidarity of the rural community.

The present-day Central Russian peasant is a very different person from his prerevolutionary counterpart. This is true not only because the substance of his way of life has changed, but because contact with the nonpeasant world is much more constant and intense for him than it was for his grandfather. Education, of course, is one of the forms which this contact takes. In fact, we might say that his ceasing altogether to be a peasant is only a question of time; this is certainly what Soviet social scientists think. They hope that the urban way of life, with its cultural advantages, can be brought to the peasant without physically or emotionally uprooting him from his environment. But evidence so far seems to indicate that industrialization means urbanization and requires the uprooting of the peasant, and this, in turn, means that those who remain on the farm (as somebody has to) get only the resources left over after payment for industrialization.

The peasant, therefore, is a man in transition, and the terms within which this transition occurs are determined not only by the point from which he starts out —the traditional culture—but by the state's attitude toward him. This is particularly true in a socialist society, with its centralized control of investment and allocation of resources. If we observe the panorama of peasant mobility on a world scale, we find that the second factor applies almost everywhere, because most of the new nation-states now coming into being are socialist in this sense at least. From the Russian experience we learn that change in peasant culture in the modern context is dependent on intensive centralized state investment. This investment must have adequate safeguards on the local level to insure its proper allocation and effectiveness. In many areas of Soviet life, and over a large part of the history of Soviet experience, such local safeguards have been lacking. Another element is no less important, however, and has been in equally short supply—internal and external peace.

Wars, the preparations for them, and periods of civil unrest, obviously place an intolerable burden on the resources which would otherwise be devoted to the development of the economy, and in an ultimate sense, to culture change. Furthermore, wars destroy in a few weeks, months, or even minutes the accumulation and accomplishments of years. This is particularly evident in the Soviet Union where, until the past 15 years, whatever social progress had been made was threatened by war, international or civil. Even now it is evident that the armaments race resulting from a tense and unstable international situation has drained and continues to drain away resources needed for the transformation of the countryside and of agriculture. And this in an era when there is a serious possibility of overpopulation on a world scale! Peasant culture change can no longer be considered, as it might have been 100 years ago, a slow, natural inevitable process that runs its course without disturbing other peoples within its own country or in other parts of the world. The "revolution of rising expectations" has created within peasant communities a force whose explosive potential social scientists are just now beginning to realize. Once the transformation of the countryside has begun, it cannot be stopped halfway. Any marked snag or decrease in the rate of change may trigger a revolutionary explosion in an unindustrialized country or, as in the Soviet case, a mass exodus from the land.

The main fact about the Russian peasant is that after nearly fifty years of revolution, civil and international war, shoving and hauling, and superhuman effort and sacrifice, he remains a man in transition. He has reached the point from which he can see a better life, but external circumstances—administrative problems, the international situation, and the resulting limitation on investment—have so far kept him from grasping it, except by leaving the status of peasant altogether.

Glossary

Artel':   a cooperative group of workers who divide up the proceeds of their work; also used for a kolkhoz (agricultural *artel'*).

Bedniak: poor peasant.

Chernozem: black-earth soil.

Desiatin: 2.7 acres (prerevolutionary measure).

Devishnik: supper for bride's girl friends on eve of the wedding.

Dvor: a household, also a homestead (dwelling house with outbuildings).

Gram: 0.04 oz.

Gubernia: province in prerevolutionary Russia.

Gulianie: courtship; in another sense, walk or outing.

Hectare: 2.47 acres.

Icon: an image of a saint or a divine personage, to which in the Russian Orthodox tradition, certain supernatural properties are attributed.

Izba: (pl. *izby*) Russian peasant cottage; in another sense, separate dwelling unit within a larger house.

Khutor: a farmstead apart from the village lands, containing the owner's dwelling.

Kilogram: 2.2 pounds.

Kilometer: 0.62 mile.

Kolkhoz: (pl. *kolkhozy*) collective farm.

Kolkhoznik: collective farm member; in this study, used to denote both male and female.

Kombed: (pl. *Kombedy*) Committee of the Poor, a revolutionary legislative body in the countryside just after the Revolution.

Kommuna: (pl. Kommuny) A form of socialist organization in which all property except items of personal use was publicly owned, and people lived and ate in common.

Kopek: one-hundredth of a ruble.

Kosovorotka: side-opening shirt worn by men.

Krai: a large sparsely settled region, usually in the borderlands.

Kulak: rich peasant, who employs hired labor.

Lapti: plaited bast shoes.

Meter: 39.37 inches.

Mir: the peasant landholding commune, in which individual households held shares.

Molokans: Old Russian sect; milk-drinkers.

MTS: Machine Tractor Station; officially abolished in 1958; until then the agency carrying out mechanized agricultural work on kolkhozy and having control, functions in the countryside.

Narodniks: Russian populists who believed that the Revolution which would transform Russian society would come from the peasantry.

Oblast: province in present-day Soviet Union.

Okrug: territorial administrative unit above the raion in size but below oblast or krai, usually in the borderlands.

Old Believer: member of any one of a number of religious bodies which rejected the ecclesiastical and ritual reforms of Patriarch Nikon, 1666.

Onuchi: linen puttees.

Otkhodnichestvo: seasonal migrant labor by peasants.

Otrub: consolidated plot on the outskirts of the village, not containing the owner's dwelling, and not subject to repartition by the *mir*.

Piatistenka: Russian two-room peasant cottage.

Podzol: type of soil.

Posidelka (variant *Posidka*): evening party given by unmarried girls and attended by young men; part of the courtship pattern.

Pridanoe: bride's marriage portion, consisting largely of clothes, bedding, and drapery.

Primachestvo: the situation of a *primak*.

Primak: a son-in-law living with his wife's family or a man living in a home owned by his wife.

Pud: 36.07 lb.

Raion: next administrative unit below *oblast* by Soviet usage.

Ruble: monetary unit; officially worth $1.11, but varying widely in buying power.

Sagene: 7 feet.

Sectarian: religious dissident; in the Russian context applied to groups such as the Molokans and Subbotniki, and sometimes to Old Believers.

Sel'sovet: township soviet.

Seredniak: middle peasant, farming with the aid of his family only.

Skhod: gathering of heads of families holding land in a commune.

Soviet: a legislative and executive assembly on any geographical level.

Sovkhoz: (pl. *sovkhozy*) state farm.

Subbotniki: Old Russian sect, Sabbatarians.

Toz: society for joint working of land; primitive form of collective farm, without joint ownership of equipment.

Tsentner: 100 kilograms; 220 pounds.

Uyezd: next unit below gubernia, prerevolutionary.

Valenki: felt boots.

Verst: 0.66 mile.

Volost: a rural territorial unit below the uyezd, prerevolutionary.

Zemstvo: agency of rural self-government, pre-revolutionary.

Zhito: the combination of barley, oats and spring wheat, considered as a single crop.

References

ALEKSANDROV, V. A. and others, eds., 1964, *Narody evropeiskoi chasti SSSR (Peoples of the European Part of the USSR)*, Vol. 1. Moscow.

ANOKHINA, L. A. and M. N. SHMELEVA, 1964, *Kul'tura i byt kolkhoznikov Kalininskoi oblasti (Culture and Life of the Kolkhozniks of Kalinin Oblast)*. Moscow.

*APTEKMAN, D. M., 1965, "Causes of the vitality of the ceremony of baptism under modern conditions," *Soviet Sociology*, Vol. 4, No. 2.
This is a good example of the Soviet approach to religious behavior, but is not particularly profound.

BELIAVSKII, P., and A. CHERNYSHOV, 1958, *Sud'ba 'Vymiraiushchei derevni' (The Fate of "The Dying Village")*. Moscow.

*BLACKWELL, WILLIAM L., 1965, "The Old Believers and the rise of private industrial enterprise in early 19th century Moscow," *Slavic Review*, Vol. 24, No. 3.
This is an interesting historical approach to the question of the Old Belief.

*BLUM, JEROME, 1964, *Lord and Peasant in Russia from the Ninth to the Nineteenth Century*. New York.
Good historical treatment.

*BOBRINSKII, A. A., 1963, "A contribution to the study of the technology of pottery in Smolensk Oblast," *Soviet Anthropology and Archaeology*, Vol. 1, No. 4.
A detailed and interesting reconstruction of one of the aspects of peasant material culture.

BONCH-BRUEVICH, V. D., 1922, *Iz mira sektantov: sbornik statei (From the World of Sectarians: A Collection of Articles)*. Moscow.

BRIGGS, L. CABOT and N. L. GUÈDE, 1964, *No More Forever: a Saharan Jewish Town*. Papers of the Peabody Museum of Archeology and Anthropology. Harvard University, Cambridge, Mass. Vol. 55, No. 1.

CAMPBELL, J. K., 1964, *Honor, Family and Patronage*. Cambridge, England.

CHEREMENSKII, P. N., 1961, *Proshloe Tambovskogo kraia (The Past of Tambov Region)*. Tambov.

*CHIZHIKOVA, L. N., 1966, "Dwellings of the Russians," *Soviet Anthropology and Archeology*, Vol. 5, No. 1.
Actually a section in ALEKSANDROV, 1964.

DANILIN, A. G., 1931, "Pervye shagi kolkhozov byvshch. Borovichskogo okruga,"

---

* Recommended reading.

("First steps of the kolkhozy of the former Borovichi okrug") *Trud i byt v kolkhozakh,* Vol. 1.

DANILOV, V. P., 1958, "Zemelnye otnosheniia v sovetskoi dokolkhoznoi derevne" ("Land relationships in the Soviet pre-kolkhoz countryside"), *Istoriia SSSR* No. 3.

DEWITT, NICHOLAS, 1961, *Education and Professional Employment in the Soviet Union.* Washington, D.C.

*DODGE, NORTON, and MURRAY FESHBACH, (mimeograph), "The Role of Women in Soviet Agriculture," Soviet Agricultural Conference at Santa Barbara, August 1965.
This article and the others given at the conference, when published, will be helpful if used critically.

DUNN, STEPHEN P., 1959, unpublished dissertation, *The Influence of Ideology on Culture Change: Two Test Cases.* Columbia University.

———, 1960, "The Roman Jewish Community: A Study in Historical Causation, *Jewish Journal of Sociology,* Vol. 2, No. 1.

*———, 1966, "Cultural processes in the Baltic area under Soviet rule." Monograph, Institute of International Studies, University of California, Berkeley.
Potentially useful contrast to this study.

*DUNN, STEPHEN P., and ETHEL DUNN, 1964, "Religion as an instrument of culture change: the problem of the sects in the Soviet Union," *Slavic Review,* Vol. 23, No. 3.
Illustrates the importance of the sects for culture change.

———, 1965*a* "Report from VIIth International Congress of Anthropological and Ethnographic Sciences,": *American Anthropologist,* Vol. 67, No. 2.

———, 1965*b* "Talks with Soviet ethnographers and some reflections," *American Anthropologist,* Vol. 67, No. 4.

FENOMENOV, M. IA., 1925, *Sovremennaia derevnia (The Contemporary Village).* Moscow-Leningrad. Two vols.

FITZPATRICK, WILLIAM H., 1963, "Soviet research in nutrition, "*Monographs in Soviet Medical Sciences* H 4. Institute of Contemporary Russian Studies. Fordham University, Bronx, New York.

FOSTER, GEORGE M., 1965, "Peasant Society and the image of limited good," *American Anthropologist,* Vol. 67, No. 2.

*HALPERN, JOEL, 1965, "Peasant culture and urbanization in Yugoslavia," *Human Organization,* Vol. 24, No. 2.
A view of the peasantry as contrast to the one taken in this study.

IAKOVLEV, IA., 1923, *Derevnia kak ona est' (Ocherki Nikol'skoi volosti)—The Village as it is (Sketches of Nikol'skaia Volost).* Moscow.

IANKOVA, Z. A., 1963, "Sovremennoe pravoslavie i antiobshchestvennaia sushchnost' ego ideologii" ("Contemporary Orthodoxy and the antisocial nature of its ideology"), *Voprosy istorii religii i ateizma,* Vol. 11.

IAROVOI, M., 1965, "Ol'gin dvor" (Olga's *dvor*), *Sovety deputatov trudiashchikhsia,* No. 6.

IVANOV, L., 1963, "V rodnykh mestakh" ("In native places"), *Novy Mir,* No. 3.

KALITS, V. IA., 1962, "Sovremennaia svad'ba na ostrove Kikhnu" ("The contemporary wedding on Kihnu Island"), in *Sem'ia i semeinyi byt kolkhoznikov pribaltiki (Family and Family Life of the Kolkhozniks of the Baltic Area),* L. N. Terent'eva and N. V. Shlygina, eds. Moscow.

*KATUNSKII, A. E., 1964, "The reactionary nature of the contemporary Old Believer ideology," *Soviet Sociology*, Vol. 3 No. 2.
More on the Old Belief today.

KAZANTSEV, N. D. and others, eds., no date, *Kolkhoznoe pravo* (*Kolkhoz Law*). Moscow.

*KLIBANOV, A. I., 1965, "The dissident denominations in the past and today," *Soviet Sociology*, Vol. 3 No. 4.
A masterful statement of Soviet attitudes and approaches toward religion.

KOGAN, D. M., 1964, "Izuchenie sovremennogo kolkhoznogo byta tsentral'nym otriadom Kompleksnoi ekspeditsii Instituta etnografii AN SSSR (kolkhozy Kirovskoi, Vladimirskoi i Gor'kovskoi oblastei)"—"Study of the contemporary kolkhoz life by the Central Detachment of the Complex Expedition of the Institute of Ethnography, AS USSR (the kolkhozy of Kirov, Vladimir and Gorky Oblasts)", *Sovetskaia etnografiia*, No. 5.

KORETSKII, V. I., 1961, "Ocherki religioznogo sektantstva na Tambovshchina" ("Sketches of religious sectarianism in the Tambov area"), in *Sovremennoe sektantstvo i ego preodolenie* [Contemporary Sectarianism and Overcoming It] (*Voprosy istorii religii i ateizma*, Vol. 9).

KRYVELEV, I. A., 1963, "O formirovanii i rasprostranenii novykh obychaev i prazdnikov u narodov SSSR" ("On the formation and distribution of new customs and holidays among the peoples of the USSR"), *Sovetskaia etnografiia*, No. 6.

KUSHNER, P. I., ed., 1958, Selo Viriatino v proshlom i nastoiashchem: Opyt etnograficheskogo izucheniia russkoi kolkhoznoi derevni (*Viriatino Village Past and Present: Attempt at Ethnographic Study of a Russian Kolkhoz Village*). Moscow.

LEPER, E. R., 1931, "Lomka byta i mirovozreniia pod vlianiem kollektivizatsii otstali derevni" ("The breakup of the way of life and the world-view under the influence of collectivization of a backward village"), *Trud i byt v kolkhozakh*, Vol. 1.

LOGUNOVA, L. A., and L. L. DESHALYT, 1958, "Vozniknovenie sel'skokhoziaistvennykh kommun i artelei v tverskoi gubernii v 1918–1919 gg." ("Formation of agricultural communes and *artels* in Tver Gubernia in 1918–1919"), in *Tverskaia guberniia v pervye gody Sovetskoi vlasti (1917–1920 gg.)*— *Tver Gubernia in the First Years of Soviet Power (1917–1920)*, M.A. Il'in and A. M. Rumiantseva, eds. Kalinin.

MALAKHOVA, I. A., 1961, "Religioznoe sektantstvo v Tambovskoi oblasti v posleoktiabr'skoi period i v nashi dni" ("Religious sectarianism in Tambov Oblast in the Post-October period and in our times"), in *Sovremennoe sektantstvo i ego preodolenie* (Voprosy *istorii religii i ateizma*, Vol. 9).

*MAYNARD, SIR JOHN, 1962, *The Russian Peasant and Other Studies*. New York (first published in 1942).
Maynard knew Russia well and was an extremely sensitive observer. His books are still the best over-all account of the peasantry just before and just after the Revolution.

MEL'NIKOV, P. I., [Andrei Pecherskii, pseud., 19th-century novelist and ethnographer] 1963, Na Gorakh (*On the Mountains*), Vols. 3 and 4 of *Sobranie sochinenii v shesti tomakh* (*Collected Works in Six Volumes*). Moscow.

MILOVIDOV, B. F., 1963, "Raspad staroobriadchestva v Riazanskoi oblasti" ("The decay of the Old Belief in Riazan Oblast"), *Voprosy istorii religii i ateizma,* Vol. 11.

MOKEEV, V. V., 1926, *Na perelome: Opyt issledovaniia ekonomika derevni (At the Turning-point: Attempt at the Study of the Economics of the Village).* Moscow-Leningrad.

MOROZOV, V. I., 1961, "Iz istorii razvitiia sel'skogo khoziaistva RSFSR, 1953–1958 gg.," ("From the history of the growth of the agriculture of the RSFSR, 1953–1958"), *Istoriia SSSR,* No. 4.

NIKOL'SKAIA, Z. A., 1961, "K kharakteristike techeniia tak-nazyvaemykh istinno-pravoslavnykh khristian" ("On the characteristics of the group of so-called True Orthodox Christians"), in *Sovremennoe sektantstvo i ego preodolenie (Voprosy istorii religii i ateizma,* Vol. 9).

NIKOL'SKII, N. M., no date, "Raskol i sektantstvo vo vtoroi polovine XIX veka," ("The Schism and sectarianism in the second half of the 19th century"), in *Istoriia Rossii v XIX veka, Tom 5: Epokha reaktsii (A History of Russia in the 19th Century, Vol. 5: The Epoch of Reaction).* St. Petersburg.

NOAROV, V., no date, "Krestianskoe khoziaistvo Tambovskoi gub. v. 1922–1923 g." ("The peasant economy in Tambov gubernia in 1922–1923"), reprint from *Kommunist,* Tambov.

PRUSAKOV, V. P., 1965, "Rasvitie denezhnoi oplaty truda v kolkhozakh i opredelenie ee ekonomicheskoi effektivnosti," ("The growth of the monetary payment for labor in kolkhozy and determining its economic effectiveness"), *Vestnik Moskovskogo universiteta, Seriia 8, Ekonomika, Filosofiia,* No. 4.

PUSHKAREVA, L. A. and M. N. SHMELEVA, 1959, "Sovremennaia russkaia krest'ianskaia svad'ba" ("The contemporary Russian peasant wedding"), *Sovetskaia etnografia,* No. 3.

SAVUSHKINA, N. I., 1963, "Ob izuchenii ispolnitel'skogo nachala v folklore" ("On the study of the principle of execution in folklore,") *Sovetskaia etnografiia,* No. 3.

SHIKHAREVA, M. S., 1964, "Svad'ba u sel'skogo naseleniia Kubani" "The wedding among the rural population of the Kuban"), *Sovetskaia etnografiia,* No. 1.

*SHIMKIN, D., 1964, "National forces and ecological adaptations in the development of Russian peasant societies," in *Process and Pattern in Culture,* edited by R. A. Manners. Chicago.
Succinct statement of problems from an ecobiological angle.

SHINGAREV, A. I., 1907, *Vymiraiushchaia derevnia (The Dying Village).* St. Petersburg, 2d ed.

*SHINN, WILLIAM T., JR., 1961, "The law of the Russian peasant household," *Slavic Review,* Vol. 10.
Sound and detailed exposition of development of customary law concerning the family.

SHUBKIN, V. N. 1965, "Youth starts out in life," *Soviet Sociology,* Vol. 4, No. 3.

SOVET VSEROSSIISKIKH S"EZDOV STAROOBRIADTSEV, 1910, *Sel'sko-khoziaistvennyi i ekonomicheskii byt staroobriadtsev (po dannym ankety 1909 goda)—Agricultural and Economic Life of Old Believers (According to Questionnaire Data of 1909).* Moscow.

TOKAREV, S. A., 1957, *Religioznye verovaniia vostochnoslavianskikh narodov XIX—nachala Xg v. (Religious Beliefs of the Eastern Slavic Peoples in the 19th—Beginning of the 20th Century).* Moscow-Leningrad.

————, 1964, *Rannye formy religii i ikh razvitie (Early Forms of Religion and Their Development)*. Moscow.

TRIFONOV, I., 1960, *Ocherki istorii klassovoi bor'by v SSSR v gody NEPa (1921–1937)—(Sketches of the History of the Class Struggle in the USSR in the Years of the NEP (1921–1937)*. Moscow.

TsSu RSFSR, 1964, *RSFSR 1963 g. Kratkii statisticheskii shornik (The RSFSR in 1963: A Short Statistical Collection)*. Moscow.

TsSU SSSR, 1962, *Itogi vsesoiuznoi perepisi naseleniia v 1959 g. Svodnyi tom (Results of the All-Union Census of the Population in 1959. Summary Volume.)* Moscow.

VISHNIAKOV, V. 1965, "Zemle—odnogo khoziaina" ("One master for the land"), *Sovety deputatov trudiashchikhsia*, No. 8.

*VUCINICH, ALEXANDER, 1960, "The state and the local community," in *The Transformation of Russian Society: Aspects of Social Change since 1861*, edited by C. E. Black. Cambridge, Mass.
An excellent historical treatment of the tension between centralism and localism in in Tsarist Russian society.

*————, 1963, *Science in Russian Culture: A History to 1860*. Stanford.
The first 100 pages of this book are extremely interesting for a glimpse of problems of culture change in Russian history.

WESSON, ROBERT G., 1963, *Soviet Communes*. New Brunswick, New Jersey.

*YANEY, GEORGE L., 1964, "The concept of the Stolypin land reform," *Slavic Review*, Vol. 23, No. 2.
A good historical sociological treatment of the ideas and economic factors leading to the Stolypin land reforms.

ZLOBIN, N. S., 1963, "Sovremennyi baptizm i ego ideologiia," ("Contemporary Baptism and Its Ideology"), *Voprosy istorii religii i ateizma*, Vol. 11.